CW00327278

Minstrels In The Gallery

A History Of Jethro Tull

by

David Rees

FIRE FLY
PUBLISHING

First published in 1998 by Firefly Publishing (reprinted 1998)

Firefly is an imprint of SAF Publishing Ltd.
In association with Helter Skelter Publishing Ltd.

SAF Publishing Ltd.,
12 Conway Gardens,
Wembley, Middx. HA9 8TR
ENGLAND

The right of David Rees to be identified as the author of this work has been asserted
by him in accordance with the Copyright, Design and Patents Act, 1988.

All rights reserved. No part of this publication may be reproduced, stored in a retrieval
system, or transmitted in any form, or by any means, electronic, photocopying,
recording or otherwise, without the prior permission of the publisher.

A CIP catalogue record for this book is available from the British Library.

Text copyright © David Rees 1998

Reprinted 2000

ISBN 0 946719 225

Front cover photograph: Fin Costello, Redferns.
Back cover photograph: Mark Colman.

Printed in England by Redwood Books, Trowbridge, Wiltshire.

To my wife, Jackie, struggling to come to terms with the fact that our sons Steven, Martin and Daniel are all fast becoming Jethro Tull fans!

Acknowledgements

Thanks are due to the following people who have helped in some way to enable me to write this book:

Martin Webb for help over the years with interviews and photos, and particularly for the research into the John Evan Band days.
Frank The Snowman, Terry The Innocent and Keef The Jacket.
Colin Harper, for continually badgering me to write it.
Kenny Wylie for keeping me in touch with the band.
All the members of Jethro Tull, past and present.
Tony Wilkinson and Chris Riley for information and photos from the very early days.
All the photographers who have given pernmission to use their work in this book.
And to all the readers of *A New Day* who keep me informed of developments throughout the world.

The publishers would also like to thank Peter Doggett.

Addresses

A New Day Records, and *A New Day*, the independent Jethro Tull information magazine.
The magazine is published four or five times a year, and covers all things Tull as well as related bands such as Blodwyn Pig, Fairport Convention, Wild Turkey, Solstice etc. For subscription details contact:
75 Wren Way, Farnborough, Hampshire, GU14 8TA, England.
Fax: 01252 372 001
email: DAVIDREES1@compuserve.com

Jethro Tull book *Complete Lyrics* is published by PALMYRA,
Bienenstr. 1, 6900 Heidelberg, Germany.
In the UK - IMP, Southend Road, Woodford Green, Essex, IG8 8HN.

Official Jethro Tull tour merchandise available from Chester Hopkins International Ltd, PO Box 1492, London W6 9PD, England.

Fairport Convention. To get on the free Fairport mailing list contact:
Woodworm Records, PO Box 37, Banbury, Oxon. OX16 8YN.

Contents

Foreword - 7

Introduction 9

Chapter 1 - Meanwhile, Back In The Year One 11

Chapter 2 - This Was, Jethro Toe 22

Chapter 3 - Sitting On A Park Bench 41

Chapter 4 - Back To The Family 61

Chapter 5 - Songs From The Wood 76

Chapter 6 - The Big Split 93

Chapter 7 - A Kick Up The Eighties 101

Chapter 8 - The Flute Is A Heavy, Metal Instrument . . . 118

Chapter 9 - Back To The Roots 133

Chapter 10 - Living In The Past! 144

Chapter 11 - In The Grip Of Stronger Stuff 152

Appendix 1 - Mick Abrahams and Blodwyn Pig 173

Appendix 2 - Discography 185

Appendix 3 - Gigography 201

Foreword

It would be nice to think that it was my gifted prose and proven track record which prompted the Publishers to ask me to write this book. Or then again, maybe it was my dashing good looks or my undisputed modesty which brought them to my door. In truth, they must have figured that having written *A New Day*, the independent Jethro Tull magazine since 1985, I must know a bit about the band. In common parlance that means I write the 'Jethro Tull fanzine'- but that is a description that I've never cared for.

Of course I am a fan; why else would I have cultivated such a peculiar hobby? But I hope and believe that I have always looked at Jethro Tull with my eyes (and ears) wide open. Over the years I have developed a (usually) very good relationship with the band, yet my outlook remains, and shall remain, most definitely independent. The greatest possible compliment I could have received came during the UK Jethro Tull Convention in 1996 when Ian Anderson said on stage, "Thanks to Dave Rees and *A New Day* for keeping things... interesting. When they think we're shite, they say we're shite – in the nicest possible way!"

That is, of course, how a fanzine should be. A book, however, is a whole different kettle of fish. Whilst I have been able to imbue *A New Day* with all manner of peripherals - jokes, politics, football anecdotes, diatribes against Athenian hoteliers and French customs officials, and a whole host of totally unrelated rock 'n' roll bands - a book had to be less a catalogue of my opinions and more a record of events. It had to be about Jethro Tull, period.

That was almost me scuppered before I'd started. But a Jethro Tull book needed to be written, for two reasons. Firstly, believe it or not, there has never been an English language book written about Jethro Tull. Secondly, several people smugly told me there was no way I'd get away with writing a book about Tull that included references to Jackie Lynton, The King Earl Boogie Band, Vikki Clayton, Solstice and the mighty Mechanics. But hey – I've already done it!

Dave Rees, March 1998

Introduction

Although Jethro Tull is a group, Ian Anderson is undeniably the leader and most instantly recognisable symbol of the band's existence. Since (almost) the very beginning he has been at the helm, writing, singing, producing, guiding and representing all aspects of Jethro Tull. Besides Anderson, there have been something like 30 musicians over the years, each contributing in various amounts to the phenomenal success Tull has achieved. Around 50 million albums sold, over 2,000 concerts played to millions of people, and 44 Platinum, Gold and Silver industry awards.

Since their first album in 1968 they have followed their own path, steadfastly refusing to imitate any musical trends, always pushing the boundaries of their music, always striving to make music that was creative and idiosyncratic. They could not be described as "influential", simply because there is no other band that sounds like them. Whatever style they have utilised over the years – and they have utilised many – the result has always clearly been Jethro Tull music. In the beginning they stood alongside the British Blues boomers such as Fleetwood Mac and Ten Years After. Later, they were often mentioned in the same breath as heavy metal specialists Led Zeppelin and Deep Purple. For some they will always be inextricably linked with the progressive scene along with Yes, ELP and Genesis. Others insist they move in the folk/rock field lead by Fairport Convention, with whom they have many links. Others highlight their jazz and classical leanings.

In short, Jethro Tull defy categorisation, and perhaps that goes a long way to explaining the incredible durability and popularity that has kept them, to borrow one of Ian Anderson's favourite euphemisms, "if not in the Premier League, at the top of the first division" for 30 years. And that's 30 years without a break. Unlike so many of their contemporaries, Tull have never retired only to make a triumphant return years later. Since they formed in '68, Jethro Tull has always been there, and thankfully for the legions of loyal fans that keep the flame burning brightly, there are no signs of Tull bowing out for some years yet.

This then is not by any means the whole story – merely the first thirty years of Jethro Tull...

CHAPTER ONE
Meanwhile, Back In The Year One

Although 1998 is officially the 30th anniversary of the group Jethro Tull, the story actually starts in 1963, when a group of school friends came together in what was to become, after many personnel shifts, one of the most enduring and creative rock groups in history. It was a time when everybody was in a band, when every town had venues for bands to play, and playing live was what bands did. Yes, it was a long, long time ago!

The Blades were formed in Blackpool by three friends with one major driving ambition, neatly enunciated by the ever articulate Ian Anderson: "It seemed like a great way to attract girls!" This notion had come to Ian and his mate Jeffrey Hammond when they went to see Johnny Breeze and The Atlantics at 'The Holy Family', their local youth club in Blackpool. Ian Anderson:

"There they were, all these fantastic birds, long hair, false eyelashes and things, crowding round this group of scabby, spotty teenagers! Jeffrey had never had a girlfriend in his life, and saw this as his introduction to some kind of feminine attachment. He bought a really cheap bass guitar, and I'd had a guitar since I was eleven, and we started as a three piece, Johnny Kidd type group, playing in front rooms. Little girls came to see us"

The sixteen-year-old Anderson, born in Edinburgh but now "marooned" in Blackpool persuaded Jeffrey Hammond that "he looked like a musician", so a musical association was formed. The third member of this trio was John Evans, then on drums but later to become a key figure in the

Tull story playing keyboards – "Drums seemed like the easiest option at the time; you just had to hit things with sticks!" Anderson was the guitarist as well as singer, but his limited technique led them to enlist the talents of Michael Stephens of The Atlantics, the band that had inspired them in the first place.

Another member of The Atlantics, later to join with Anderson and Co, was Chris Riley, who remembers those early days well:

"They (Ian & Jeffrey) used to come and see us regularly, just as we were getting into R&B and blues, and they too became very interested in it. There was a bit of rivalry and kidology between us, because with all due respect, we were better players than they were at the time. But it never came to fisticuffs or anything. We were just kids. The next thing I knew they formed a band called The Blades. Our bass player Michael Stephens had started palling out with them, so he joined them as guitarist and we had to find another bass player.

I kept in touch with Michael, and we went to see The Blades when they got a gig at a local coffee bar. There was Ian – just singing, I don't think he had a guitar – Michael, John Evans on a tiny drumkit, and Jeffrey Hammond on bass. Jeffrey was kind of like Stu Sutcliffe from The Beatles. He really had to concentrate on pointing his fingers in the right direction. Actually Jeff was sort of on the fringes of it all at the time, I don't think he played very much. Ian wasn't up to much as a player either then, hence the addition of Michael. They used to do a lot of Pretty Things songs, copying almost everything off one of their albums the first time I saw them. They also had a harmonica player in the very early days, a guy called Harry Hartley. He was Bob Dylan before Dylan was – he used to write weird poetry and stuff. He's a bus conductor in Blackpool now!" [One would like to imagine on Route 61.]

We (The Atlantics) were the big band in the area then, playing six or seven nights a week, but I was getting really bored with the material our management insisted we play. Everything was changing then, The Beatles and The Stones were leading the way, and I wanted to play more R&B and blues stuff. I left the band and formed The Hobos with Chris Wooton which featured Glenn Cornick on bass. He was actually Glenn Barnard in those days, but [just to confuse things further] he used to call himself

Glenn Douglas. Douglas was his middle name, and he much preferred that because everybody used to call him Barnyard! I liked Glenn a lot, but we never really hit it off, perhaps because we were too alike. We were both fiery characters, and a bit moody too; we used to have some ding-dongs, me and Glenn. I remember kicking him up the backside on-stage once because he was pratting about. But he was a very good bass player, in a different class to Jeffrey, with all due respect to him. The Hobos used to get some good gigs, playing with people like The Walker Brothers, The Hollies, The Yardbirds etc.

We battled on with The Hobos for a couple of years, then we just ground to a halt, working a lot but with no recording contract. It kind of fell apart. Then in March 1966 I got a message asking if I'd be interested in joining The John Evan Band. I hadn't actually heard them, but we had heard through the grapevine that they were pretty good. They had improved greatly as players, and the music was right up my street. They'd gone from The Blades four-piece to having a rhythm section with a sax and trumpet player, and I was delighted to join them."

The John Evan Band is where the ingredients for Jethro Tull really started to gel - many of the early characters were re-enlisted into the ranks once Tull had hit the big time, including Barrie Barlow who had answered an advert in the *Blackpool Evening Gazette*. How the band arrived at the Jethro Tull moniker shall be revealed in due course, but why 'The John Evan Band?' – recollections vary...

"It wasn't John's band" recalls Ian Anderson, "it was more of a sop to John's mum because she paid for the van and a lot of the equipment". Not so according to Chris Riley who maintains that John was the driving musical force behind the band at the time, and John himself tells a different story:

"It's true that my mum paid for the van and more, but that's got nothing to do with the name. It was Jeffrey who suggested it, I'm quite sure about that. And we decided that The John Evan Band sounded better than The John Evans' Band, so I lost an S from my name! And I was undoubtedly the one who knew most about music in a formal kind of way – keys and harmonies and things like that. I'd been taught to play the piano since about the age of four by my mother. And the headquarters of the band

13

centred at our house; the practice room was our garage. Surprisingly we didn't get many complaints from the neighbours, and in fact many people now claim to have stood outside the garage for hours listening to us. It was different in those days; now the slightest noise will have the Noise Abatement Society on your back, but back then you couldn't walk down the street in Blackpool without hearing guitars and drums coming from every other house."

Chris Riley has fond memories of those practice sessions:

"Mrs Evans still lives in the same house; I pass it twice a week and never fail to think about those sessions – we made quite an impressive sound. John had wanted to get off drums and play keyboards, so Barrie Barlow had arrived on the scene. Barrie and I were the only ones who had a job, and therefore money. Needless to say we bought the beer and the fags. Ian was forever tapping fags off people – he was as tight as a duck's arse, never putting his hand in his pocket!"

With the new line-up and a handful of gigs, the John Evan Band roped in a local electrician as their agency manager, one Johnny Taylor. The official studio photo of the band, taken before Riley joined, was doctored with the addition of his head and shoulders, and was christened "the seven heads and twelve legs" picture! One unfortunate chap who was not in the photo was Ernie Robinson, who had declined an invitation to join the band with the classic comment "I'm sorry Ian, but I can't see myself making any money with you!"

The seven piece John Evan Band were in demand in 1966, sometimes playing seven nights a week. Hits of the day were played grudgingly, but the bulk of the set was the blues and R&B that had brought them together in the first instance; Sonny Terry and Brownie McGhee, James Brown and Graham Bond were among the main influences, although as sax player Tony Wilkinson recalled:

"It often didn't work when we played the stuff we wanted to play. Most of the time the music was just a backdrop for the local girls to gyrate about to with their boyfriends, so we had to play current material. I remember doing a lot of Tamla Motown stuff like "Knock On Wood", which we thought was crap. There were a few gigs that were great, where we would get a really receptive audience, but until we graduated to the university circuit we had to play stuff we didn't like. I do remember though the three boat clubs in Nottingham – The Britannia, The Trent and The Union – where we shared the stage with people like Graham Bond, Jack Bruce, Dick Heckstall-Smith and John Mayall. They were heady days, and big news for us because they were doing the material that we really admired."

Tragically, Tony Wilkinson was killed in a motorcycle accident in 1990, but a year earlier he had recalled some of the adolescent characters in the band.

"Jeff Hammond was a bit odd, I thought. He was hard work because he wasn't very forthcoming, and a lot of his eccentricities seemed to me to be simply due to bad manners and an inability to communicate – as it is with most eccentrics. He never did anything particularly constructive or useful or profound in any way. He just arrived, played, moped about very moodily and then we dropped him off at home. That was it."

John Evans was never an easy character – in fact, like Jeff, he was hard work. He perfected the art of being rude, and he always played gormless. But he was very placid; he'd just go along with things. He did all the driving, everywhere we went, which was the cause of some concern on several occasions. The van was always breaking down, it would take for-ever to get to some gigs, and we'd be on a motorway when we heard him snoring – whilst driving! Nobody was allowed to drive this bloody van except John – he was obsessed with it. He was absolutely like a man pos-sessed when driving that van. The only things he reacted to were traffic lights and policemen, and then there was some response! He was very docile in lots of other respects, and very, very intelligent. He was grossly underestimated and dismissed by the majority of people, us included, be-cause it was just too difficult to actually get through to him.

Barrie Barlow and I never really got on; in fact we used to hate each other with a passion. Perhaps we were just too young at the time? We had some stinking rows, and he was like a little terrier, he just wouldn't let go. He was quite a handy little lad actually. I remember one night driving to the Club A Go-Go in Newcastle; I was in the front of the van and he was behind me. We were passing remarks as usual and we eventually ended up having a fist fight across the two seats while John was trying to drive the bloody van! Barrie was a confused little bugger really. He had family problems at the time and lacked security, which manifested itself in basic aggression. I didn't understand what that was all about, so I was aggressive back to him – a real base reaction. And also, because I was the biggest in the band I was always the one who went to whoever was paying us to actually get paid. A big balls ache with being in a little band is that no bastard ever wants to pay you, and I'm sure Barrie thought I was working the cash, and that John, "Elvo" and myself were doing a three-way split and giving the rest of them the change!

But Barrie was a knockout drummer. He was very inventive, and never afraid to try anything new. He used to practice really hard, which none of the others did really; we were always too knackered!"

"Elvo" was not a mysterious new member of the band, but none other than Ian Anderson, who had gained said nickname after an enthusiastic punter had burst backstage at the Warrington Co-op Hall to enthuse to Ian – "Man, you sound just like Elvo!" A puzzled band asked for elucidation, and they were rewarded with "Elvo – the King.... Elvis!". The name stuck for years afterwards.

Barrie Barlow had held down a 'proper' job for the early part of his time with the band, but the constant gigging and subsequent late arrivals at work forced his hand to decide between a steady job and a career as a musician. He chose music.

"I think we were on the princely sum of £2 a week then, and I became a full-time part of the various versions of the band – The Blades, The John Evan Band, The John Evan Big Band Sound, The John Evan Smash and so on. I can't remember how and why The Blades became The John Evan Band.... around that time there were a lot of organ orientated bands – Georgie Fame, Graham Bond, Brian Auger – and it just seemed that all the bands were named after their keyboard player. So we got a Hammond organ and called ourselves The John Evan Band. Simple as that!

The reason I'd started playing was because of The Beatles, it was a sort of a fashionable thing, and when I met these guys it was bluesy stuff. Then along came this album with Ginger Baker, Dick Heckstall-Smith

16

and Jack Bruce on it, called *Sound Of '65* by Graham Bond. We learned that entire album and used to play three quarters of it in the set. That was when I really became serious about playing. The band lasted for a few years, with so many line-up changes, but I can honestly say that at any given time it was a pretty good band. When we were playing other people's material it was a truly collective band, with no leader as such, though of course later on Ian's talents really emerged.

I actually left the band for a while when Tony Wilkinson joined, because it seemed like he took over everything and was calling the shots. We didn't get on anyway, and I couldn't see that he deserved to be calling the shots, because he wasn't very good musically. Ian was, John was, but not Tony. I only realised much later the reason for our conflict was that he had the hots for the girl I was dating at the time; he married her eventually! So I can understand the problem now."

Jeffrey Hammond left the band in 1966 to go to Art College, and his place was eventually taken by Glenn Cornick. Chris Riley departed soon after - "When the van blew up and all our money went on repairing it I'd had enough!" - and another Scot, Neil Smith, answered the ad. in the *Manchester Evening News* and duly took up the guitarists slot after watching them play at the Bolton Beachcomber. Neil Smith:

"Ian Anderson showed me the chord sequence of a Jimmy Smith song called 'The Cat', and I just played along and improvised. They were playing the kind of music I really liked, and it felt great playing with them, so I was in the band. Two other guys that were in the band then, Bo Ward (bass) and Ritchie Dharma (drums), left shortly after I joined, and they actually approached me to join them in forming a new band with a different singer; they didn't think Ian was commercial enough! I thought they were crazy, but they went ahead and left, so Barrie Barlow was quickly recruited again, and then Glenn Cornick."

The band continued to gig constantly, and even managed a "Firstimers" TV appearance for Granada on 24th May '67, performing an early Anderson composition "Take The Easy Way Home", earning themselves a glowing and somewhat prophetic tribute from John Hemp, then head of Granada's light entertainment: "These boys are certainly the best I have heard so far, and I think they stand a good chance of making the grade". If only Decca had employed him in their A&R department when The Beatles were touting....

   They also recorded a handful of songs in various studios, some of which still exist somewhere on an acetate, but no records were released. [One of the tracks, "Aeroplane", was released as the B-side to the first Jethro Tull (Toe) single, and another, "Letting You Go", eventually surfaced many years later on a Derek Lawrence compilation CD, having been retitled "Blues For The 18th"]. Ian Anderson remembers one of their first studio sessions, at Studio 2, Abbey Road:

> "Going into a studio was actually very frightening. We arrived there in the van at midnight so as not to be late for the session. We actually spent the night sleeping in the van, which was parked outside the main door in front of the studios. At the crack of dawn the commissionaire scuttled us in through the back door. I think that session was for Derek Lawrence. He kept telling us about this guitarist that he really wanted us to get together with. He kept on and on at us to work with him, telling us what a great player he was, and it felt like we were being promoted to be some sort of backing band to this whiz kid guitarist. Anyway, we'd never heard of him, so we didn't take much notice. Ritchie Blackmore was his name!"

   In a bid to break into the big time the band decided it was time to head south to London. It was "a last ditch attempt to make a living playing music", recalls Anderson. "We owed a lot of money to friends and relatives who had helped us buy equipment, and it was getting a bit serious. We had come to the end of the road in the north of England, and we had to have a crack at the emerging blues scene in London". It was a commitment that Neil Smith was unwilling to make, and he reluctantly decided to hang on to the security of his home and job rather than risk the uncertain future of the John Evan Band. Neil Smith:

> "After I left, I felt a real sense of freedom after being ground down, playing the same stuff over and over again and trying to work five days a week. Part of the problem was that I was based in Bolton and most of the others were based in Blackpool, so we never got to rehearse, we were not

a close unit. I think it might have worked out differently if I'd developed with them, and we'd hit it off better. I did admire Ian as a singer and a writer, and I always knew he would make a success of something. I wasn't actually sure it would be in music, though I should have known it I guess. He was always in control of things, he always knew what he was doing, and he had a plan to create a more English sound rather than just follow the American styles. And of course he eventually did just that!"

He didn't know it at the time, but Neil Smith would become involved in the Jethro Tull story many years later. In 1990, after discussions with *A New Day*, a limited edition CD was produced of a John Evan Band concert in 1966, which Neil had taped "to learn the songs properly". The quality is not great, but it is a remarkably fascinating insight into the origins of the band.

The early days in London were grim. Glenn Cornick was living in relative luxury with his parents who had moved to London themselves and were able to offer him his home comforts. Anderson however found himself living in a bed-sit for three months "on the verge of starvation". A part-time job, cleaning the toilets in the Ritz Cinema in Luton for £1 per day, kept him in rent money until his fortunes changed within the music business, with the band which was about to emerge as the first line-up of Jethro Tull.

A new guitarist was required, and Smith's replacement was to prove a crucial element in the establishment of the band's reputation as a hot live act. By this time they had been picked up by the management team of Chris Wright and Terry Ellis, and it was Wright who pointed them in the direction of Mick Abrahams, a guitarist who had established a fine reputation already. Abrahams was playing in the three piece called McGregor's Engine, when bassist Andy Pyle suddenly decided to take a three month break, so he was easily persuaded to join the band, and they subsequently based themselves in his home town of Luton. After just a few weeks most of the guys had had enough and went back home, and Mick drafted in his friend and former colleague in McGregor's Engine, Clive Bunker on drums. Abrahams was a major influence on the music the band were playing, and John Evans became disillusioned with it:

"I loved the original black artists, but I felt uncomfortable trying to play it myself. And I was fed up living in bed-sits, and I couldn't see any way in the foreseeable future that I'd be earning enough with the band to improve my lot. Ian was becoming quite single-minded in his purpose of making it in the rock business, but I wasn't so committed. I took the cowards way out and went back to live with my mum, and back to college to make up for the fact that I'd failed all my 'O' levels because we were out driving all over the country every night."

Tony Wilkinson stuck with the Anderson/Abrahams/Bunker/Cornick line-up for a few months, but recalled the moment he decided to leave:

"I remember thinking even then – and I was only 17 – that one way or another Elvo was going to make it, because it was impossible for that much talent to remain undetected for any length of time. I thought that as a band we might have some success, but I knew that I wasn't good enough to be in a band of that standing. It takes more than just musical ability. It takes a great deal of basic acumen and durability and determination to achieve any level of success, certainly in the music business. And I wasn't the creative influence in the band, Elvo was, and I think it was obvious to all of us. He wrote the material, he came up with what was effectively the melody. He would draw on the variability and creative ability of the rest of the band, but in truth he could have drawn on another half dozen people in some other band and still achieved the same level of success. So it wasn't to do with us, it was to do with him in its entirety; the band was purely peripheral to his abilities.

Not only from a composing point of view, but also from a consistency of performance point of view. You've got to turn out immaculate performances on every occasion. Elvo was able to do that, but I wasn't. Other members of the band were able to do it too.... John Evans was, Barrie Barlow certainly was, and Neil Smith too. Mick Abrahams was a brilliant guitarist, better than anyone we had previously experienced or seen. Had I stayed with what was then the transition band from The John Evan Band to Jethro Tull it would not have been long before either Elvo and the rest of the band, or some management team or recording manager would have decided that the baritone sax player was not an asset to the band! I knew I had to leave."

The four remaining band members decided to fulfil the bookings outstanding for the John Evan Band, even though they were now a blues band, playing soul gigs originally booked for a seven-piece. Anderson would visit the Ellis/Wright agency several times a week to "sit in their office and embarrass them into finding us a few gigs. They were still selling us as the seven-piece band, and they didn't find out for several weeks that we were reduced to four!"

CHAPTER TWO
This Was Jethro TOE!

The change of name to Jethro Tull was not immediate. Ian Anderson maintains that their management used to book them under different names because they were so bad that they could not get a return booking under the previous name! All the evidence of course suggests that they were not bad at all, but it's certainly true that the band was blessed or cursed with tags such as "Navy Blue", "Ian Henderson's Bag o' Nails", "Bag o' Blues" "Candy Coloured Rain" and many more. As Ian recalls, "We never knew what we were called from one night to the next. We would arrive at the gig, check the names on the poster, and whoever we didn't recognise had to be us! If we were booked to play a club that had booked us a couple of weeks before, we tried to make sure we wore different clothes in the hope they wouldn't recognise us!"

However, they were certainly good enough to encourage the producer Derek Lawrence to get them into a studio to cut their first single, a Mick Abrahams song called "Sunshine Day", backed by an Anderson/Cornick composition (wrongly credited to Anderson and Len Barnard), "Aeroplane", which was actually one of the John Evan Band studio cuts with the saxophones mixed out. (It is a little known fact that vocals on "Aeroplane" were shared between Anderson and Tony Wilson of Hot Chocolate fame). They had to have a name for the band to go on the record, and from a very long list they eventually chose Jethro Tull, a name suggested to them by a Chrysalis booking agent. Abrahams recalls that the booker explained who Tull was (an 18th century agriculturist) and all agreed it was a good name. Bunker, on the other hand, remembers that after hours of debate "any old name would do!". They differ too on the reason behind the bizarre mis-credit on the record label to Jethro Toe. "We had all agreed on Jethro Tull" says Mick, "but Derek Lawrence obviously misheard it as Jethro Toe – it was simply a mistake on his part". Clive Bunker – "No, Derek heard it right, but he said Jethro Toe would be better, so that's what he put on the record. It wasn't a mistake.... well, not in the sense that he'd mis-heard it! But the actual production of the record, that's another matter!" Glenn Cornick concurs – "Derek Lawrence didn't like the name Jethro Tull. He knew what it was supposed to be but he didn't think it was cool enough. I remember arguing with him about it. It wasn't a misprint. We recorded some other tracks with him, when we were using the name Candy Coloured Rain; "My Green Tambourine" and "The Man" were two I remember, and some others with titles that escape me now".

The truth is that it was partly a mistake and partly deliberate, as Derek Lawrence explains:

"It was my fault. They gave me the name over the phone and I thought they'd said 'Jethro Toe'. That was the name I'd heard and liked, so when the mistake was discovered I didn't really want to change it. It was too late anyway really, because all the details had gone to MGM and it was all ready to go."

MGM released the single in February '68. It sold so few copies that the name change debacle did not matter anyway. Derek Lawrence's associa-tion with the band began and ended with that first single when he was sub-sequently "blown out by Terry Ellis and Chris Wright", but not before he had imparted some good advice to the fledgling group. "I told them to stop trying to be Sounds Incorporated and become a proper rock band!" Inci-dentally, Derek has searched high and low for the other five tracks re-corded under the name Candy Coloured Rain but has so far unearthed nothing. He is convinced they are somewhere within the vaults at EMI, and Tull fans everywhere live in hope that he might one day rediscover these lost gems.

Undeterred by this spectacular first failure the band continued to play anywhere and everywhere they could throughout the year, securing a coveted residency at the Marquee Club along the way, and building up a strong following throughout the country. Ian Anderson was already blossoming into a great songwriter, and his stage persona became ever more prominent, with the trademark manic acrobatics and one-legged flute playing wowing audiences everywhere. Nobody can actually recall the exact moment when Ian picked up on the flute, but Ian remembers why he did it:

"There was a school of thought that said Mick Abrahams should be the front man, and I should shuffle off to the back of the stage and play rhythm guitar. I wasn't having that obviously, but as Mick was clearly a far better guitarist than I was, I had to find something else I could do. I thought about a violin or a flute. I was assured the flute was easier to play, and of course I could fit it in my pocket which meant I didn't have to lug a load of equipment about with me, so that's what I went for!"

Glenn Cornick relates a different, more pragmatic story:

"Someone in Blackpool owed Ian some money. I went with Ian in the van to collect the money, but the guy couldn't pay up. He did have a flute which he offered to Ian in lieu of cash, and that's how he acquired his flute."

Another striking aspect of Anderson's stage persona was his shabby overcoat, an ever-present item of attire both on and off stage. "It was more a way of life than a stage image. The fact that I was living in a freezing cold bed-sit, and the coat kept me warm. I would have to sleep in it sometimes so it wasn't so unusual to wear it through the day, even when we were performing".

All the hard work paid off when, just one week after recording their first radio session for John Peel's *Top Gear*, Tull played the Sunbury Jazz and Blues Festival that August, spectacularly stealing the show from the heavyweight name bands on the bill. The reception they got on the day was rapturous, and the music press followed suit with glowing reviews. Glenn Cornick remembers it well:

"Before that festival we must have played 300 gigs in a year, never getting more than £20 a night, all over the bloody country playing all those little clubs that were around then. We played every club in Britain. We got to play face to face to everyone who was interested in that kind of music and we became very popular on that scene, and it was as if they had all turned up to see us at Sunbury! Nobody in the audience knew who was going on in what order, but before we were even announced John Gee walked on-stage with a carrier bag full of Ian's flutes and claghorns and so on, and the whole audience stood up and cheered. It was one of the best moments of my life. Before then we were a small band, but from that moment on we were a big band. There was no question in any of our minds after that, we were going to make it".

Anderson concurs:

"We hadn't realised, until we went on stage, just how popular we really were. We had not realised that all of those people out there had seen us two or three times before in the months preceding the festival. It was terrifying going out to play to such a huge audience, and it was overwhelming to find that most of them already knew us. I can honestly say we got the most genuine reception at the festival, simply because we played to those people 'in the flesh' more often than the bigger names on the bill".

One member of that audience was Martin Barre, who was later to become a major player in the Tull story:

"Tull were without doubt the group of the festival simply because nobody else was doing anything like it. They were absolutely astounding to watch, both musically and visually. As a guitarist myself I was there mainly to see and hear Mick Abrahams, who was a great player and had a great, magnetic on-stage persona, but Ian too was such an amazing performer it was obvious they were destined for great things".

Another witness on that day also destined to star in this story, David Palmer, arrived at the opinion that, "There is something that is really unique... if ever a band is going to do something, it is Jethro Tull".

Palmer soon found himself working with this very special band, much to his surprise. He was an established musical arranger with a classical background, and had started to work within the pop music field. In the late summer of '68 he was working as a ghost music writer for an English filmmaker at Sound Techniques in Chelsea. Ian Anderson and Terry Ellis were checking out the studio, and asked the engineer there if he could recommend a music writer to help with their debut album. Ellis subsequently called Palmer and commissioned him to write some parts "for horns". As David explains – "Horns, to me at that time, meant French horns. So I thought he wanted French horns for music by Strauss or Mahler and so on. When he told me the name of the group – Jethro Tull – I could have fallen through the floor!"

David met Ian and Terry Ellis, played them a selection of horns and trumpet sounds, and having found what Ian was looking for went into the studio to put horns on Mick Abrahams' song "Move On Alone". Bizarrely, Mick didn't know horns had been added to his song until the finished album came out! Palmer recalls how Anderson impressed him at that first encounter;

> "We did the first take and went upstairs into the control room to listen to it. There was a wrong note somewhere, and Ian spotted it immediately. I knew then he was OK, I could work with him".

A few weeks later David was called in again, at only a few hours notice, to write a string arrangement for "A Christmas Song", which was later released as the B-side to their third single. It was the start of a long-standing musical relationship, though David did not actually become a fully-fledged band member for some years after.

Island Records had won the race to sign this hot new band, as Cornick recalls:

> "Before Sunbury nobody had ever written a bloody word about us. After Sunbury every music paper was tearing the doors down to get to us and every record company in Britain made us an offer. We had already talked to Island, but nobody else had shown an interest. Spooky Tooth had recommended to Island that they come and see us, and it was through that we signed for them, because they were closest to what we were trying to do".

This Was, the first Tull album, was released on Island Records in October 1968, and helped by their outstanding reputation on the live circuit, it
was an instant success, reaching number 10 in the UK chart. A heady mixture of rock, blues, jazz and (comparatively) virtuoso playing, it was further distinguished from the contemporary sounds of the day by Ian's
extraordinary flute playing, given full reign on the album with the cover of
Roland Kirk's "Serenade To A Cuckoo". The stage favourite "Cat's
Squirrel" had become Mick Abrahams' tour-de-force, and Clive Bunker
got to have a good thrash on "Dharma For One".

It was a strange mixture, and perhaps already pointed to tensions and
musical diversities within the band. Sure, it was 'the blues', but then it
was so much more than that too. Ian Anderson claims, with some justifica-
tion, credit for foresight in naming the album *This Was,* for very soon Tull
were making music which was a million miles removed from those early
blues roots. Another far sighted aspect of the album was the strange cover
photo, featuring the band made up to look like very old men – how many
other bands can honestly claim thirty years on to look younger than they
did on their first album?

"A Song For Jeffrey" was taken from the album for a single release,
backed with "One For John Gee", a tribute to the manager of the Marquee
Club who had shown such faith in them previously. It didn't chart, but the
follow up in November, the non-album track "Love Story" slipped in at
number 29, the first of a series of hit singles in the early stages of the
band's career. It was also the final contribution from guitarist Abrahams.

Relationships within the band, particularly between Abrahams and Anderson, had been strained for some time. With two such strong personalities pulling in opposite directions something had to give. The years have
perhaps dulled the memories of the circumstances surrounding Mick's departure. Anderson claims he was sacked from the band because he was not
committed enough to breaking the band, refusing to work more than four
or five nights a week, and blowing out a couple of gigs for no reason. He
recalls one particular incident when Mick had called them at the last m-
inute to pull out of a gig due to illness, only to be spotted by the rest of the
band outside a cinema later that evening. The crunch came with the offer

of a US tour, which was not greeted with great enthusiasm by Mick. The other members decided they had to think about finding another guitarist with the same degree of commitment as themselves, and an acrimonious split ensued. Abrahams pleads guilty to some, but not all charges:

> "Yeah, I got the boot, but I was about to leave anyway. Terry Ellis found out I was going to quit, so he called me into his office to fire me! I've never forgiven him for that. But looking back, maybe I wasn't committed enough. I've never been one for being away from home for a long time, and I never fancied the thought of gigging every night of the week. But I did want to break the band, go to America and all the rest of it.... but maybe I just didn't want to do it with Ian. Initially I liked Ian a lot, but after a while it became obvious that there was no trust between us, and our relationship deteriorated dramatically. I think it was caused more by him than me, but in an effort to get my own back I did do one or two stupid things.
>
> The worst thing, the most wrong thing I've ever done in my life, was when I actually refused to go to a gig. I had to put my foot down because I was so pissed off with all the bullshit and the whole attitude that I just said 'Right – bollocks! I'm just not going to do it!' It was the only way I could think of at the time to fight back, but it was a pretty nasty way of doing it. And that one thing got me branded with a whole lot of other things".

That incident had occurred after the Sunbury gig but before the album was recorded. Within two months of the release of *This Was* Abrahams had left, picking up the blues theme that Tull was leaving behind with his new band Blodwyn Pig, leaving Tull without a guitarist on the eve of their first American tour. Hasty auditions were held, with Tony Iommi, later of Black Sabbath, landing the job. Tony and his band Earth, who later became Black Sabbath, had done a show with Tull the night Mick Abrahams left, and he had noticed that something strange was going on:

> "They were passing each other notes on stage - Mick was giving Ian notes saying 'I'm leaving' and so on! They asked me that night if I'd be interested in the job. I told the rest of the lads in Earth, and they all said I should take the job, and not worry about them. Later, I got a call to come

down to London for the auditions, just as a formality. I went, and it was packed with people - I remember seeing Martin Barre there, and Davy O'List from The Nice. There were so many people there I couldn't stand it, so I actually walked out to go back home. One of the group ran out after me to get me back in, promising they would get to me in a minute. So I did the audition and got the job".

Inaccurate press reports at the time claimed that O'List had joined Jethro Tull, but clearly that was not the case. Anderson has since claimed that Iommi was only ever taken on to stand in for a TV special that was imminent, but that's not how Tony remembers it:

"I joined the band as a full member, there was no question of being a stand-in. But it just didn't work out. We had started rehearsing, and Ian was writing loads of stuff, and although I liked all the lads in Jethro Tull it felt a funny situation to be in after being with a load of people I knew so well. Geezer Butler had come with me to the rehearsals, and I told him that I felt uncomfortable in the new surroundings. He said to give it more time, but after a few days I spoke to Ian and told him I didn't feel right about it. It wasn't a problem with the music or the guys in Tull, but I just felt uncomfortable within myself, being in such a new situation. I was so used to hanging around with everyone, but the Tull lads seemed to be separate in some ways. Clive and Glen would be together, but Ian would be sitting at another table which seemed alien to me. The first time we went to eat, I sat at a table with Ian, thinking we were all together - but apparently we were not! I don't like situations like that. If it's going to be a band, it's got to be a band together.

Ian was very polite to me and we had no problems at all, but there was a vibe with him and the other guys at the time. We'd all be talking away together, and then Ian would walk in and they would all shut up. I saw the same thing happen some years later when Sabbath did a gig with Tull in America. It was very strange.

Anyway, I told Ian I wanted to leave and he asked me to give it a bit more time. I told him I knew it wasn't going to work out, I just didn't feel comfortable with the gig. He said OK, but asked me to stay on to do the Stones TV thing, which of course I did".

So his stay was a short one, but was captured for posterity when he 'played' guitar with Tull on the Rolling Stones' *Rock 'n' Roll Circus* TV special. In fact only Ian was singing live, the rest of the band miming to a pre-recorded backing track of "A Song For Jeffrey". So whilst Tony Iommi's influence on Jethro Tull was ultimately non-existent, his brief presence within Tull helped shape Black Sabbath into the hugely successful band they were to become, as Tony explains:

"I am actually grateful to Tull in a lot of ways, because it taught me a lot of things about the way our band worked. We had been a bit half-hearted about rehearsals and stuff. Tull were so strict about rehearsals - "Be there at 9 am or else!" - I'd never experienced that before. But it was a really good attitude, and I went back to Sabbath with that same attitude. So my time with Tull taught me a sense of responsibility and authority which I was able to pass onto the rest of the lads to get ourselves on the way. It really helped us a lot."

The permanent replacement was finally found after an almost surreal audition by Martin Barre. Although he had not landed the gig at his first attempt, Ian Anderson had been sufficiently impressed to invite him back for another audition when Tony Iommi left. He turned up with an electric guitar but no amplification, and Ian tried to listen to his playing by putting his ear as close to the guitar as possible! His playing must have been impressive, for in spite of the bizarre circumstances Barre was invited to join the band.

His baptism of fire started on 30th December 1968 at The Winter Gardens in Penzance, and three weeks later they were in New York supporting Blood Sweat and Tears, having sandwiched a couple of gigs in Stockholm the week before (recorded for radio and TV), supporting Jimi Hendrix, apparently at Jimi's insistence. As Martin puts it, "It was terrifying anyway stepping into a band as big as Tull, so imagine being a guitarist in that situation playing on the same bill as Hendrix! It's possible that I was so nervous that I stopped worrying about what I was doing, and just got on with it through sheer terror".

"He was certainly terrified of me", says Anderson. For the first year he was with us, he thought I was a homosexual, because of the way we would camp it up to tease him!"

The following months were taken up with extensive touring, supporting the likes of Led Zeppelin and Vanilla Fudge. It was an important stepping stone towards the big time, but it was not a pleasant experience as Anderson recalls:

> "It certainly wasn't the glamorous life that people might imagine. We supported a lot of very good groups, but in the thirteen weeks we were there we had a lot of bad luck. We were all ill at various times, and we never had any money. We couldn't go out, we couldn't even eat properly. But of course it did us a lot of good in the long term, particularly when we were supporting Led Zeppelin on a lot of shows. They were very good to us and for us, and it's fair to say that without them we would not have had the success we did. Of course later on we were able to help other British bands in the same way, like Yes and Gentle Giant for example, which was a pleasure to do".

Eventually they took time out from touring to record that all important second album. In the interim, whilst in America the Ellis/Wright agency – or Chrysalis, as they were now titled - had told Ian to "write a hit single". The result, the classic "Living In The Past", was released in the UK in May, duly reaching the dizzy heights of number 3 in the charts. There were the inevitable cries of "sell out" from the precious underground movement, but Tull were delighted with the apparent crossover success of their music. Ian Anderson:

> "We are not ashamed to have a hit single and do *Top Of The Pops* – if it brings our music to a younger audience it can only be a good thing. It's good to have our singles played on the radio. We don't care if people don't like what they hear, but at least they will have the opportunity to hear it and to make up their own minds. But despite our current single success, they are not our priority. Playing live is the most important thing for us, then the albums, and then singles."

Anderson re-iterated that opinion some years later, when reflecting on the string of hit singles that Tull had enjoyed:

"We never, ever saw ourselves as a singles band. We had several hits, but then all of the other 'serious' groups had them as well. Family, Spooky Tooth, Fleetwood Mac, John Mayall etc. It wasn't a case of picking songs that were specifically aimed at the commercial singles market. We all had hit singles because we had a lot of fans, and they wanted to buy those songs. But for us, and those other groups, it was not important, we never thought we needed to have a hit single".

In June they made their first, memorable appearance on *Top Of The Pops* alongside more clean cut types such as Cliff Richard, who later confessed to the music press to being "very impressed with Ian Anderson, he's a very intelligent guy. We got on really well". Older viewers were not so impressed with their outrageous appearance, giving further credibility to Jethro Tull in the ever-present generation wars and thus enhancing their teen-appeal!

In July 1969 the second Jethro Tull album, *Stand Up*, entered the UK chart at number 1, giving Island Records their first chart-topping album. It was an amazing collection, still broadly based in the blues idiom but reflecting a bewildering array of influences. Martin Barre showed himself to be a worthy successor to guitar hero Mick Abrahams, and Anderson's songwriting had matured incredibly in the few months since *This Was*. The departure of Abrahams meant that Jethro Tull was now indisputably Ian Anderson's band, and he demonstrated a clarity of vision in his writing that was to take Tull where no other band was heading. All the material was written by Anderson, with the exception of J.S.Bach's "Bouree". This was not credited as such on the original album, an omission which a slightly embarrassed Anderson was to justify latterly with the observation that a blues/rock band in '69 couldn't own up to playing classical music!

The hectic touring schedule was hardly interrupted by recording commitments, and Tull continued to shuttle back and forth across the Atlantic to consolidate and build upon their growing reputation, to the extent that they were soon able to say goodbye to support slots and undertake their first headlining tour of America. Strangely, this breakthrough was not greeted with great enthusiasm by the band. Ian Anderson:

"We were actually very reluctant to headline a tour. We preferred to be second on the bill because it was fun, and the possibility of playing better than the top group was exciting. When you're top of the bill the only way is down and you find yourself facing the possibility of being blown off-stage by the support". And some of the audiences in America were not to his liking; "I wasn't prepared for people who were out of their minds, flaked out on the floor or dancing around like lunatics. I didn't like strobe lights in my face, and I hated hippies! Of course people who saw me jumping around on-stage thought I was on every drug under the sun, but that was not the case."

It is certainly true that his stage antics, the wild cavorting and twirling, the bug-eyed glares, and the mass of unkempt hair, horrified parents the world over, but beneath the stage persona there was always a very intelligent and articulate artist with an intense respect for his art. In complete contrast to his overtly hippy and bohemian appearance, Ian became evermore introverted and distant from the other members of the band. Clive Bunker:

"In the three years I was with the band he certainly went into himself more, which is understandable really. I would hate to have been in his position where he was the front man, the key man. All the pressures of the band were on him, because he wrote all the stuff. On a tour he'd be the one that would supposedly go to bed early, but in fact he would go back to his hotel to start writing so that we would have a store of stuff ready for when we got back."

One important gig that summer was at the prestigious Newport Jazz Festival, playing alongside such legends as Ray Charles, Woody Herman and Roland Kirk as well as other major rock bands like Zeppelin, Jeff Beck, Ten Years After and Blood Sweat and Tears. Initially Ian had not been over keen on the idea:

"I'm a bit worried about it. I'm not really sure what they are trying to do. It will be really good, but I don't think you can mix it up that much. Seeing us might upset the people who have come to see Woody Herman or Roland Kirk, and they might upset the people who are there to see us and the other rock groups. It is good to bring new and old music together, but I'm a bit worried about it all".

He need not have worried, for it was a tremendous success. Glenn Cornick:

"Yeah, it was a great gig. I remember playing on the same bill as Roland Kirk, who Ian was always accused of copying. Roland Kirk was really thrilled to meet us, and pleased that Ian was doing all that stuff because it had made him famous! We had a good time with him. The Newport Festival was interesting because it was the first year they'd had any sort of rock music on, so we were breaking new ground there.

The way America worked in those days, you established yourself on the coasts – New York, Boston, San Francisco and Los Angeles – and then worked inwards from there. Hence we played a small club in Boston called The Tea Party, but it was a very important gig. Once you had those first four places covered you could spread into the other markets and get a little buzz going about you. But it was tough at first. Touring if you're not working every day is shitty, depressing. There was no momentum at all to that tour, and I guarantee we lost money, but it broke us in certain markets so that we could go back the next time and do better. Later tours were a lot more fun".

In September, Tull went to Ireland for the first time, and during the show in Dublin, Anderson's famous old greatcoat, a home-leaving present from his father and now a Tull trademark, was stolen by fans. It was to be many, many years before Tull returned to Ireland!

In October of '69 Tull released another single, "Sweet Dream"/"17", which again charted in the UK, at number 9. Significantly it was the first release on the fledgling Chrysalis label, founded specifically for Jethro Tull. The relationship has continued to the present day, a remarkable association in the music industry, although the dilution of Chrysalis in recent years into the EMI group means that Jethro Tull themselves have outlasted one of the major independent labels of the last three decades!

The next Tull single was also a significant landmark, as it marked the reappearance of John Evans as guest keyboard player. "The Witches Promise"/"Teacher" hit number 4 in the UK chart, as did the third album, *Benefit* in April. John Evans was again invited to play on the album, which was another shift in direction for this increasingly eclectic group. The blues influence had all but disappeared, and although it was clearly a rock album there was a further leaning towards introspection from Ian, where he expressed through song his feelings of growing up amongst a generation he felt he didn't belong with. The music did indeed benefit from the presence of, and the extra dimension afforded by, John Evans on keyboards, and the complex and intricate arrangements hinted at the genesis of future grandiose concepts.

Another noticeable addition to the Jethro Tull sound was the use of electronic gadgetry to produce artificial synthesised sounds, with varying degrees of success. Anderson reflects on those experiments with the experience of an older and much wiser musician:

"It was actually a bit silly really. It was at a point where we thought we might be drying up, and tried to come up with something different. We fell into the trap of using the studio to make 'clever' noises, which were actually not that good. And if they were good, The Beatles had done it before anyway. It's too easy, when you are young, to get carried away in the studio and to do things that really aren't worth doing just because you can".

After "Witches Promise" Tull decided to stop pursuing hit singles, claiming they were not having the desired effect. Ian told the *NME*:

"We sell more albums than we do singles and we have found that most of the singles were being bought by people who had already bought the album. So we were not reaching two different audiences, they were overlapping. And we don't want to get caught up into thinking that we have to have hit singles because it becomes a burden to remain alive in terms of chart success. We will still issue singles from albums so that radio has

35

something to play, but they will be to promote interest in the album – we would rather they didn't make the singles chart"!

His wish was granted when "Inside"/"Alive and Well and Living In", both taken from *Benefit*, failed to chart. The addition of a keyboard player was a major step for the band, and came as something of a surprise after Anderson's comments in *Melody Maker* late in '69:

> "I'd hate to add a piano or organ. I want to learn them anyway, and if we had a proper musician I'd have no reason to learn. I'm learning piano, organ, balalaika, mandolin and guitar, and so we already have a sufficiently large variety of musical instruments to use".

Clearly he had something of a rethink, perhaps realising that as the singer, flautist, writer, acoustic guitarist and now producer it might not be such a bad move to leave the keyboards to somebody else! The fact that John Evans was "a musical virgin" as Ian announced him in the press was as significant as was the long-standing friendship between the pair.

> "If John hadn't joined I can't think of anyone else we would have asked. We would have remained a four-piece. I would feel uncomfortable about getting in a 'name' keyboard player who had played with lots of other groups. If people already knew him, knew his music, I would have to try to accommodate his style into the group, whereas John hasn't really changed the sound too much because most of the new songs were written for guitar and keyboards. That's what Martin Barre has been playing until now. We have been heaping a lot of responsibility onto him, having to play chordal accompaniments and solos as well. Martin has improved so much since John joined, just through having to play only what he wanted to play, and having more time to think about his own playing within the music as a whole in the live context. He is certainly a lot freer, and so am I. Everyone can relax a little bit more with the addition of one more player, one more solo voice."

John's association with Tull was not initially intended to be permanent. He was studying, and excelling, at the Chelsea College of Science, and his only connection with the band then was that he was living in the same flats as Ian. He was therefore ideally situated when Ian asked him to guest on the album, adding overdubs in the evenings after studies. It was during rehearsals in Germany that Anderson decided to offer John a full role in the band:

"Ian called from Germany and said they really wanted to play some of the new songs on stage, but they couldn't do it without keyboards – would I do it? I didn't know what to do. I was doing really well at college, I'd come top in all the exams, won all the book prizes and so on, and for once in my life I seemed to be doing something successfully on my own efforts. I spoke to my tutor about it, and he convinced me I should go for it – 'Look, it's pop music, there's a lot of money in it! Do it for a couple of years, make some money and invest it or buy a house, and come back and get your degree'. So I joined, supposedly for a year or two. It was a fantastic experience, and I went a little crazy initially. I'd never been outside of England before, and suddenly, just weeks after taking my Easter exams as a student, I was playing to thousands of people at the Long Beach Coliseum! For weeks I was bubbling, talking too much (with excitement) and drinking far too much. This was the life!"

Inspired by one of the Marx Brothers, John bought his famous white suit, perfected his clown-like stage persona, and his "year or two" became ten years with one of the biggest bands of the 70's. Fortunately his debut gig with Tull in Nurnberg was a happier occasion than Tull's first appearance in Germany a couple of months earlier, which had ended in a riot!

The 1970 *NME* readers poll saw Jethro Tull voted 'Best New Group' by a massive margin as their popularity continued to spread. They made a triumphant return to the UK at the massive Isle Of Wight Festival, and a gig in America, a benefit at Carnegie Hall for a centre for the rehabilitation of drug addicts, was recorded and subsequently released in part on an album. In view of Anderson's anti-drugs stance, it seemed an unlikely choice for a Tull benefit - and indeed it was, as Ian explained later:

"We were asked to do it, and although I agreed, it would not have been my first choice for a benefit concert. Perhaps I was persuaded by interested parties at the time that it would be a good thing to do, politically. Of course I feel sorry for people who get themselves into that state, but to be perfectly honest I do feel there are much more urgent and worthy causes to support".

The constant touring began to take its toll on band morale. Martin Barre resented having to spend six months of the year in America:

"The thought of it honestly depresses me. At first just to go there was exciting and to play there was such a big thing, but now I don't think any of us are looking forward to it. We have no time to do anything ourselves and our personal lives are suffering; I'm going through a stage of depression. This past year has been like a conveyor belt thing, making records, touring through America, it's endless, but we haven't the time to get off the conveyor belt because our schedule is so tight. I still love playing concerts, but it would be nice to go home every night after the gig!"

Clive Bunker summed up the hectic schedule more succinctly as "six months in America, fly to Europe, then back to America with just enough time to collect a change of underpants!" Ian Anderson enjoyed the concerts but hated every other aspect of touring, "It seemed such a terrible way of life. My only recreation was writing the songs, which at least injected some meaning into a lonely hotel room existence, but during every tour I vowed I was going to leave the band at the end of it." Glenn Cornick recalls the nightmare of playing rock festivals through 69/70:

"We had some great gigs, but we'd show up at these rock festivals to play at 7 or 8 at night only to hear they were running eight hours late, and we'd end up having to go on-stage at four in the morning. It would be freezing on-stage, and I had to try to play bass guitar with my fingers dropping off! We were in New York when we were invited to play at the Woodstock festival. Ten Years After were there so we called them and asked them what it was like. They said, "It's pissing down with rain, it's out of control, it's one of the worst effing gigs you've ever seen!" So we decided not to go, which may or may not have been a good move. In some ways it would have been nice to be there, but missing it clearly did us no harm".

The 'nightmare' was soon ended for Glenn Cornick when he was sacked from the band at the end of another American tour in November 1970.

"Ian kicked me out. We finished the tour in New York and went to Kennedy airport the next day to fly home. We were just about to check in at the gates when Terry Ellis asked me to come and have a coffee with him. As we sat down he said, 'Ian doesn't want you in the band anymore. I've cancelled your reservation; you have to fly home tomorrow.' They got on the plane without me because they didn't want to have to talk to me. That's short and sweet! I know what the problem was – it certainly wasn't my playing, it couldn't have been, because they replaced me with Jeffrey (Hammond)! I mean, Jeffrey's a great bloke, I've always liked him, but he's not a great bass player – and Jeffrey would tell you that himself. The problem was that Ian didn't respect my morals at the time, chasing girls and socialising. I was definitely a bit of a party animal, I enjoyed myself and enjoyed the rock'n'roll lifestyle, and Ian didn't approve of my general mode of behaviour. But I was never out of it on-stage, I always did my job well. It's all a long time ago now, I've seen Ian since and we get on fine, but I will never forgive him for not having the guts to speak to me personally that day".

Glenn bounced back with his own band, Wild Turkey, having a degree of success with their two albums on Chrysalis Records. The band split in the early '70's, but were reunited in 1996, returning with a great new album *Stealer Of Years*.

The touring might have been an unpleasant aspect of building a rock legend, but their incessant gigging in America paid great dividends when *Benefit* went to number 11 in the US album chart, giving Tull their biggest hit so far.

Jeffrey Hammond was the next ex-Blade to be reunited with his erstwhile colleague, again largely through being in the right place at the right time.

"I was just leaving art school, I was in a dead end situation where I wanted to carry on painting but couldn't see it as a profession. I'd kept in

39

touch with Jethro Tull, and I'd actually gone to the studio with John Evans when he did the "Witches Promise" single. When Glenn Cornick left the group I was living in Ian's house – in fact I was decorating it for him – and so he asked me if I wanted to join the band. I was very fortunate to be there and to have the old-boy network working in my favour. It was a tremendous opportunity and exceptionally exciting.

As soon as they came back from the tour we started recording the album *Aqualung* and getting ready to tour again. I remember buying some unusual stage clothes, flying goggles and so on. I very clearly remember the first concert I played in Odense in Denmark. It was a long time since I'd been on-stage anywhere and I hadn't realised how hot it was. I was wearing these goggles which steamed up halfway through the first song – I couldn't see a thing! It was very much a case of in at the deep end."

The dramatic change in Hammond's lifestyle was accompanied by an odd change of name, when, on Ian's suggestion, he added another Hammond to his name to become Jeffrey Hammond Hammond. "Ian just thought it sounded better, and I quite liked the idea. It actually wasn't too much of an affectation because my mother's name was Hammond before she got married!"

CHAPTER THREE
Sitting On A Park Bench

Tull's fourth album *Aqualung*, released in March 1971, was, and perhaps still is, *the* definitive Tull album. The title track and "Locomotive Breath" have remained constant factors both in the live Tull set and AOR radio in America to this day, and sales have exceeded 5 million to date. But it was not a pleasant album to make as Ian recalls:

"As usual the recording sessions were squeezed in between live work, and we had a lot of problems with the studio, which was then new. We couldn't get things to sound the way we wanted them to, and that put a lot of stress on the band. We were all very tired, physically and emotionally drained after being on the road for so long, and we were on a very tight schedule to get the album finished. It had to be finished by a certain time because we were off on tour again. We had also just recruited Jeffrey on bass, and he was almost completely incapable of playing his instrument. He was not a real musician, so we had to teach him to play as we were recording. He was talented enough to pick it up quickly, he could play exactly what we told him and showed him to play, but he didn't understand any musical principles at all – he did it all from memory rather than 'feel'. So it was a strange recording experience; on one hand we were in a new, state of the art studio, but on the other hand we couldn't get the sound we wanted and our bass player couldn't yet play bass! Even Martin Barre had problems, with the result that I ended up playing some lead guitar on 'Locomotive Breath'. He just couldn't get the sound I wanted and didn't understand what I wanted him to do, so eventually I grabbed his guitar and did it myself!

Aqualung was the album where I started to take myself half seriously as a songwriter. Prior to that songs were just something that you had to have, you had to come up with them in order to justify being on-stage and getting paid for it. I had put things together to justify being there, but I didn't take it terribly seriously, and I didn't think for a minute that I was a very useful songwriter, or a musician for that matter. On *Aqualung* I started to make more of an effort to write songs that were not the kind of songs other people were writing. The subject matter is clearly well away from the standard pop or rock songs of the era. Being different did not of course mean it was good.... but at the time being different was good enough!"

Cynics and indeed realists might well argue that it was something of a self-inflicted wound to enlist a bass player that could not play, but it was characteristic of Anderson's methodology to continue to work with people that he knew personally rather than looking for proven but personally unknown musicians. Jeffrey, in spite of his self-confessed limited natural ability, proved to be a quick learner and skilful player of the bass parts he was given, and with his striking appearance (later including his famous black and white striped bass, costume and even stage zebra!) he soon became a great favourite with the fans. In a way he was already known to Tull fans, having been mentioned in earlier Jethro Tull song titles on each of the three previous albums ("A Song For Jeffrey", "Jeffrey Goes To Leicester Square", and "For Michael Collins, Jeffrey and Me"). There had also been a very early attempt at a Jethro Tull newsletter, *Jeffrey's Journal*, purportedly written by Hammond, though he denies any involvement with it now!

Aqualung was recorded under the working title of "My God", the epic, anti-religion song that opened side two of the album and which had featured in the live set for some time previously – apparently the change of name on release was to avoid confusion with a recently issued popular bootleg album of the same name. Heavy rock songs were interspersed with some solo, acoustic pieces from Ian, and most of the songs were clearly distinct, unrelated pieces. However, the way the songs were split over the two sides of the vinyl still gave the overall impression of two mini-albums, the "Aqualung" set and the "My God" set, particularly as side two was made up of songs with a religious.... or anti-religious theme. Subsequently *Aqualung* was interpreted by critics as being a concept album, although Ian Anderson has always denied it: "It was just a bunch of songs, some of which just happened to have a common theme. It was never intended as a concept, and I still don't see that it is. *Tommy* was a concept album, *Sgt Pepper* was, but *Aqualung* certainly wasn't."

The savage, biting attacks on organised religion on songs like "My God" and "Wind Up" struck a chord with many a Catholic Grammar schoolboy, as Martin Allcock was to recall many years later when he too joined the band. "I will never forget the first time I heard 'Wind Up'... the lyrics, the anger, it summed up exactly the way I felt about things at the time... and still do". The meaning and the passion is still there too for Ian Anderson almost three decades on, as anyone will attest if they've seen his still powerful performance of those songs in recent live sets:

> "Those songs still mean as much to me as when I first wrote them, although I hope if I was to write them now they would be rather less naïve
> – I was still a very young man when I wrote them. They were not, as some perceived, an attack on God, but more on organised religion, the hypocrisy of organised Christianity. I don't mean that to sound as heavy as it might, and I have no arguments with anyone's personal religious beliefs. I'm sure there is a God, but nobody can possibly know what form he or it might take; 'God' could be a rock in the middle of a desert somewhere.... 'God' could be anything at all."

Social issues were also a central theme of the album, the sordid side of life featuring child prostitute "Cross-eyed Mary" and the "Aqualung" character himself, based on a project that Ian's first wife Jennie was working on. She had been photographing homeless tramps and vagrants, and some notes scribbled on the photos inspired Ian to write what was to become Tull's most famous song. Incidentally, the cover painting of the character "Aqualung" bore an uncanny resemblance to the early appearance of Ian Anderson, even though he insists it was not intentional!

"He was initially created by an artist who had been told to come up with a figure that looked something like my early stage image, but 20 years older. It was a little in-joke that got out of hand, with the result that he ended up looking more like me than he should have, leading people to believe that those songs were of an autobiographical nature, which of course they weren't. I couldn't possibly write a song from the point of view of a tramp. The best I could do was to use the knowledge I had from what I had seen on the streets around me. He had to have a name, I didn't want to call the song "Old Tramp" or something, so I wondered what such a chap might be called, what would his nick-name be? 'Aqualung' came simply from the wheezing noise that an Aqualung makes."

It was almost a costly choice, for Anderson thought the underwater breathing apparatus was simply an aqualung, not realising it was actually a fully registered, copyright brand name! Fortunately the Aqualung Corporation was magnanimous and a possible fortune in royalties remained with the band!

Once again the album reached number 4 in the UK album chart, but this time no single was taken from it, although one had been planned and scrapped at the last minute. "Lick Your Fingers Clean", a non-album track, was to have been coupled with "Up To Me" from the album, but was withdrawn with the implausible reasoning that it was "too close to the album release date"! "Lick Your Fingers Clean" remained unreleased until the 20th Anniversary box set 17 years later, although basically the same lyrics were utilised in a vastly different song, "Two Fingers" on the *War-child* album in 1974.

Tull graced the singles charts again later in the year, on both sides of the Atlantic, though with different records. "Living In The Past" was a rare hit for Tull in America, where the audience was fast catching up with the UK, and in July the UK fans were treated to a five track EP featuring "Life Is A Long Song" as the leader track, which got to number 18 in the chart. None of the tracks were included on album at the time. The EP marked the recording debut of Barrie (renamed Barriemore) Barlow, who had joined Tull when Clive Bunker decided to leave the band just after the release of "Aqualung". Unusually, it was an amicable split. Clive Bunker:

"I left the band to get married, simple as that. We were just about to do the first world tour – I think we had one more American tour to do, then we were planning to tour the world and then going to live in Switzerland for tax purposes. In a gap in the tour prior to that I met the girl who was to become my wife, and during the rest of the tour I decided to get married and knock it all on the head. I didn't know quite what to do, and I had regular chats with Eric Brooks, who was then like a father to all of us, about what I should do about it. Ultimately he told me just to tell Terry Ellis how I felt and get it all sorted out. I put it off until the last moment, with a view to speaking to Terry on the plane home at the end of the tour, but Terry flew off on holiday so I didn't get to talk to him. It all got a bit iffy.

Back in England Eric told Ian, and Ian came to my house to talk it over. It was a bit awkward, a traumatic time really, because then Tull were about as big as it gets. But Ian understood why I wanted to leave, and he didn't try to pressure me into staying. We parted as friends, and we still are friends. There was no falling out, and none of the usual 'musical differences' etc. Ian was, and is, a musical genius, and I always enjoyed the wonderful music he wrote. Luckily for all concerned Barrie knew the guys and the music and was easily able to step into things and do the next tour."

Bunker went on to form the short lived 'supergroup' Jude, with Frankie Miller, Robin Trower and James Dewar, but they split after record company pressure who wanted to project them purely as a guitar dominated band. He continued to play in various bands in semi-retired mode, but recent times have seen him returning to music in a big way. Clive is currently a member of prog-rockers Solstice and The Vikki Clayton Band, and has recently recorded his first solo album.

Barrie Barlow got the invitation to rejoin his old friends in the John Evan Band via an unusual visitation from John Evans. Barrie:

"It was Cup Final day. I was at my mate's house who'd got the colour telly, we'd got some cans in – like you do for the cup final – drawn the curtains, got rid of the women and so on. And suddenly Evans comes screaming up the road, drives over a couple of gardens, completely pissed out of his head. He'd just finished the American tour, and he had come back as brown as a berry with hair down to his arse. And he just walked into this mate's house, Ziggy Shaw.... Stormed in and said 'What the fucking hell are you doing with this bunch of cunts? Come on, you don't want to associate with these cunts!'.

Because he was drunk, and he was getting a bit arsey, so I had to usher him out the door. 'It's great to see you John, but I really want to watch the cup final', you know. So he said 'come and watch it at my mother's. Come on! Come on!' And he dragged me, still in my slippers, away from my mates and a big colour telly to watch it on a tiny black and white thing! So I'm sat there right in front of the telly, not talking to him because I'm trying to concentrate on the game, and he just kept talking and talking. I wasn't listening, I didn't hear anything until he said 'Clive is leaving Tull. Do you want the gig?' I heard that alright!"

A trip to the record shop to buy the last three Tull albums, and a guided tour by John Evans through the required learning helped Barrie through the audition, and he was catapulted from his life as a lathe turner and part-time musician into the heady world of what had become one of the most successful bands around. The EP was recorded in a couple of days before the rehearsals for the US tour. Barrie:

"It was a strange experience; very peculiar indeed. Clive was a great player, very well known, and an integral part of the original Jethro Tull, so I felt obliged to try to do my best to play the songs like Clive played them. But I had been to see Tull about six weeks before that, at the Opera House in Blackpool, and I actually couldn't understand it. With all defer-ence to all concerned, I couldn't understand what was going on then be-cause they weren't playing together. It was like five different people playing in five different bands, and it wasn't as good as lots of bands I'd seen. The tightness had gone – it wasn't the great band I'd seen a couple of years before at Mothers. Mind you, I don't think they liked playing in Blackpool; I think Ian has an aversion to Blackpool.

Anyway, one of the first things Ian said to me when I joined was 'Don't worry. Nobody can keep time in this band'! That was really en-couraging! From then on it was like absolute madness for me; I quit my job and headed for the big city. We did the EP thing, and then rehearsed for the tour. It was insane, crazy for me, because I had been in this work-work-work routine and then it was suddenly..... heaven, because now all I had to do was play!

Having said that, I had to work really hard just to cut it in the band, because there were lots of good players around then who could have taken the gig, and they could easily have looked elsewhere. Michael Giles from King Crimson was doing nothing at the time, and he had been *the* guy for years. He would have been great with Tull. So three weeks after playing The Gaiety Bar with Ronnie Ogden I was doing a 10,000 seater in Salt Lake City! I was scared to death. I went down to the sound-check on my own, and it was like standing in Wembley Stadium, it was totally intimidating."

His memories of his first gig are hazy, but the second night at Red Rocks in Phoenix will never be forgotten. 20,000 fans turned up for the 12,000 seats available, and the unrest and subsequent heavy rioting, tear gas et al, not only gave Barrie a memorable induction into the downside of life in a major band, but also led to rock concerts being banned from the venue for many years afterwards. The Casino Ballroom in Hampton Beach suffered a similar fate the following month, having sold far more tickets than the venue could accommodate. On a brighter note, that same month brought the accolade of the front cover of *Rolling Stone* featuring Ian Anderson. Tull had well and truly arrived! And it just kept getting better for Tull as the tour rolled on, as they continued to smash audience figures and house records wherever they went, confirming their status as one of the biggest live attractions in the world.

To top all the drama now heaped upon Barrie Barlow, his first serious recordings with Tull – i.e. album – were on what was by far the most ambitious musical project thus far undertaken by the band; the epic concept album *Thick As A Brick*. One continuous piece of music spread over both sides of the album, with an album cover every bit as complex and intricate as the music itself, it was, in Ian Anderson's own words, "The mother of all concept albums!" But... was it really all that serious, or was it all just a joke? Ian explained the origins in a recent interview, some of which was included on the 25th anniversary CD edition of *Brick* in 1997:

"It came about primarily because *Aqualung* had generally been perceived as a concept album, whereas to me it was just a bunch of songs. So with *Brick*, I said let's come up with something that is really the mother of all concept albums, and really is a mind-boggler in terms of what was then relatively complex music, and also lyrically was complex, confusing, and above all a bit of a spoof. It was deliberately tongue-in-cheek and meant to send up ourselves, the music critics, and the audience perhaps.... but not necessarily in that order! This was the period of Monty Python and a very British sense of humour".

The first joke was the suggestion that the whole piece was a poem written by a twelve year old boy called Gerald Bostock, and set to music by the band. Although Ian once suggested that the very first line came to him in a letter from a fan (Gerald, perhaps?), Ian Anderson was of course the writer of both the lyrics and the music, but even now there are many who believe Gerald Bostock is real. Even EMI it seems, who still co-credit him on the recent CD! I wonder where they send the royalty cheques? Ian:

"I thought we steered a very good line between making it sound vaguely plausible as a concept and being quite silly to the extent that most people would get the joke. Looking back it was certainly silly, and some might say quite adolescent, but I can only plead that I was a late developer and only 23 at the time, so it was the voice and the brain of a youth there, trying to do something that was different. In that sense it was the kind of thing that I'm still trying to do 25 years on."

Once again, the album was written and recorded under the constraints of a very tight timetable, having booked the recording studio for a mere two weeks after first rehearsals – for which the music had not even been written! Ian:

"The day would normally begin with me getting up really early in order to have two or three hours in which to write some music, which I then presented to the band as material that I'd written weeks before! We'd run through it, with the band adding their thoughts and ideas as we went along, and we developed it along with the music we had rehearsed the day before. So it built up sequentially day by day. It started at the beginning, and every day we added a bit more, sometimes reprising one of the earlier ideas in some way. By the end of about two weeks we had the whole thing rehearsed from beginning to end, in the way we were actually going to record it. Because of that, because we all knew it as a band, we recorded it in only about a week, which was really quickly. In fact the recording was so much easier than putting the cover together!"

Indeed, *Thick As A Brick* is remembered as much for the elaborate cover as it is for the music. Presented as a spoof local newspaper, *The St Cleve Chronicle*, with pages of letters, small adverts, and typically parochial news items, it was a bold attempt to create something new and different on every level within the rock album format. The humour was, typically for the time, very Pythonesque, very bizarre.... and somewhat hit and miss. But it certainly gave the fans something to mull over whilst trying to fathom the meaning of the lyrics, and for quiz enthusiasts the answers to the crossword were a source of some new and exotic words!

The sleeve design also brought on major headaches for Chrysalis, who protested to Anderson that it would be far too expensive to package the album in such a way. That argument that was shot down with his usual level headed reasoning that if a real local newspaper could be printed every week and all but given away, so could a spoof newspaper!

Most of the writing was done by Anderson, John Evans and Jeffrey Hammond, whilst the job of putting the thing together convincingly was given to Roy Eldridge, one-time music journalist and now newly arrived at Chrysalis. Thus he had the possibly unique experience of leaving a newspaper to work for a record company only to find one of his first tasks was to compile a newspaper!

Once the music and the cover were finished, Jethro Tull were presented with the really difficult part – the prospect of having a song lasting over forty minutes that they would have to play live.

"We were petrified by the thought of playing it live" recalls Martin Barre. "The first time we played the whole thing live was a terrifying experience; there is so much to remember, so many odd time signatures, 7/4's and 6/8's.... it was all done on adrenaline. It's amazing what fear can do!"

As the show developed, the forty minutes became almost an hour, as various little jokes and activities were added to *Brick*, in order to make it more of a show rather than merely a musical performance. It was simply an extension of the humour in the album cover, and whilst the audiences benefited from seeing something that really was unique, the band enjoyed it more because they had in-built breaks in the music rather than having to play it all the way through!

As with the record cover, the on-stage humour varied from very funny to frankly embarrassing. The show started with five elderly chaps walking onto the stage to check out the instruments, generally looking puzzled by the whole set up. An equally puzzled audience then watched as the old-timers removed their old overcoats to reveal themselves as Jethro Tull. The opening announcement from Anderson was simply *Thick As A Brick*, his last pronouncement until they had played the whole album through, which Anderson would back-announce as "a little twelve-bar thing we like to knock off before we start the show". A telephone would ring during the song which Ian would answer, stopping the band in full swing, starting again after the call as if nothing had happened.

"Aqualung" was introduced by a roadie in full wet suit and flippers. John Evans read the local news and weather reports half way through *Brick*. There was even a urinal attached to John's piano, which he would apparently utilise during each performance. By and large, the humour worked, although Anderson remembers that the Japanese audiences, enjoying their first glimpse of Tull in '72, just did not get it! The bewildered responses over there eventually prompted Terry Ellis to have placards made up with a Japanese translation of the vocal jokes – but to no avail, apparently! Maybe Monty Python humour was not the in-thing in Japan?

Jeffrey Hammond does not agree with the Monty Python comparisons, "But I can see why people might make the comparison. The humour wasn't forced or contrived. It all seemed completely natural. Stage performances since then have gone completely over the top, but at the time I suppose it was fairly innovative and different. Jethro Tull was always about more than just the music".

Brick was another huge success for Tull, reaching number 5 in the UK and topping the US chart for three weeks, having been hyped into the public consciousness with an intriguing pre-release advertising campaign in the press. There was no single released, but in June fans got an unexpected vinyl bonus with the release of the *Living In The Past* double album. It was aimed largely at the fans who had discovered the band after they had really broken big the previous year, and included the many non-album tracks which had appeared on singles, including all five tracks from the "Life's A Long Song" EP. But a few previously unreleased tracks and the first official live recordings, along with the superbly illustrated and detailed packaging, made it a highly desirable item for long time fans as well.

In August of '72 the band took up residence at the Chateau D'Herouville studio in Paris to record the follow up to *Thick As A Brick*. Yet again, the recording sessions are remembered as a nightmare experience by the band, but this time things proved to be so bad that the recorded work was actually scrapped. Ian Anderson:

> "The Chateau had such a good reputation, and lots of famous people like Elton John and Cat Stevens had recorded very successful albums there, but we found it a complete nightmare. The equipment was extremely dodgy, everything was going wrong technically every day, and we were really struggling to make this album. We did eventually get three sides of a double album recorded with great difficulty, but then we finally became so disenchanted with it we just jumped on a plane and went back to England. We scrapped the whole thing and started again."

Those tapes were long believed to have been destroyed, but were eventually discovered by Ian many years later and duly mastered and released after tremendous pressure from fans, but back in 1973 Tull had the arduous task of starting from scratch to make an album. It would seem that the second attempt at recording the album was a far more productive and rewarding experience, because as late as March '73 Tull were playing music from the aborted sessions in concert, yet the finished album surfaced in all its glory in July. If it was hurried it was not evident on the album, for from the ashes of those Chateau D'Herouville sessions – renamed Chateau D'Isaster by an obviously still disgruntled Anderson in 1988! – Tull went on to make perhaps their finest work to date - the classic *A Passion Play*.

It was a follow up to *Thick As A Brick* in every way. Another continuous track spread over both sides of the album, similarly complex music, but with even more obscure lyrical themes this time around. A spoof theatre programme packaging replaced the newspaper sleeve from the previous album with the members of Jethro Tull being pictured as the actors in a play. Interestingly, Ian Anderson, credited as Mark Ridley, in the programme, was said to have "made his West End debut as 'Elvoe' in Ron Read's social critique The Demo, an obscure in-joke reference to Ian's old nickname from the John Evan Band days, and Don Read, their first manager.

The one major change in the Tull sound was Anderson's heavy use of saxophone, although he did not of course abandon his trusty flute, and John Evans utilised synthesisers much more than on previous albums. Perhaps the most outstanding feature of the album though was the incredible singing of Ian Anderson, reaching new heights as a vocalist.

Many hailed it as a work of genius. Others, including the vast majority of the music critics, most of whom had previously held Tull in high regard, saw it as a concept album too far. *A Passion Play* was and is very much a watershed in the Tull story in many ways, but particularly regarding the relationship between the band and the press.

Perhaps the big mistake was the decision to premiere the full work in concert. Opening the shows with a brand new piece lasting an hour is not universally regarded as a safe option, and Tull paid the price for their boldness with almost universal slatings in the press. Ironically it was Chris Welch, a huge Tull fan then and now, who almost single-handedly started the landslide of press maulings with his *Melody Maker* review of the UK premiere. He reported, "more in sadness than in anger", on "a failure", highlighting his review with the pointed by-line "It began to occur to me that this was very poor music indeed".

The consensus in the press was that Tull, or more pointedly, Ian Anderson was taking himself far too seriously. "Pretentious" suddenly became the catchword when describing Jethro Tull, and 25 years on it still sticks in certain areas of the press. Surprisingly perhaps, Ian Anderson agrees that the band were indeed taking themselves too seriously at the time.

"*Thick As A Brick* was very successful, and when it came to the next album I guess we all fell into the trap of thinking we should do the same kind of thing again, but instead of being silly about it maybe we should take it seriously. I think the problem with it was that the humour that was there on *Thick As A Brick* was not there on *A Passion Play*. And I think that's because a lot of the humour had been knocked out of it by the circumstances leading up to the making of the album. A year of being on tour, living in Switzerland, rehearsing, recording it in France then finally coming back to England to start it all over again, rehearsing and recording virtually all new material. That really took the humour out of it! The result is that *A Passion Play* is too deadpan, it doesn't have those slightly irreverent and humorous little interludes or moments of light relief that would have made it more listenable."

Martin Barre is more positive about it:

"More people still talk about *A Passion Play* than most of our other albums. It is an important album, but the problems that we had with it originally do tend to taint the overall memory. But it is a good album, and the tour and the theatrics that went with it made it a very memorable period for us".

Anderson's opinion that the album lacked humour is surprising given that within the heart of the music the band decided to include a bizarre, surreal story narrated by Jeffrey Hammond. "The Story Of The Hare Who Lost His Spectacles" was clearly included as a humorous interval, bearing no relation whatsoever musically or lyrically to the body of work that was *A Passion Play*. Again the inspiration was Monty Python weirdness that either delighted or irritated the listener, and further annoyance was caused by placing the track at the end of one side and the start of the second side of the vinyl, thus completely destroying the continuity of both the music and the interval story.

Jeffrey Hammond 'shoulders the blame' for the controversial track:

"It was rather extraordinary I suppose. You see, *Thick As A Brick* had been quite a departure from what had gone before, and it is always difficult to follow something like that. I know a lot of people thought *Passion Play* struggled to keep up with it. I don't think so myself, but I think maybe things did get out of line where one felt one had to do more and more of it. It became almost manic in a way. In fact I probably wasn't a very good influence on the band after that, in the sense that perhaps those kinds of things got too important in relation to the music. Eventually of course they dropped away quite naturally, but it did take time. 'The Hare' was just a bit of whimsy, but it's very difficult to measure how much of that kind of material should be allowed to creep in. Perhaps that was a bit too much!"

The track was set to film starring the band members dressed in animal costumes, which was shown during the live performances, further bewildering the audiences who had not yet had the opportunity to check out the album.

Fans in the UK had already become somewhat disenchanted with the band when Tull controversially cancelled two shows scheduled for April citing Ian Anderson's 'nervous exhaustion'. Eighteen thousand disappointed ticket holders were shocked to read reports in the *NME* that Tull were in fact rehearsing the new show in Canada at the time the UK gigs were to have taken place. An embarrassed press officer was forced to admit that Tull were scheduled for rehearsals, and that "Ian Anderson may have gone along for an hour or two if he was feeling up to it". Whatever the truth, Tull made amends when they re-scheduled the shows to include the full *Passion Play* show that had been designed for America, despite the enormous expense of flying the elaborate equipment to the UK. The two shows at The Empire Pool Wembley, in June were the only UK shows on the *Passion Play* tour.

The live shows were an incredible experience, lasting almost three hours. It must have given Anderson a certain amount of pleasure to announce, an hour into the set, "And now for our second number....", but with hindsight it was perhaps somewhat over ambitious to expect 10-20,000 eager fans to fully appreciate such a large slice of completely new material in one hit. And the audience frustration was only added to by the clever opening devised by Anderson, a simple device to grab the attention of the audience which ultimately backfired.

A tiny white dot was projected onto the huge screens, which pulsed to a heartbeat, which got louder as the dot grew bigger. The 'dot' eventually started to move, transforming into the ballerina as pictured on the album cover, who then crashed through a mirror to herald the start of the show. The effect lasted for about 30 minutes, and those fans who had actually noticed what was going on understandably had become rather bored with the whole thing, not realising it was never intended to be a part of the show. Anderson had reckoned that the audiences were never in their seats when the show was due to start, so instead of simply doing nothing they might as well put on something that might intrigue the fans while they were waiting.

He was particularly annoyed that his brilliantly conceived opening was singled out for heavy criticism by the fans and critics alike:

"It wasn't even part of the show. It came before the show, during the time people were meeting up with their friends, finding their seats, buying a drink and so on. It was supposed to be an interesting little extra for them, and I for one thought it was very exciting. Every night I would watch the audience, to see who would be the first person to notice that that the dot had actually started moving. The audience never had to wait longer than they would have normally, we always went on-stage when we were supposed to, and it really annoyed me to hear people complaining about the boring opening. I think people didn't like it because it was confusing, they never really knew when the show had actually started".

Even if *A Passion Play* live was not the resounding success Tull were hoping for, the live shows were still very well received by the fans, not least because "Play" was practically a bonus hour before Tull played another full set of favourites, including a good slice of *Brick*. The album went to number 1 in America, and everything seemed to be going well, apart from the barrage of press abuse heaped upon the album and the live shows. Never before had Tull received such a unanimous hammering in the media. Steve Clarke in the *NME* bemoaned "the slide from *Stand Up* to *Thick As A Brick* culminating in the fall that is *A Passion Play*. A shame, because Ian Anderson is so much better than this". His live review was no better, declaring *A Passion Play* to be a failure both musically and visually. Chris Welch in *Melody Maker*, under the headline 'Enough Is Enough', cut much deeper with a thoughtful, heart-felt, and biting continuation of his earlier concert overview:

> "It gives me no pleasure to report upon this recording. In fact I can not recall an album by a British rock band that has given me more pain to endure. After studying this album at great length, stewing my eyes out over the lyrics, bending an ear to each nuance of the music, I am left with the feeling of never wanting to hear another British rock group album again. If this is where ten years of 'progression' has taken us, then it's time to go backwards".

Ouch! And let's remember, Chris Welch actually liked Jethro Tull! And Rob Mackie, reporting on the first Wembley show, reserved judgement on the music but took issue with the presentation: "The style of presentation of *Passion Play* seemed to be just another reflection of Tull's apparent lack of concern for their audiences in the UK. Pete Townsend launched 'Tommy' by explaining the story, talking about it both on-stage and in the press. Anderson launched straight into 'Passion Play' in a void, without a word of explanation to anyone and barely even time for applause between sections of it."

And so it went on. But even those press critics were astonished when Jethro Tull issued a press release announcing their retirement from live performances due to the mauling they had received in the press. Tull's manager Terry Ellis tried to explain the group's decision thus:

> "The group have been working continuously for nearly six years, during which time their total break from concerts has not been more than one month. In particular the effort they have put into preparing their concert appearances has been immense. The preparation of the music and production of *A Passion Play* began a year and a half ago and it is, in their opinion, the best thing they have ever done. The abuse heaped upon the show by the critics has been bitterly disappointing to the group, and illogical as

it may be to identify the opinions of reviewers with those of the public, it has become increasingly difficult for the group to go on-stage without worrying whether the audience are enjoying what they are playing. This has been a great burden, and in the circumstances – with the film already in the planning stages – the group thought it better to cancel all concert plans and to concentrate on the film, and to reconsider the situation after that".

It is difficult to imagine what response Ellis was hoping for with such an announcement, but not surprisingly the same press were unsympathetic to this frankly odd reasoning. Realising the P.R. faux pas, Anderson quickly disassociated himself from the announcement, blaming 'an over zealous press agent'. He has since gone into more detail about the most ludicrous chapter in Tull's long history, displaying an acute awareness of the absolute folly of the exercise:

"It was a thing that the record company did, as a PR exercise, and it went terribly wrong. It was an attempt to put on record the fact that we were really unhappy about the press abuse we'd had. The idea being that the following week they would come back with the news that Tull weren't retiring, they were in fact making a film, and so they could keep the press guessing from week to week, to keep the band in the news. The guys in the group knew nothing about it. I knew the story was coming out, but I was very unhappy about it. I knew it was a very silly thing to do, and looking back I know I should never allowed it to happen.

It backfired terribly, as it was always going to, and simply made us look very silly. Of course we had taken the criticism to heart, and would do again if it happened again, but the record company's response was the completely wrong way to fight back. It goes on all the time - Rod Stewart, Elton John, everybody tries to manipulate the press to their advantage now and then. Jethro Tull have never done much of that kind of thing, but whenever we have it has backfired on us dramatically! It should not have happened, and I think the record company learned enough from that experience to ensure that it never happens again!"

Nevertheless Tull played their last gig in '73 in Boston at the end of September and took their first extended break from touring since the formation of the band.

The plan was to spend the time working on a number of ideas, including the film project mentioned by Ellis in the 'retirement' announcement, tentatively titled *Warchild*. An orchestral score was written and partly recorded, but subsequent lack of time after a series of delays meant the film never got off the ground.

One of the first projects undertaken by Ian Anderson during the brief sojourn was his first music production outside of Jethro Tull. English folk-rockers Steeleye Span had supported Tull at many concerts, and Anderson had taken an interest in their music. One particular song, "Thomas The Rhymer", had struck him as being an obvious choice for a single, and during conversations with the singer Maddy Prior, he agreed to help with the production. In due course he actually mixed the whole album, which was released in March '74, entitled *Now We Are Six*. It was a fruitful collaboration, giving Steeleye their biggest hit album to date, charting at number 13.

Anderson also became involved with Captain Beefheart's Magic Band, although this time on a purely financial level. The Captain had supported Tull on an earlier US tour, and Ian had struck up a good relationship with his band, though not particularly with their leader:

"I had been quoted as saying I didn't like much American music at the time, with the exception of Captain Beefheart and Frank Zappa. He obviously heard about it, and rang me one day asking to support us on our next tour. I was a bit nervous about it because although they were a very interesting band and I personally enjoyed the things they did, I could see that Tull fans might not like it. Particularly in America, where he was hardly known, although through the efforts of John Peel he had become something of a cult hero in the UK.

In the end we agreed to have him for at least part of the tour, and they did die a death pretty much every night, the audience really didn't like them at all. We were all fairly chummy with all the guys in the band, but Beefheart was a tyrant and a bully with his own boys, and a very insecure

man. Very charismatic, but used to total domination which was a cover
for very deep seated insecurity. If he didn't feel he had manipulated and
totally controlled you, he was desperate to try to do so.

He was a strange, very intense guy. He used to ring me in the middle
of the night and say, "Can we rap?" I would point out that it was 3 am and
I had a show to do the next day, but he would argue the point, "Hey man,
I need to talk to you now..." "Sorry Don, I can't talk now, I'm going
back to sleep, see you tomorrow", and so on. So he had a strange relationship with me where he was trying to make me one of his 'followers', and
I was singularly unimpressed by it.

The rest of the guys were really nice fellas, but he was a bit hard with
them. I've seen him reduce at least two of the band to tears by publicly
humiliating them as to their performance on-stage. He was a real bully
boy. Music is much the richer for Captain Don, but like a lot of people
with that particular sort of naïve talent, he was not an easy man and he
was doomed by his own personality to destroy everything around him.

His relationships with his record companies particularly suffered. He
would get advances and go and spend all the money, and he had no concept at all of running the group and the business side of it. He would take
the money from the record company and spend it all on himself, while the
other guys had no food, nothing. Some of the stories they told us were
just awful. He had a giant chip on his shoulder, and it became insufferable
really. His attitude was that everybody was against him but he was a true
artist, but we all knew that. He was a talented, special guy, and he didn't
need to keep telling people about it all the time.

I saw him a couple of times after the tour, but we kind of lost touch
when he split with his guys and formed another Magic Band. I actually
got the old Magic Band together, flew them over, put them up for a couple of months and gave them the studio time to make an album, saying
they could pay me back when they had sold some albums and made some
money.

I said they should call themselves The Magic Band, because of course
they were the Magic Band. We researched it legally and felt they would
be perfectly justified in using the name, but they chickened out and decided to call themselves Mallard. Foolishly, in my opinion, instead of just

doing it themselves they brought in a new front man to try to replace Don, and it wasn't a great album. It didn't sell, and I never got repaid!"

CHAPTER FOUR
Back To The Family

Before Jethro Tull could release any more albums themselves, or indeed films, the decision was taken to try to put an end to hostilities between group and press. A press conference was called in Montreux, where *A Passion Play* had been conceived, and the world's music press was there in force. So important was it seen to be that it even warranted a report on the TV news that night. Anderson spoke of the plans for the film and soundtrack album, and another group album of the same name, but could not resist the temptation to fight back against the critics over their handling of *A Passion Play*.

"The thing that annoyed me really was that people dismissed it when it was obviously a record you had to listen to many times. It took a long time to write, and a long time to make, and to us on stage, at it's best, it was a very fine performance. It just seems sad that somebody should dismiss it in one sentence by saying, 'This is clearly bad music', because it seems a little unreasonable. If we actually made a bad album I would welcome criticism, but *A Passion Play* was the best and probably most commercial album we have made. But it was not easy to get into first time around. People seemed to object to the fact that they actually had to sit down and listen to it more than once, and qualify the statements of their criticism. They seemed unwilling to do that, preferring simply to dismiss it, which I do find unfair. It certainly doesn't reward me in any way for months of work, and it's not a very constructive method of criticism. Criticism ought to be, first of all, to the artist. Unfortunately though it seems to be aimed at the audiences, and seems to have an effect on what a possible audience might believe, might buy, and might come and see, because they have no other source".

He also defended the presentation and the total lack of any kind of explanation of the album:

"I rather like the idea of offering the individual the opportunity to read into things what they will. People listen in different states of consciousness and they will, whatever you say, make their own interpretations. I would much rather put the ball firmly in their court and say, 'Right, we've done our bit, now it's up to you.'"

It seems extraordinary now looking back on that statement, that Anderson actually believed that a music critic was employed to speak to the artists rather than the audience, the very people who bought the music papers. And that a critic should spend hours listening to his work before offering their opinion on it, no matter what other work-load or deadline was involved. In a perfect world of course, he might have had a point. But even though in the 70's music critics did largely consider the music rather than image, it was asking a lot of them to sweat blood over every review. Terry Ellis went even further with his novel views on the role of the critic:

"They are a bunch of hypocrites who take themselves too seriously, without realising how important they are in terms of influencing opinion. And they don't identify enough with the people they are writing for."

Possibly very true, then and now, but another theory was perhaps just a bit too radical: "The music papers are not there to criticise"! In spite of the attacks on the press, the press conference was a success in terms of at least partially rebuilding relationships, although Tull were never to fully regain their place as the critic's favourites. The backlash had started, and continued with varying degrees of savagery for many years.

Although Tull made a triumphant return to the public domain in 1974, it was with the group album only, the film (and therefore the soundtrack album) having been abandoned. David Palmer had been heavily involved in the soundtrack:

"We recorded a lot of music. Martin Barre wrote a little acoustic guitar piece, which we developed into something much longer. There was one particular piece that Ian wrote, called 'Waltz Of The Angels' I think, that was really very good. He played it on the guitar, and it was almost like Benjamin Britten or Tchaikovsky. It was a very, very good piece of music. We had a tape of that but sent the only copy to London Weekend Television because they wanted some music for a series they were planning.

I felt very sad about that film, because Ian and I had worked very hard on it. We had a meeting with Sir Frederick Ashton at his home in Chelsea. We invited him to do the choreography, and after he heard the music he was up for it. John Cleese, who is a friend of mine, was to be the humour advisor. But then the big mistake was made when we asked Bryan Forbes to direct. Then it was hurry-hurry-wait. Hurry-hurry-wait. Until eventually, within the time frame of a major touring band like Jethro Tull it had to be shelved. Ian might say now for the better, because we were all young and eager to become involved in a movie. But Ian wanted to do it, and he had it in himself to pull it off.

He might not have made a movie that would have got glowing critiques from those people who hold themselves up as film experts, but he would certainly have been capable of supervising the whole thing himself. It's all part of the development of a musician's life. I remember starting to write an opera when I was at the Royal Academy; I mean, I hadn't got far past Mozart's operas, let alone Wagner, Verdi and the other lot. I was a mile out, but I still desperately wanted to do it, to keep moving onwards. And I'm sure that was the motivation behind Ian wanting to write that film."

Aside from the time factor, a major stumbling block proved to be getting finance. The UK film industry at the time was almost non existent, so Anderson had to look to America for backing; "Well I certainly wasn't going to put any of my money into such a ludicrous project!", joked Ian some years later. Money was offered, but not without severe strings attached, which would have robbed Anderson of final control, and the studios demanded big name stars that were not in his original plans. Reluctantly, he decided to abandon the project.

The group album was recorded in tandem with the orchestral film score, and *Warchild* was released in the UK in September 1974, charting at number 14. The title was taken from a song by Roy Harper, another refugee from Blackpool who Anderson had always admired – and still does. The two actually recorded together that year when Anderson played flute on "Home", the only studio track on Harper's otherwise 'live' album *Flashes From The Archives Of Oblivion*. It was the first time Anderson had played on somebody else's album, and it came about after a typically unorthodox approach from the erratic genius Harper. Ian Anderson:

> "He called me at two in the morning and said, 'I'm in the studio and I really need you here to play flute on this song. I need one of those wild, breathy solos you do'. I told him I'd be there in the morning to see what I could do. It wasn't even the kind of song for a flute solo, but I was pleased to be of service!"

Warchild was a return to single song format, although Anderson insisted it was not a deliberate attempt to deflect the criticism of 'the excesses' of the previous two albums. Indeed *Warchild* was something of a continuation of the basic theme behind *A Passion Play*, that of the possible choices to be faced after death. The main characters in the abandoned film were to have been the not insignificant personifications of God and The Devil, with the possibly controversial premise that somehow their two roles might be interchangeable!

> "I was trying to say that it's not necessarily always the case that God is good and the Devil is bad. God was not averse to turning people into pillars of salt, whereas the Devil has often given people a good time, with the odd Pagan festival here and there! I'm not a Satanist or anything like that, but it seemed like an interesting concept for a film. The album dealt with similar ideas, but without the film to back it up it seemed sensible to wash over the concept and let the music stand on it's own. The music was initially built around the film, so the songs had to be constructed in more orthodox lengths as opposed to the lengthy *Passion Play* structure".

The music was very much in the style of *A Passion Play*, still featuring Ian's sax playing alongside the flute. The connection with *Passion Play*

Minstrels In The Gallery

even extended to two of the tracks - "Solitaire" and "Skating Away On The Thin Ice Of The New Day" - being salvaged from the aborted Chateau D'Herouville sessions. This was not generally known at the time, and "Solitaire" was incorrectly assumed by many to be aimed at the critics who had savaged *A Passion Play* the year before.

Many years later Ian's memories are at odds with his talk at the time of not being influenced by the flak aimed at *A Passion Play*, particularly regarding the return to the shorter song format. Ian Anderson:

"We had to come back with an album that was a little bit more to the point, less pompous and overbearing than *Passion Play* had been, so it was just a bunch of songs. There were some pretty good songs on *Warchild*. It was a good fun album, and we did lots of tours with it, going to back to Australia and New Zealand for the second time. [*Incidentally, the city of Melbourne was the backdrop to the cover of the album*]. But it was a funny record because it came about almost by default. I was in Switzerland writing music with David Palmer with a view to making some kind of musical or something, and whatever it was became the 'Warchild' album. I always thought about it being a movie as well. It was a most peculiar time for me – I was always thinking about music that wasn't going to be just an album. It was either going to be a movie, or a stage musical, or something else. It was OK, but I think it would have been far better if we had just concentrated on making decent records".

Jeffrey Hammond:

"I was never involved in the film project, but I remember it was a serious project which just seemed to disappear for some reason. But I liked the album. They were good, short songs, and again very different to what had gone before. I particularly liked the string section we used, and they complemented the subsequent live shows very well also. I don't think they enjoyed it quite so much though because they were generally seated next to my bass speakers and were continually asking for the volume to be turned down. It used to make them bounce up and down on their seats, and they were probably stone deaf by the end of the tour!"

Martin Barre:

"That was a lot of trouble. They couldn't hear what they were playing on-stage, and I never heard them…. but they looked good!"

 Anderson agrees:

"It wasn't the best thing in the world to take on. They were lovely girls and terrific players in the classical context, but they didn't find it easy translating their way of playing into the rock context. I think they enjoyed it but they were a little fretful sometimes. It's not easy trying to play a violin when you can't hear yourself! It worked pretty well, but I think they perhaps didn't realise just what they were letting themselves in for, getting caught up in such a long tour. And of course we hadn't realised what we were letting ourselves in for, because we completely forgot that they would all have periods! And they all managed to have their periods at different times, so there was never a day when one of them wasn't in a foul mood!"

For the first time in three years Tull lifted a single from the album, the unrepresentative and surprisingly simple "Bungle In The Jungle". It failed to chart in the UK, but did reach the top 20 in America. Anderson was surprised by the success of the almost disco-friendly single, and joked that he was slightly disappointed by it: "I'd always been fond of the idea that Jethro Tull was a group that nobody could dance to, except me!"

The album got a reasonable press reaction: "Jethro Sensation! Journalist Enjoys New Album", screamed *Sounds*. The *NME* announced that, "Jethro Tull retrieve, if not all, then much of their floundering critical reputation with an album that echoes the triumphs of *Stand Up* and *Benefit*."

The live show was even more impressive than the album, with Tull reaching new theatrical heights and expanding the visual humour ever further. Chris Charlesworth in *Melody Maker* was ecstatic: "Rise Sir Ian of Flute, for thou hast indeed redeemed thyself. The critics have had their way, the *Passion Play* has been forgotten, and Jethro Tull are back once again playing the kind of music that won them their hard earned reputation as brilliant showmen and inventive instrumentalists."

When Tull finally returned to the UK for a proper tour in November, the first (apart from the two Wembley shows) since March '72, they had surrounded themselves with women! The all-girl band Fanny were the support at the London shows, the all-girl dance troupe Pan's People entertained during the interval, and when Tull hit the stage they had four new members – an all-girl string quartet. And Ian's personal roadie was the wonderfully attired Shona Learoyd, later to become Mrs Shona Anderson.

Visually, Tull were stunning. Anderson's stage costume was a brightly coloured medieval minstrel's costume, complete with his now legendary silver codpiece. Martin Barre's floral costume was the epitome of garishness, and his on-stage persona became more animated than ever before as he jumped and skipped across the stage. Jeffrey Hammond Hammond was dressed in a black and white striped suit and hat, playing black and white striped guitars, including a black and white striped double bass! During the latter part of the tour the theme was expanded to include a two-man pantomime zebra which came on-stage to defecate black and white striped tennis balls which Jeffrey caught and juggled.

The members of the string quartet were resplendent all in black, with identical platinum wigs. A moving tree shared the stage with a wooden dog who 'duetted' with Jeffrey on "How Much Is That Doggie In The Window?" Perhaps they didn't take themselves too seriously after all?

Incidentally, the fans at those *Warchild* shows did in fact hear at least a part of the aborted soundtrack album; the whimsical instrumental that was played immediately prior to Tull hitting the stage was a piece called "Quartet", which did eventually surface on the *Nightcap* CD set in 1993.

The *Warchild* tour continued through most of 1975, including an unprecedented sold out five night stint at the Los Angeles Forum, which drew a record 93,000 fans, prompting headlines in the press like "Jethro Tull – Now The World's Biggest Band?"

The tour was briefly interrupted with a two month break to record the next album, *Minstrel In The Gallery*, which was recorded in Monte Carlo on their newly purchased mobile studio. It was the first (released) Tull album to be recorded outside of the UK, for a number of reasons. They were not overly enamoured with the British studios available, and there was also a desire to get away from the annual schedule of touring and recording, so their own mobile studio brought a feeling of freedom to record whenever and wherever they wanted to. Perhaps more significantly though, it was a course of action strongly recommended by their tax accountants!

Minstrel came into being in a different manner to previous Tull albums, most of which had been written whilst the band were on the road. It was written by Anderson during a month of isolation either side of Christmas, and the resulting material was a wonderful collection of deeply personal reflections, of anger and sadness. Anderson put that down to the environment, which clearly had focused his mind on the constant pressure he was under as the lynch-pin of the whole Jethro Tull enterprise:

> "It's harder to go somewhere and write specifically because it's much more of a self-conscious effort. It made me sick getting up in the morning and watching all these people lying on the beach with their amazing vanity. Most of them are really ugly people, physically grotesque. The women are unattractive and the men are obscene. They lie there in the sun getting a tan, and they do nothing. I get very aggressive in that sort of situation because I've got a lot of things to do".

Anderson does not have happy memories of the recording sessions, recalling that much of it had the feeling of a solo album, having been recorded by him remote from the band.

> "Technically, it was a very good album, one of our better ones. We managed to get a great sound, having had the luxury of being able to set up the studio exactly the way we wanted it. But again it's a bit humourless, a bit too introverted. It didn't have the input from the band that the three previous albums had. I think the band was suffering at the time of *Minstrel*. Jeffrey was a great guy, and a great bass player in the context of what he did, but he wasn't a real musician's musician. John Evans had gone off the boil. He had completely lost interest in rock music and was playing Beethoven stuff endlessly on the piano. He was generally not a happy guy at the time, and was drinking far too much. And Barrie, who is

a bit of a dissident type, was always picking fights and arguments. The band was still playing well, but it lacked real harmony."

That may be Anderson's view, but *Minstrel* has always been regarded by fans as one of the band's finest albums, encompassing as it does all that was good about mid-70's Tull.

David Palmer was again heavily involved, enriching the album with delightful string arrangements for the ladies in platinum wigs. The heavy rockers were catered for with the blistering title track, and the progressive concept album lobbyists were satisfied with the mini-concept "Baker Street Muse", a truly magnificent collection of connected songs, which ran for most of side two on the vinyl. (That song suite was based on Ian's time spent living in the Baker Street area of London, with several allusions to his pursuit of a young lady. The lady in question later became his wife, so the album does at least have some happy associations for him!) And "Black Satin Dancer" stands as one of Tull's greatest songs, although typically Anderson was self-critical even then. "It's the sort of song that Led Zeppelin would write if they could write lyrics, but had they done it I'm sure it would have had a much better riff, and it would have been heavier. With my lyrics and Led Zeppelin's music we might arrive at something halfway there!"

Naturally Zeppelin fans were offended by that remark, despite the fact that Anderson has always claimed to be a fan of Led Zeppelin. Maybe Robert Plant was also offended, but a real row blew up via *Melody Maker* in May the following year when Anderson publicly attacked Plant for 'misleading the British public' with his claims of excessive taxation. Plant had slammed the system for taking 98% of his earnings, making it pointless to release records. Anderson countered that the maximum tax payable would be around 70%, a big proportion but still leaving a healthy slice of a very big cake. "I earn as much as a bricklayer who works really hard – and that's a lot of money". Plant had the last word in the following week's *MM* – "Yes, well he writes songs like a bricklayer too!"

The album title was a literal reference to the recording location. "We placed the studio in a gallery, as pictured on the back of the album. We were literally Minstrels In The Gallery". But whilst there were indeed minstrels (plural), it was a singular minstrel in the album title, and the dominance of Ian Anderson, with much of the material performed by him alone, gave rise once more to calls from fans for a long awaited solo album of acoustic material. He dismissed the idea out of hand. "I am the flute player and acoustic guitarist in Jethro Tull, and I'm happy in that role. I think it would detract from the band if I were to make a whole album of those little acoustic things that I do within Jethro Tull. They fit well within the context of a group album, they are an important part of what we do, but I would not like to take it any further. We are a rock group, and I am a rock musician who happens to play acoustic instruments". Even so, it is remarkable that 20 years and two solo albums on, he has still not made the acoustic album that everybody has been expecting and hoping for ever since.

Minstrel In The Gallery continued Tull's uneasy rehabilitation into the pages of the music press. "Ian Anderson is a hero once more" proclaimed Barbara Charone in *Sounds*, and a major review in *Melody Maker* praised "Tull's breath of fresh air... It's not a perfect album, but here they come as near as they ever will to former glories". Yet again they managed to register in the top 20 album chart, but just as predictably the title track released as a single from the album failed to make any impression on the chart.

Minstrel marked Jeffrey Hammond's last involvement with Jethro Tull, and indeed with music, period. "At the end of the tour he just burnt all his stage clothes, hung up his guitar, and never touched it again", says Anderson. Jeffrey's version is slightly different:

"Well, that sounds like a nice story, but it was a final thing. I had to leave because I needed to be able to express myself, and I couldn't do it through music. I was not a great player, as anybody will testify. I could do what I had to do within the group, but I was not a naturally gifted player. I was perfectly happy with nearly everything that Ian wanted to do, but I have a personal drive that I have to express in my own way. If I'd been a good musician I might have formed another group, but as I wasn't I had to look to other ways of self-expression. I've always known that I've had things to say, and it's important for me to carry on my journey. Ian is a very persuasive character, and there were many times when I felt I couldn't contribute as much creatively as I wanted to. I wasn't capable of doing so within that sphere, and it became very frustrating.

The frustration got worse as time wore on, and whilst I knew I could have gone on for another couple of years, I realised it was better to make the break as soon as possible. It was very hard to do, because Ian and I were great friends, and had been for years. I had to do it in a rather blunt way, and sadly it was just blurted out one day during a meeting. It wasn't a pleasant thing to do, but I had to do it that way for fear of Ian persuading me to stay. But the band definitely got better musically after I left, so it was certainly for the best".

Jeffrey's replacement was John Glascock ('Old Brittledick' as Anderson used to introduce him), a wonderfully gifted player who had previously played with the exciting flamenco-rock band Carmen. They had supported Tull on several American shows the previous year, and John had often watched the Tull set from the side of the stage. Although he and Ian Anderson had hardly spoken to each other on the tour, Ian had been impressed with his playing, and as Carmen had since split up, John was the first choice for Hammond's replacement. He was delighted to get the gig, and in turn his fluid, natural style was a great boost for the band. Ironically, his first recordings with Jethro Tull were on the band's least creative album, the stodgy and uninspired *Too Old To Rock'n'Roll: Too Young To Die!*

Anderson had clearly had high hopes for this album when he had talked to *Melody Maker*'s Harry Doherty the previous year: "In the latter half of 1976 Jethro Tull will become a much more hugely popular group. By the time the next album comes out it will contain a number of songs which will reach a lot of younger kids again". I suppose he was right in the sense that they actually got onto TV a couple of times which did reach a lot of kids, but whether Tull reached them to any lasting degree with 'Too Old' is debatable. Chrysalis probably fared better with a compilation album put out three months earlier, the oddly titled *M.U. – The Best Of Jethro Tull*. A straightforward, simply packaged single album, but with the irritating inclusion of just one previously unreleased track designed to grab more money from die-hard fans. M.U. stood for Musicians Union, and the album came with a poster of almost all the members of Tull, past and present, reunited for an afternoon for the pose. The one notable absentee was Mick Abrahams, who was pointedly not invited!

As with *Warchild*, the original thinking behind *Too Old To Rock'n'Roll* was a far more ambitious project than merely another Jethro Tull album. Ian Anderson and David Palmer had started writing it towards the end of 1975, with a view to presenting it as a stage musical, with Adam Faith starring as the 'hero' of the play. In December of that year, Anderson told the *NME*, "We are recording 18 new songs, from which the best 10 or 12 will be selected. All the songs are about people from different walks of life; an ageing rock-star, a housewife, an artist, and so on". It seems the ageing rocker took over though, to feature in a concept album that was, for once, by no means incomprehensible.

Of necessity, the plot was pretty straightforward, with the message that the cyclical nature of fashion means that if you don't change your image, it will one day be fashionable again. Young rocker Ray Lomas (allegedly a real person, a friend of David Palmer) becomes old rocker Ray Lomas, while his erstwhile mates grow up in more conventional fashion. A typically rebellious ton-up on the A1 results in the inevitable motorcycle smash, almost killing Ray who was, after all, Too Old To Rock'n'Roll. But because he was also Too Young To Die he not only survives, but against all the odds becomes a fashionable teen hero once more. Bravo!

Just in case the songs didn't tell the story clearly enough, the album sleeve carried a comic strip to follow the plot with. Well, it might have made for a good stage musical, but within the confines of a studio album, which was all that eventually came of the idea, it was less than thrilling. Ironically, the advent of punk rock just after the albums release justified the idea of the stage play, yet at the same time made it redundant, as far as Anderson was concerned:

"Punk rock has really said it all. It is like watching the story unfold in real life. The new punks are doing what the old rockers were doing years ago. They were playing rock and blues, now it's punk-rock, but it's essentially the same thing, both in terms of the music and the attitude. I started out doing what the Sex Pistols are doing now. OK, I didn't actually spit at people when we played the Marquee, but I certainly insulted them a lot!"

The title track was released as a single before the album came out, and as a single it worked well. A nice little story set to simple, accessible music, it could have been a hit. But as with most hit (or should-have-been-hit) singles, the novelty soon wore off after repeated listening. But at least long time fans who had refused to stump up for the *M.U.* album just to get one new track could now find it (Rainbow Blues) on the B-side of the single. Maddy Prior sang backing vocals on the title track, returning Anderson's production favour of a couple of years before. Backing vocals on two other tracks on the album came courtesy of Angela Allen, who had been in Carmen with John Glascock.

The album itself had too many straightforward, obvious 'pop' songs on it, without the required good tunes to accompany the songs, and the lyrics were largely just not up to Anderson's usual standard. And because the songs had originally been written with Adam Faith in mind, as if singing in character Anderson forsook his hitherto superb vocal style, coming on as some kind of cockney geezer on many of the tracks. Indeed in a couple of UK TV appearances to promote the album he was that character, famously attempting to sing and drink beer simultaneously on *Supersonic*, commercial TV's short-lived answer to *Top Of The Pops*. It was good, sloppy fun, beating The Sex Pistols by some weeks in the TV rock-yobbo stakes, but it was lightweight, and not the stuff that had made Tull what they were. And while the boot's going in, the lacklustre production didn't help much either. If ever a Tull album warranted a remix when the time comes, this is the one!

It was not all bad news though; amongst the also-rans, Anderson slipped in some fine songs, though curiously two of the best tracks ("Salamander" and "Bad-Eyed and Loveless") were almost solo pieces from Ian. Lyrically and musically, they were closer to the Jethro Tull that the fans knew and loved. Another highlight was the touching "From A Deadbeat To An Old Greaser". Almost spoken harmonised vocals from Ian, and a cool late-night sax solo from David Palmer made this remarkable track a real one-off in terms of Jethro Tull music before and since.

At least this time there are no horror stories about the making of the album. Simply having a bass player that knew exactly what to do, without having to be shown, made life in the studio so much easier. And a lasting legacy from *Too Old* is that song's frequent and triumphant place in the concert repertoire ever since. Incidentally, it was also one of the songs chosen by the CIA when they tried (and succeeded) to flush out General Noriega from his diplomatic stronghold by playing very loud rock music to him. Or rather, at him!

Another, less fortunate legacy, is the ready wrapped gift of a cliché headline from Anderson to unimaginative music critics, who have since been more than happy to write off a live performance from the band who are not only Too Old To Rock'n'Roll, but are also Living In The Past. And isn't it wonderful that Tull rhymes with Dull?! It has to be said that *Too Old* is an albatross that Anderson placed firmly around his own neck!

The *Too Old To Rock'n'Roll* tour was very short by Tull standards, and like the very lengthy *Minstrel* tour, ignored the UK completely. The one compensation for the home-based fans was an Independent Television broadcast, produced by Mike Mansfield, who had also put the band on *Supersonic*, of a filmed studio performance of the whole album. Fans in London were also able to tune into a simultaneous FM radio broadcast courtesy of Capital Radio; it was the first time ever that the independent TV and radio networks had worked together in such a way.

In a press interview after the release of the album, Anderson made the extraordinary statement that, "I have decided to write another hit single this year. It's about time we went on *Top Of The Pops* again". This when the music papers had just seen the future of rock'n'roll in The Sex Pistols, before they had even released "Anarchy In The UK". It was a bold and possibly foolhardy prediction, but against all the odds, he did it. "Ring Out Solstice Bells", a 'Christmas' single in celebration of 22nd December (well, it is Jethro Tull we're talking about!) slipped into the chart at number 28, and when Rod Stewart had to drop out of *Top Of The Pops* at the eleventh hour an emergency call went out to first reserves, Jethro Tull. The record company was obviously delighted, until they realised they didn't know where three of the band members were, including Anderson. The saga of the scramble to get this famously and perennially progressive underground group onto the country's most commercially important music show was gleefully reported in the *NME* by Tony Stewart:

"Superstar Ian was shopping in Oxford Street. Guitarist Martin Barre was driving up to London from Wales, and drummer Barrie Barlow was attending his uncle's funeral in Birmingham. Up at the Tull office, a scramble button was pressed. A distress call for Martin Barre to phone the office was broadcast by Capital Radio, and luckily he heard it. Barrie Barlow was located by telephone after the office had phoned every Barlow in the Brum area. But Ian Anderson was still adrift, and failed to respond to tannoyed calls in every major department store in Oxford Street. Eventually, after Tull's accountant's wife heard the Capital distress call and telephoned her husband, who had just been with Anderson, he was located in a boutique. A hurried recording session was arranged to lay down a backing track, and with only minutes to spare all members of Jethro Tull made it to the *Top Of The Pops* studio."

It was clearly worth all the effort, for it was a well-known fact that an appearance on *Top Of The Pops* was guaranteed to greatly increase sales of any record. And sure enough, the following week it had gone from number 28 to.... err... number 28. Can't win 'em all I guess!

CHAPTER FIVE
Songs From The Wood

The pre-release publicity for "Solstice Bells", which was in fact a four track EP, had stated that it was a stand-alone release that would not be included on an album. However, the relative success of the song prompted a change of heart, and "Bells" was indeed included on *Songs From The Wood*, which was released in January '77, charting at number 13. The two other new tracks on the EP, "March, The Mad Scientist" and "Pan Dance" (the instrumental written for the Pan's People dance routine on the *Warchild* tour) were not available again until the 20th anniversary box set in '88.

Songs From The Wood heralded yet another on-stage image for Anderson, which had gone from medieval minstrel to leather-clad rocker to some kind of blue uniformed space-man in the years since Tull had been seen in the UK. The return home saw Ian Anderson, country squire, resplendent in red bowler hat, waistcoat and sports jacket, with an album of distinctly English music to accompany the image. The one-off experiment of *Too Old* out of their system, Tull were back with a gentler, more acoustic sound, utilising all manner of exotic sounding instruments to create something that almost resembled folk music. In truth the folk-rock tag that Tull picked up in some quarters with this album was very wide of the mark, because it was the subject matter of most of the songs, rather than the actual music, which gave the album a rustic feel. Anderson's vocals too had an earthier twang to them, lending English authenticity to tales of pastoral legends like "Jack-in-the-Green", "the little chap who looks after this green and pleasant land". Anderson reflects with hindsight on the possible shortcomings of the album:

"We had gone off the idea of being tax exiles hiding in Switzerland. We had come home, paid our taxes and settled down. I had got married, bought a house and we had a baby, and I was generally speaking very happy with life. The album obviously reflects the way I felt at the time, and consequently there is no anger, no social critique at all, which is probably what is wrong with the album! It's a nice album, I do like it a lot, but it might have been a little bit quaint and twee, and dangerously close to folk music, which I loathe! But importantly, that album did bring the guys in the band together again. It was one of the albums which benefited from a lot of input from all the other band members".

It was an important album too for David Palmer. The string quartet, now disbanded, had made a significant contribution to the Tull sound in the previous two or three years, and when the decision was made to replace those elements with another keyboard player, he was the obvious choice. So after many years of invaluable service as musical collaborator and arranger, he became a full member of Jethro Tull, giving them the unusual luxury of having two keyboard players in the line up. Naturally it was within the live context that the twin keyboard set-up was most notably beneficial. Visually the contrast of David Palmer cutting a dash in black tailcoat, and John Evans in his ice-cream salesman's suit, was typically Tull. Musically their styles were not so different, but playing the incredibly and deceptively difficult music live was made far simpler with two keyboard players – in the days when everything was actually played live rather than sequenced and sampled!

The consensus of opinion amongst the fans was that *Songs From The Wood* was a wonderful return to form, and a new generation of fans picked up on this unique band through the album and subsequent tour, but many critics did not concur. Tull-baiting by the music press was fashionable, and Anderson was clearly annoyed by it, fighting back at the critics with continuous sniping from the stage throughout the tour, thereby in turn eliciting ever more savage reviews. The taunts didn't stop with the press either, as the dreaded punk rock phenomenon also became the butt of his abuse and jokey asides to the audience.

It was a common affliction of many established rock musicians (and fans) at the time, though of course time and the eventually perceived reality that some of it was really rather good suffered Anderson to modify his opinions drastically. He now cheerfully admits to being a major fan of the early Stranglers, and has cited, on several occasions, The Ramones as being his favourite rock band. Curiously, Joey Ramone is also a fan of Ian Anderson, even daring to dedicate songs to Ian and Tull during Ramones gigs. Perhaps the wheel had turned full circle in 1990 when Anderson guested, with great and obvious enthusiasm, on an album by The Six and Violence, an outrageous punk hard-core band from New York.

In 1977 such a musical collaboration would have been unthinkable. The New Wave was out to get the Dinosaurs, and Anderson was fighting back. And how else would you expect a band such as Tull, with an already long history of musical idiosyncrasy, to fight back against the heavy metal guitar thrash of Cook and Jones, and the sneering whine of Johnny Rotten, other than with mandolins, lutes, marimba, glockenspiel, nakers and tabor, and David Palmer's portative pipe organ?! If you can't beat 'em, ignore 'em!

The UK leg of the *Songs From The Wood* tour at last brought Jethro Tull an appearance on the BBC *In Concert* programme. An established radio show, it had featured almost every major (and minor) band at least once, with the noticeable exception of Tull. In fact Tull on the BBC network had been a rarity since 1969, when an argument between Ian Anderson and John Walters, the producer of the great John Peel's radio show, had signalled their last appearance on his programmes.

When the call did come, Tull fans had the bonus of sound and vision, as the BBC experimented with the short-lived *Sight & Sound In Concert* series. The one-hour show was filmed on Feb 10th at The Hippodrome in Golders Green, and broadcast a week later. There have been many rumours since of a possible CD or video release, but sadly as yet it remains locked in the BBC archives.

78

In October 1977 Ian Anderson, having at last "planted some roots" after living out of a suitcase for years, cemented his new relationship with the land by purchasing the 15,000 acre Strathaird Estate on the Isle Of Skye. The residents of the Scottish Island were understandably concerned, fearing it was merely another legendary rock-star excess, but Anderson, as always, had a clear vision of what he wanted to do. An article in an in-flight magazine had suddenly inspired him to move into salmon farming, and very quickly he transformed what had previously been a rich man's folly into a thriving business concern. With the integrity and professionalism that he brought to his music, he set up the farm on the estate, and smoking and processing plants in Inverness, eventually creating 400 jobs locally. His 'hands-on' approach earned him the hard-won respect from the islanders, and the music press had a result too; Anderson now had the official title of 'The Laird Of Strathaird', a definite no-no in the halcyon days of punk rock!

Later in '77 Chrysalis released another compilation, *Repeat – The Best Of Jethro Tull Volume 2*, again with the rip off of one previously unreleased track, "Glory Row". This time however, unlike the one 'new' track on *Volume 1*, it has never been made available as a B-side or on any subsequent compilation album.

The start of 1978 saw the release of "Woman In The Wings", a remarkable album from Maddy Prior that featured almost the full Jethro Tull line-up backing her. Although no one song caught the whole band playing together, there were contributions from Martin Barre, Barrie Barlow, David Palmer, John Glascock and Ian Anderson, and even Shona Anderson turned up as backing vocalist. Ian Anderson played flute and co-produced the album (with Palmer and long time Tull engineer Robin Black), and was duly credited. However there is no mistaking his rich vocalising on "Rollercoaster", which was strangely not credited.

The next proper Tull album, *Heavy Horses*, released in April 1978, was almost 'Songs From The Wood Part 2', to such an extent that they could have been paired as a double album and nobody would have seen the join. Except perhaps Ian Anderson:

"It is a rather more menacing album than *Songs From The Wood*, in a positive way. And I think the guys in the group are playing better, probably due to the different ways we used to record the songs. Some of the songs were already worked out completely before we recorded them, and we did them very quickly after a lot of rehearsal. Others were actually built from scratch in the studio. I might have gone in with an idea, or some lyrics and a basic tune, and the rest of the guys have added their ideas to it. Others have come from the groups' ideas, and I've developed them in the studio. There's a lot of imagination and creativity gone into the album, driven mainly by the desire to follow no set formula for making a record - which is why it took a long time to make.

We probably recorded about 20 songs, many of which were discarded or not finished. And the songs were written in different environments. I wrote some as usual in hotels on tour, another one on the train, which I tend to do a lot. And some were written at home surrounded by animals. Writing songs at home, rather than on tour or on holiday, tends to give you a more objective look at your life, so obviously the subject matter is going to be more personal and possibly relevant to most of the people who listen to the songs."

The title of the album was a reference to the heavy working horses, a dying breed with the advent of technology. Anderson joked:

"I suppose it's almost an equestrian *Aqualung* in a way. Once powerful and majestic creatures find themselves on the scrap heap, forgotten by society and replaced by machines. I'm not particularly obsessed by the animals, and it's not intended as a heartfelt campaign to bring them back into service, but I do have a soft spot for horses."

The fascination with the countryside on the previous album was joined by an apparent obsession with animals, with horses, dogs, cats and mice all getting a song devoted to them.

"I'm pleased to say that all of the songs are actually about something. The worst thing in the world is finding that you've written a song that is not really about anything at all, it's just an excuse for opening your mouth while the group rock out. To me that's pointless rock and roll. Some people would say it's not pointless, and that that is what rock and roll is all about, but unfortunately I do insist that songs should mean something, on some level. Johnny Rotten sings about things, and so do I, although they are quite different things!

I like animals, particularly my cats. What I really like about them is that they appear to be such passive, loveable creatures who just lie there doing nothing, when in reality they are nasty, vicious animals that do terrible things to other furry little animals. People always have this idea that nature is lovely and fluffy and cute, but the truth is nature is actually too tough for almost all of us. That's why we live in towns, in nice warm houses. The natural, animal world is a horrific place, and I've tried to put that across on "The Mouse Police", which is my collective name for my cats, who think nothing of devouring a mouse, head first, for pleasure."

Once again, this was not folk music by any stretch of the imagination, but it wasn't rock music either for the most part. And where they tried to rock out, most notably on long songs like "No Lullaby" and "Heavy Horses", it became evident that Tull were getting stuck in a rut. Where once the odd time signatures and unexpected shifts in tempo and direction had made Tull a fascinating and unique band, now it was becoming something of a cliché. The listener was no longer surprised by the sudden changes in a song; it was almost a case of waiting for it to happen. Some of the magic was still there, with works of genius like "The Mouse Police" and the wonderfully simple "Moths", but the insistence on stopping the groove seemingly just for the sake of it was becoming tiresome, and a good song like "Heavy Horses" was rather spoilt by not knowing when to call a halt.

The massive fan base nevertheless lapped it up, and *Heavy Horses* remains one of the most successful and popular Tull albums. Once again though, the release of "Moths" as a single failed to make any impression on the charts, but it did create something of a mystery for the fans. Originally it was to be coupled with a song called "Beltane", recorded for the album but not used. That was mysteriously cancelled at the last minute and replaced by "Life's A Long Song". "Beltane" was finally made available on the box-set, and proved to be one of the better songs from those sessions, begging the question why was it not on the album in the first place? Incidentally, although "Moths" is, on the face of it, another song about animals, it was conceived as a love song, inspired by a possibly fictitious game described in a book by John Le Carré.

The album's success was even outstripped by the always huge demand to see the band live, and concert audiences continued to snap up tickets whenever and wherever they went on sale. In 1978 Jethro Tull played five consecutive sold out gigs in London, two at The Rainbow and three at The Hammersmith Odeon, and three sold out nights at the massive Madison Square Gardens in New York. It is widely accepted that Tull were at something of a live performance peak, so what better time then to release their very first live album? Five months after *Heavy Horses* came the magnificent *Live – Bursting Out* double album, successfully capturing Tull in all their live glory. A new studio track, "A Stitch In Time", was also released as a single to coincide with the live album. For some reason the single was released in two different versions; packaging and catalogue numbers were identical, but it came as a 3min 30secs track or 4min 20secs, both on white or (rarer) black vinyl. Another mystery was why they bothered with the single at all. It was a good enough Jethro Tull song, but hardly natural hit single material, and had no connection with the live album it was supposed to promote, except for the cover photo. Anderson was pictured stage front, legs apart as on the album, but this time with a discernible rip in his trousers. So was "A Stitch In Time" just a very expensive joke to tie in with the cover photo? No matter, it was another welcome addition to the collection in a very productive year for Jethro Tull.

Fans the world over had another opportunity to both see and hear them live when one of their Madison Square Gardens concerts in October '78 was broadcast live across the globe. The BBC broadcast it simultaneously on TV and radio (commandeering a no doubt irritated John Peel's radio slot!), once again setting a broadcasting first, as it was the first transatlantic live hook-up for a rock concert. On TV and radio it was a great success, although the punters at the gig itself were less than impressed with the changes made to the set to create the illusion for TV. Forty minutes into the set the viewers were watching 'the encore', thinking they had joined the show towards the end!

One memorable feature of the broadcast was Anderson's typically reckless welcome to the watching millions throughout the world: "Hello to the Krauts, the Frogs, the Wops, the Eye-ties, the Sprouts" etc.etc. He should have been a diplomat, our Ian Anderson! Another feature was the UK audience's only glimpse of Tony Williams on bass. Tony was an old friend from the early days in Blackpool, (a member of The Executives) who had been drafted in for the US tour when John Glascock was taken ill. Chris Riley recalls watching the broadcast and being amazed to see Tony playing his bass guitar! "All the power and glory and money that Tull had, and he had to borrow my bloody bass! Actually Tony was not a bass guitarist, he played lead guitar, but he took his chance and did a good job". Williams recalls the invitation to step in:

"Barrie Barlow called me at the shop I was working in. He said, 'I've been waiting five years to give you this call – do you want the Tull gig?' I said, 'No, not playing the bass'. There's no way I could handle it. But he wouldn't take no for an answer, and so we both went through the set, over and over, until I'd learnt it all. Martin remixed the tracks for me with the bass brought right up, and I learnt it parrot fashion. We rehearsed for about two months, so I had plenty of preparation for it. But it was never going to be my gig, I just learned John Glascock's parts. He was a great player, and I enjoyed playing his bass parts. I'd never really been a Tull fan, it wasn't my scene really, but I knew them all personally and we got on well, so it was an enjoyable experience. But even then I could see that something was going on within the band. The seeds had been sown, and it was clear that there were going to be changes. Of course nobody knew at the time what those changes would be".

Like the *Sight and Sound* broadcast, there have been numerous reports of a future CD/video release of the Madison Square broadcast, but so far only the live version of *Thick As A Brick* has made it onto CD (on the 25th anniversary *Brick* CD). Parts of the show were also included on the 20th anniversary video. In truth, the similarity between the show and the *Bursting Out* CD makes it an unlikely choice for a further CD.

Anderson saw *Bursting Out* as a double-edged landmark album. It was after all the 10th anniversary of Jethro Tull, a good enough reason for a live set. He also saw it as marking, "The end of an era, and of course the start of a new one. We have gone as far as we can with the styles of music we've been playing so far. I think we will be moving in different directions from now on". He was almost spot-on, although before the start of the new era there was the small matter of *Stormwatch*, the third in the trilogy of folk-influenced Tull albums, in 1979. Before that though Jethro Tull – or parts of it – were to reach out even further into hitherto uncharted waters, eschewing folk, blues, rock and everything else that had gone before, when they accepted a commission to write for The Scottish Ballet.

The invitation may have been extended to Ian Anderson because he was a Scot and had been seen wearing what could be described as ballet tights on-stage, but more likely because the director of The Scottish Ballet was none other than Robin Anderson, Ian's brother. And to keep things strictly within the Anderson clan, Jon Anderson of Yes (but not related to Ian and Robin) was commissioned to write a second piece. To be fair, the family tie was not necessarily the main credential for the commission. The ballet wanted 'two very distinguished rock music composers' to write new pieces for the company, and few classic rock aficionados would deny that the Andersons were probably the front runners for the job, related or not.

Ian Anderson turned to David Palmer for assistance, and naturally his vast experience of classical composition was an invaluable asset both during the writing and orchestration. Martin Barre also collaborated on the work, though to a much lesser extent. Ironically, 'The Waters Edge', as it was titled, which was by far David Palmer's most significant contribution (in terms of volume) to the Tull legacy, is the source of his only unhappy memories of his time with the band:

"It was commissioned, and Ian wrote some themes, and Martin wrote a couple of pieces. Martin wasn't entirely aware, I think, of the structure of astrophic song, or the more complex structures of developed balletic sequences. They have to be conceived as what they are, and not just as little pieces of music. It has to be constructed, not contrived."

Ian wrote one particularly good theme, and lots of very interesting pieces that I developed into balletic sequences with Robert North, who is now one of the most celebrated choreographers in western ballet. We were recording *Heavy Horses* at around that time, but I gave it all I had. I think Ian thought it was taking me a long time to write, because I write so quickly, but I was actually giving it the complete works. It's a bloody enormous score – it's BIG, nearly an hour long, for a full symphony orchestra. I gave it my all.

And then we had a press conference in London to launch the ballet. I walked into the room, which was full of the leading London ballet critics and so on, and I picked up one of the handbills on the table. It announced '*The Waters Edge* – a ballet written by Ian Anderson'. I walked out. Maybe it was petulant, but I think it was merited. I walked out, got a cab home and thought 'Well fuck that!' I was distressed, having worked so hard on it. Ian apologised for the error, but it should never have happened. Consequently my memories of *The Waters Edge* are tainted, which is a great shame."

The Waters Edge was performed in Glasgow and Edinburgh, but the rest of the country missed out, although a piano only performance did eventually reach London. Such a short and limited life might indicate that it was something of a musical failure, but it was actually a fine piece of music that deserved greater exposure. The subject matter was archetypal Jethro Tull fare for the time, dealing as it did with the myths and legends of the ancient Kingdom of Scotland, nasty wee beasties, kelpies, mermaids et al. The subsequent total disappearance is as mysterious to Tull fans as is The Loch Ness Monster! Unfortunately the only recording that survives was made on a hand held tape recorder. Suggestions that it should have been properly recorded for posterity provoke something less than enthusiasm from Ian Anderson:

"No, no, it was awful, hideous! The Scottish Ballet Orchestra, as with all ballet orchestras, were not very good. They are OK if they are playing Swan Lake or something they've been brought up with, but they are not really musically equipped to play something that's a bit strange to them. They did struggle very badly with it, and it was embarrassing. There were bits in it, time signatures and things, that they just could not cope with at all. And given that rehearsal was probably no more than half a day for live performance, you can't expect them to be able to play it properly. Swan Lake for the thousandth time is fine, but to run through something completely new just once or twice before you have to play it live to an audience is likely to result in a mess. And it was a mess, it was really embarrassing. The actual pieces themselves were OK, but if you were going to record them now you probably wouldn't try to do it with an orchestra. You would use a lot of machinery to get something that sounded quite nice."

Contrary to Anderson's opinion, *The Waters Edge* was almost resurrected in 1993 when the original director of the ballet, now elevated to the lofty ranks of Director Of The Winnipeg Symphony Orchestra, asked David Palmer to present him with an orchestral suite of the ballet for performance and recording. It is one of many projects that Palmer hopes to complete, but sadly his hectic schedule offers little hope for an imminent rebirth of *The Waters Edge*.

After the interesting diversion of the ballet, it was business as usual for Tull as they finished work on 'that difficult twelfth album'! And yes, in many ways it was difficult. *Stormwatch* was an unusual album, in the sense that it seemed to be struggling for an identity. It was a shift away from the folkier themes of the previous two albums, but the folk element was still there, bubbling underneath. Musically it is difficult to fault, but there was a certain lack of energy and inspiration that indicated that Tull were merely treading water, a criticism that could never have been (justifiably) levelled at them before. It had its moments though; the cracking "Something's On The Move" recalled Tull of old, and the beautiful "Dun Ringill" remains one of Anderson's finest moments.

Another highlight was David Palmer's "Elegy", the only surviving piece of music from *The Waters Edge*. It was remarkable not only for it's simple beauty, but also for the fact that it was the first track that had not come from the pen of Ian Anderson to appear on a studio Tull album since *This Was*. As the second instrumental track on *Stormwatch*, it again echoed *This Was*, the only other Tull album to bear two instrumentals. But the previous worrying traits of *Heavy Horses* were even more evident this time around, with lumbering neo-epics like "Flying Dutchman" and "Dark Ages", more good songs slightly spoilt by being over-long and too clever by half. It was a good album, but nothing to write home about; something had to be done to rescue Tull from the slide into mediocrity. Within a year something had been done, but the scale of the changes, and the manner in which it was done, rocked the loyal fan base and caused such bad feeling within the Tull ranks that the ripples of discontent are still evident in some quarters today. But before all of that, the most tragic chapter of the Jethro Tull story was about to unfold.

John Glascock had returned to the fold after his illness, to start recording the album. Sadly his health deteriorated rapidly during the sessions and he was forced to cry off, leaving Ian Anderson to play most of the bass parts himself. ("And to record his bass parts too loudly" as Barrie Barlow was later to opine – but that's another story!) A new bass player was required for the tour, and Anderson had his sights set on what Barrie Barlow clearly reckoned to be the wrong guy:-

"Ian wanted this guy who had been at Harvard Music Academy or something in Boston, a sort of pseudo-funk player. He was a very good player, but he wasn't the right guy for Tull, and I was quite surprised that Ian wanted him. So I said 'Look, Richard Thompson is playing in Reading tonight. I'm gonna go and check Dave Pegg out'. So I went, and thought Peggy would be absolutely ideal. I got him down here for an audition, and he got the gig."

Well, yes, he did get the gig, but it wasn't quite as straightforward as Barrie suggests. Ian Anderson had called Pegg, the long time bass player with folk-rock legends Fairport Convention, several times to get him to come along for an audition. Pegg had not returned the calls, thinking it was he-who-shall-forever-be-known-as 'The Other Ian Anderson', writer, broadcaster and folk musician. The Ian A. Anderson who edits *Folk Roots* magazine has never had the greatest of relationships with Dave Pegg, and it nearly cost him the biggest break of his career! And whatever chance there may have been of improving their relationship was probably lost forever when Dave Pegg listened to an album by Anderson's English Country Blues Band with a view to booking them for Cropredy. He was singularly unimpressed, and unfortunately Ian A. Anderson called Pegg just as he had finished listening to the album whilst imbibing fairly meaningful quantities of whisky. The demon drink having done its job of enhancing brutal honesty whilst relaxing diplomacy, Pegg tactfully informed Anderson that it was "the worst album he'd ever heard and there was no way he would put them on at his festival". Curiously, 'The Other Ian Anderson' has also held a grudge against Mr Tull since 1968, claiming he was responsible for Island dropping the second Anderson for fear of creating confusion, a claim dismissed as pure paranoia by our hero.

The *Stormwatch* tour, which started in October '79 and finished with an unprecedented five-night sell out stint at the Hammersmith Odeon was another slightly lack-lustre affair, though strangely it was not the new material that was at fault. On the contrary, Tull played almost all of the new album from the outset of the shows, until the familiar strains of "Aqualung" allowed the fans to revel in a bit of the customary nostalgia. The live performance breathed new life into the *Stormwatch* material, and it was a tremendous musical success.

Oddly, the second half of the set was where it started to show the strain. The familiar material had become, well... too familiar, and the little oddities served up as a special live treat were not up to par. "Peggy's Pub", a jolly jig from new boy Dave was OK, as was "Pastime With Good Company (King Henry's Madrigal)", featuring David Palmer's Portative Pipe Organ. "Elegy" too was a very nice piece. But all together in a Tull set it was just too much distraction from the main course, genuine Jethro Tull songs. This writer remembers the uncomfortable realisation at the Hammersmith Odeon that, for the first time ever at a Jethro Tull gig, he was bored!

Just after the tour Tull played a short acoustic set live on Capital Radio, as a favour to Richard Digance. Digance was a good friend of Barrie Barlow, and had supported Tull on their 1978 UK tour – the last time Tull used a support in the UK – and was now hosting a weekly show on London's major commercial radio station. Tull played an excellent acoustic set in the foyer, including the unreleased "Peggy's Pub", and even brought in Francis Wilson, TV weatherman, to reprise his spoken intro to "Dun Ringill". Highlight of the show though must be Digance's retort to Anderson's statement that they had just "spent five nights at the Hammersmith Odeon". "Blimey" replied Digance, "it must have been a good film!"

Good or bad, the *Stormwatch* tour was completely overshadowed by tragedy with the untimely death of John Glascock, aged just 28. His close friend Barrie Barlow:

"We were like brothers, John and I. He couldn't do anything other than play the bass and guitar, that's all he ever wanted to do. He lived a fairly 'rock'n'roll' life before joining Tull, and he was a shot in the arm for the band, a marvellous player. He loved being a part of Tull, and the band were all the better for his involvement. But although he was a great player, Ian didn't really like him, and I think he got a really bad deal all round. And I used to get really angry on John's behalf, to see the way he was treated. And you know, he was the best player Tull ever had, in my opinion. He would work really hard – at the end of every gig Ian and I had to wring out our clothes, and John was the third person to do that when he joined Tull, he'd put everything into it.

We used to share a dressing room, and he sat down one night with his hand on his chest, complaining of heartburn. I put it down to him not eating or something. Anyway, we finished the tour and went back home, and after a couple of days to recover I called Jackie, John's girlfriend, and she said, 'This lazy sod's been in bed for two days!' And John was renowned normally for staying up all night. Some hotels in America, he wouldn't be there in the morning because he was still out rockin' and rollin'. So she got the doctor out and they rushed him to hospital, and he had to have open-heart surgery. I was shattered!

But, we had another tour to do. I got Tony Williams in for the tour. John did come back, but his circulation had been affected and the feeling in his fingers wasn't right. He could still play acoustic guitar though, and we started to write some things together.

When Peggy joined Tull as full-time replacement for John, he was great, learned everything very quickly and so on, but he brought that folky element into it which was not the closest thing to my heart. A very nice man, a great player, and added something to the band, but I missed

John. I couldn't help it, I missed him. So we did an American tour, and towards the end of it I called John from L.A. I asked him if he fancied joining me and David Allen (from Carmen) in forming a new band. He was absolutely elated, so I called David Allen and he was up for it. I met him, we had lunch – he had booked his flight that very day! – and the next day, John died!

We had one more gig to do on the tour, and I didn't want to do it. But the management bludgeoned me into doing it, and I cried all the way through the gig. I was like a zombie, and must have been like a zombie for months and months. It hurt, it really did. And the hurt was multiplied by the way he'd been treated. I really don't want to say too much more – I have always admired Ian, and he is unquestionably a musical genius. We were friends for a very long time, and I don't want to make waves, but I can never forget the way he treated John. I think he despised the ladishness of John, the fact that he was a working class lad".

Although this is an extremely sensitive subject, and a desperately sad chapter to dwell on, it is only fair to try to put both sides of the story. Ian Anderson has rarely spoken about John's death, other than the obvious expressions of sadness and regret. But in recent years it has become clear that Barrie Barlow is still very bitter about what he saw as the bad treatment John Glascock received from Ian Anderson when he was with the band. Late last year, one Martha Klassanos asked Anderson for his comments on Barlow's accusations, as part of an article she was writing on Glascock. This was Ian's full reply, printed with permission of both Ian and Martha:

"No, there were no bad feelings at any time between me and John Glascock. Indeed we always got along very well although it is true to say that I did my best to discourage him from smoking, drinking and late nights following his first heart surgery, and during which time we hoped he could fulfil his on-going activities with Jethro Tull.

I don't know the nature of Barrie's gripe, but I suspect that he may be developing some natural feelings of personal guilt since he, more than anybody, was close to John during his time with us.

When Jeffrey Hammond Hammond left the band, John Glascock was an obvious choice since we knew him from Carmen's support tour, and we were aware that the band had consequently broken up. John was a natural and easy musician, and although he had little musical theory, he coped happily with everything thrown at him, both past and present material.

He was an amiable and invariably cheerful character who never had a bad word to say about anybody and, although he liked to 'party', he could always be relied upon to fulfil his professional duties as required.

John Glascock never appeared as an 'outsider' since he came from the same musical background as the rest of us, and had the easy going personality that allowed him to fit in from the start.

The real tragedy of John's short life and untimely death was that his illness was not brought on by lifestyle related provocation, but was a congenital defect which was probably going to catch up with him sooner or later. But, like many people in similar situations, he found it impossible to modify his lifestyle to accommodate the realities of precarious health. I rather wish that everyone around him had echoed my occasionally stiff and warning tones instead of actively encouraging him in his return to late night party life with the usual attendant health risking social activities.

I may be cruel to reflect in this way after the fact, but I feel there were a number of people present at his funeral who were nursing a sense of guilt at perhaps not having done more to keep John on the straight and narrow path towards recovery and on-going stability.

You are quite right in that none of us chooses to openly talk or reminisce about John's short time in the band. I think that all of us who knew him and worked with him have rather private and unanimously fond memories of him, and feel that the sad and possibly unnecessary nature of his demise is best left in the realms of private sorrow rather than to be publicly aired as a sad reminder of wasted life.

I have no objection to you publishing this or discussing it with others, but I rather doubt that this, or any words will serve to usefully adorn the more tangible and strong legacy of the music he left behind him, both on record and in people's hearts.

Ian Anderson, December 1997.

David Palmer remembers the night John died as one of the strangest personal experiences he has ever had.

"We were in San Diego, and the band had played like the Mexican Tramways Orchestra. It was an appalling, dreadful gig. And afterwards we were called into the food room and I thought 'Ah, good. We are going to get a bollocking! We are going to be told to get a grip'. I thought it was late in coming, that it should have happened a couple of weeks before. Ian came in and said, 'Is everybody here?' and I thought 'Oh, it's gonna be a major bollocking!' I honestly thought he was going to say we were playing like crap, and if we didn't sort it out, he was off. Because he didn't have to say we were fired; if he went, the band was finished. But Ian said 'John Glascock died tonight'. That was such a strange experience, having expected him to say something else, and then he said something that actually really did completely demolish us. I know that's life, something like that happens once to all of us at some point, but that was salutary, for sure."

CHAPTER SIX
The Big Split

The events of the following year, 1980, still beggar belief even with almost two decades worth of hindsight! In an interesting prelude to the events that shocked the fans, *Arena* on BBC2 had broadcast a documentary featuring Jethro Tull on the road. Possibly the two most telling moments came during interviews with John Evans and David Palmer. Evans clearly displayed all the symptoms of being completely 'out of it', confessing to camera that due to his lifestyle most of the time he didn't know his 'arse from his elbow'. The erudite Palmer told the audience that Ian Anderson was Jethro Tull; "Ian could take any other bunch of musicians and have them sounding exactly like Jethro Tull". An honest and modest compliment to Ian, it was to prove more prophetic than originally intended. Barrie Barlow remembers things very clearly:

> "Well, I had definitely decided to leave Tull and start up another band. It was going to be me, John Glascock, David Allen and a great guitarist called Robin Hill. Tragically, John had died, but we decided to go ahead anyway, and eventually enlisted Chris Glen on bass. I had to do another Tull tour, which Ian had announced would be the last for some time because he wanted to concentrate on his fish farms. Tull rehearsals at Shepperton were from 10 till 6, and then, with everyone's permission, David, Robin, Chris, myself, and Tommy Ayres on keyboards, would rehearse until midnight. So I was getting this band together before I left Tull, to make it smooth, you know? So everybody could be friends.
>
> We did the Tull tour – my last Tull tour – came back, and I had a meeting with Ian. We shook hands and agreed to go our separate ways, all

very amicably. Everything was fine. I called Terry Ellis within a couple of weeks to see if he was interested in the new band, and he promised to come to see us. Then the next issue of *Melody Maker* came out, and I just could not believe it...."

'SACKED!' was the screaming front-page headline that greeted the readers, a reference to Ian Anderson's apparent summary dismissal of Tull stalwarts Barlow, David Palmer and John Evans. Barlow:

"I went fucking mental. Ian had sent a note of apology before it came out, but I thought 'hell, it can't be that bad', but of course it was! And David Palmer.... his daughter was at school and the kids were taking the mickey out of her in the playground. That's how David found out he'd been sacked from the band! And John Evans was really shattered. He just didn't know what to do. When you are on the road with a major band everything is done for you, and suddenly to take that away from him was a shock to the system. He didn't know where to start. He came to live with us for about six months. He brought his piano with him and practised all the time; he nearly drove us crazy!"

John Evans admits to being in a bad way at the time, having suffered from depression for several years before the big split:

"Things changed over the years. I really kept myself to myself in the last three or four years with Tull. I just told myself I had a regime to live by, and I used that to stop having depressions. I was in the aftermath of the initial rush, the 'I'm so clever because I'm up here in the big time' kind of thing, and you get a bit disillusioned when you realise you're not. It is not you that people admire. Not who you are, but what you are. It's just people looking up to a pop-star. So I was going through a stage of 'What is in there? What am I doing? What does it all mean?', you know. I used to spend a lot of my time just staring at the hotel bedroom wall, gradually hyperventilating, and eventually losing the feeling in my fingers and my hands.

But I was surprised when it all ended. I got the news in a letter. At the end of tours we used to go our own ways, and people would get in touch with us when something was organised. After the last tour it was agreed we would have a decent break rather than the usual few weeks, to give us a chance to go off and do our own thing for a while.

At the time I was in a sorry state financially, having just got divorced coupled with some bad business ventures. I was generally feeling a bit low. But now I had some time on my hands, I thought I'd realise one of my ambitions and try to play a Mozart concerto, which I thought was just about within my technical grasp. I kept in touch with David Palmer, who was at the time experimenting with synthesisers, and we decided to do something together. We decided to give a little concert, and spent the summer practising for it.

Then in July I got a letter – it was a carbon copy from a typewriter. It said 'Dear Barrie, David and John. I'm sorry this is so rushed, but basically *Melody Maker* is coming out tomorrow and the story in it – which I couldn't prevent, I didn't want it in but Terry Ellis put it in without my knowledge – is that the group has split up. Really, I'm going to do something on my own, maybe called Jethro Tull, maybe not. But I am using different people and I thought I ought to let you know'. I can't remember if Ian had signed it or if that was a bloody carbon copy as well. I was stunned by this, and really hurt. And after it had sunk in I thought 'I'm broke, I have no career, no qualifications. I'm 32 years old, and I get this totally impersonal, duplicate letter telling me it's all over. It was, to put it mildly, a bit of a shock!"

Once he was over the shock, more positive thoughts came to him as he pressed on with the plans for a concert with David Palmer. Dave Bristow, another fine keyboard player, joined John and David, and flush with the success of their concert they decided to form a group, called 'Tallis' after Thomas Tallis, one of Palmer's favourite composers. Tallis actually recorded an album, but could not find an outlet for it. Dave Bristow decided he did not want to pursue it any further, and the project simply fizzled out. David Palmer:

"It fell victim to a necessary time-scale. Because I had not long left Tull it was very easy for me to go into any record company and play the tape to the A&R man, not some minion who would play ten seconds of it and move on. And there was uniform appraisal – 'It's very good, very forward looking, but where can we sell it?' I said we would go out and play it to people, to which they replied 'Yes, go out and play live, get some fans, then we'll go with the album'. But then I would have been in the position where five guys, myself included, would have been depending on the success of my band for their livelihood. They needed guarantees before they could commit themselves, and of course there are no guarantees. So sadly it never happened".

The album remains unreleased to this day, although at last there are tentative plans to release it on CD in aid of charity fairly soon.

With the demise of Tallis, John Evans turned his back on the music business. An unexpected influx of royalty money (a mistake, as it turned out) put him back on his feet. He bought a boat ("a disaster!"), and spent six months "playing at being a farmer". Eventually he fell into building work, initially out of necessity because he could not afford to pay anybody to renovate his old house. He discovered that he enjoyed doing it, and was soon running his own business.

For David Palmer however, his exit from Tull was the springboard to massive personal success in the classical/rock crossover market. Since leaving Tull he has toured the world conducting the major symphony orchestras, and has released a number of albums of orchestral versions of classic rock music. Jethro Tull, Yes, Genesis, Pink Floyd and The Beatles *Sgt Pepper* have all been given the classical treatment by David – with varying degrees of artistic success. Of the three recipients of the infamous carbon copy letter, he alone bears no bitterness over the split:

"It was time. It was time for me to move on, that's for sure. With all artists there is a need to involve oneself with other artists. Tull was, not incestuous, but familial perhaps. It was time for that to stop, and for new horizons to be looked at. The fact that the result of having a new Jethro Tull was an album called *A* which fell far short of what I had certainly been striving for and wanting to see preserved, is incidental. There is clear evidence of artists going off tangentially, in pursuit of rainbow's ends, and not finding them.

I would say that the best Jethro Tull was the band that existed in the mid to late 70's. That band produced live performances together with recordings that were pretty damn good! I'm certainly very proud to have

Above: The John Evan Smash 1967
l-r: Neil Smith, Ian Anderson,
Neil Valentine, (seated) John Evans,
Barrie Barlow, Tony Wilkinson,
Glenn Cornick.

Left: Ian Anderson at
The Surbiton Toby Jug, early 1969
(photo by Graham F. Page).

Above: Ian Anderson, Lund. Sweden 2/12/74. **Below left:** John Evans and canine friend.
Below right: Jeffrey Hammond-Hammond in his infamous striped suit (photos by Per Ekstrom).

Above: Ian Anderson, Copenhagen 1974 (photo by Lars Hegndal).
Below: Ian Anderson, David Palmer and John Glascock, *Heavy Horses* tour,
Houston, Texas 1978 (photo: Lindsey Davis).

Above left: David Palmer, Cologne 1977
Above right: David Palmer and Dave Pegg, Cologne 1980 (photos by M. König).
Below: One of the classic Tull photos, taken by amateur photographer Frank Smith in Manchester 1991, and later used by Tull for the cover of *In Concert* in 1995. By an amazing stroke of luck, it was actually frame 37 in a roll of 36.

Above: Dave Pegg, Ian Anderson and Martin Barre, Pullman Washington, Oct 24 1992.
Below: Martin Barre (photos by Mark Colman).

Above: Ian Anderson and Martin Barre (photo by Mark Colman).
Opposite top: Ian Anderson, 1993 Ruisrock Festival, Finland (photo by Jyrki Myllyla).
Opposite bottom: Ian Anderson (photo by Mark Colman).

Above left: Mick Abrahams onstage with Blodwyn Pig in 1990.
Above right: Glenn Cornick and his famous headband return for the reformation of Wild Turkey in 1996.
Below: Mick Abrahams, Maart Allcock, Ian Anderson and Clive Bunker at the 1990 Jethro Tull Convention in Milton Keynes (all photos by Martin Webb).

been a part of that. But I think I have always known the direction in which I was headed, though only time would tell if I would ever achieve those objectives. You can't predict success; it's like doing the pools. But to have a pencil in your hand, and to be one of the quickest writers in the west, with an understanding of orchestral and rock music was something that I had to move on with. And I suppose, looking at what I do now, my credentials are impeccable. I am conducting major symphony orchestras around the world, performing rock music of the 70's and David Palmer music of the 90's, and I have a credibility factor on two counts.

I am the product of a celebrated music establishment, taught by some of the finest brains in western music, and I've been a member of one of the biggest and best rock'n'roll bands in the world. They are credentials which should get me into the White House! I am certainly a very proud ex-member of Jethro Tull".

Although as of the *A* album Palmer ceased to be involved with Jethro Tull, their paths have since crossed on more than one occasion. In 1985 he was commissioned by Channel 4 to write the music for a major historical series, *The Blood Of The British*. His music was used throughout the series, and the haunting theme tune, sung by Ian Anderson, was later released as a single. Ian Anderson and Martin Barre also helped out – albeit slightly reluctantly – on Palmer's first classical/rock album, *A Classic Case* of Jethro Tull. There is even a cameo appearance from Anderson on the subsequent Genesis album. And in 1997 Anderson finally joined Palmer on-stage at the London premiere of his *Queen* classical album, playing flute and singing several Tull standards to an audience that was clearly there to see and hear Anderson rather than orchestral Queen songs.

Barrie Barlow's musical venture after Tull floundered at first.

"I carried on working with David Allen and Robin Hill, rehearsing in our cottage near Blackpool, but then I had to go away to do an album with somebody. And when I came back David Allen had gone and tried to get a deal for himself. Everybody wanted to kill him!"

Barrie then got together with Zal Cleminson (of the Sensational Alex Harvey Band) and formed Tandoori Cassette, a very creative but sadly short-lived band. As Barrie says, it was a band that was ahead of its time.

Barrie is now a very sought after producer and session player, having worked with Robert Plant and Jimmy Page in recent years.

So, what of the album that had brought about the demise of Jethro Tull as was? Had David Palmer hit the nail on the head with his theory that Anderson plus anybody would still sound like Jethro Tull? Well, no, that's not quite the way it went.

Clearly Anderson saw the need to try something different after hitting a slightly stodgy patch in recent years. He has since stated that Tull as a unit almost ceased to be at the time of the big split, but I firmly believe that the split was the saviour of the band, even if the first new steps were not universally popular with Tull fans. *A* was an uncertain step, not necessarily in the right direction, but certainly away from the wrong direction. He wanted to make an album that didn't sound like another Tull album, hence the desire to work with different musicians. Many of the traditional Tull trademarks remained of course, including the unmistakable guitar playing of Martin Barre. Despite the countless personnel changes over the years, Ian Anderson insists that if Barre was not in the band, it would be the end of Jethro Tull. "To use another guitarist after all this time would be like getting divorced and then marrying again the next day". Dave Pegg was also retained for *A*, for although he was a member of Jethro Tull he had not yet recorded with them.

The new sounds came courtesy of the violin and keyboards of 'special guest' Eddie Jobson, once of Roxy Music and UK, both of whom had opened for Tull in the past, and drummer Mark Craney, the first American to join the ranks, recruited on the recommendation of Jobson.

It was always intended as a one-off line up, confirming that *A* started life as an Ian Anderson solo album. Indeed, the very title was taken from the 'A' for 'Anderson' written on the master tape boxes. And as a one-off, it was a successful and interesting diversion, the new instrumentation allowing the band to experiment once more with new styles of music. The apparent modernisation of the Tull sound was mirrored in the new on-stage image; gone were the colourful and varied costumes, replaced by uniform white jump suits. It must be said, the new look suited some band members better than others. Jobson looked cool. He was, after all, once in

Roxy Music! Craney and a still hirsute Dave Pegg did not look out of place, and Anderson moved around enough to carry the image, but Martin Barre – the pre-Marathon Runner version – looked, frankly, rather odd. "That was probably the least flattering of all our stage costumes" opines Martin, with no lack of understatement!

Another innovation due to new technology was Anderson's use of radio mic and electric flute, leaving him free to wander out into the audience whenever the mood took him.

As with *Stormwatch* before it, the new material was far more successful in live performance than on record, but conversely the new line-up struggled to play the old standards convincingly at times. Or was it simply that the shock of the new image would not allow the older fans to adjust to the new interpretations of their favourite Tull songs? Jobson, a highly talented musician who had plenty of his own good ideas to offer, was nevertheless treated with suspicion by much of the fan base, perhaps being seen as the villain in the drama of the brutal dismembering of the much loved late 70's line-up. John Evans had, after all, become a firm favourite of the fans, most of who only knew of Jethro Tull with him in the band. He was a hard act to follow, emotionally rather than musically; a fact that has been evident to all others who subsequently took up his former position. It is strange but true to relate that for countless Tull fans the keyboard player in Tull has been judged less on his overall musical prowess than his ability to precisely copy Evans' famous piano introduction to "Locomotive Breath"!

Tull toured America and Europe with *A*, again granting only two concerts to the UK audience, and again both in London. A major recompense came in the form of *Slipstream*, the first commercially available video from Jethro Tull, which featured lots of footage from the *A* tour, along with several well made studio promos. It was an exceptionally well produced video, making good and creative use of the mixture of live and studio footage, but for many it came at the wrong time, and featured the wrong line-up.

A had some fine songs and wonderful musicianship, but lacked heart. The futuristic, environmentally concerned subject matter of many of the songs did not leave much room for the subtle humour and warmth that is found in the greater works of Tull, and as a result it is seen with hindsight by many to be one of Tull's least important albums. That's a pity in many ways, for although it was from easily the shortest lived line-up, and is a proverbial 'sore-thumb' in the Tull catalogue, it was a vitally important stepping stone out of the 70's and into the new decade; a decade which was to herald the creative re-birth of Ian Anderson and Jethro Tull.

CHAPTER SEVEN
A Kick Up The Eighties

Fourteen months passed before Jethro Tull surfaced again, and they were fruitful months indeed for Anderson's songwriting. Something like twenty tracks were recorded for the next album, with only a dozen making it on to the finished article. The quality of the rejected tracks only became evident when many of them were included on the 20th Anniversary box set. *The Broadsword And The Beast*, released April '82, showed Tull well and truly back on form.

Gerry Conway, a veteran of the folk rock scene, had replaced Mark Craney on drums, and Eddie Jobson's departure, initially to pursue a solo career and then into the ranks of Yes, necessitated the recruitment of another keyboard player. Ian Anderson and Martin Barre were pointed in the direction of a young Scottish band called The R.A.F (Rich And Famous), and were mightily impressed by the incredibly talented keyboard player, Peter John Vettese. He was to become a very influential member of Jethro Tull over the following four years, initially breathing new life into the Tull sound, but eventually almost inadvertently destroying it!

The turmoil within the ranks, and the evident unrest amongst a large part of the audience, had focused Anderson's attention on the need to haul Tull back from the brink. *Broadsword* was in many ways a very calculated manoeuvre to return to the traditional qualities that had endeared the band to the fans from the outset. He had seen the need for change, and also seen that the initial redirection was not true to the spirit of Tull. Anderson:

"It was a much more deliberate attempt to make an album that sounded like a Jethro Tull album. It more or less embodied things about the group that we felt would give us a broad-based audience. And we used a producer so that he could give us an independent view, an objective mind about making it work in those terms."

If that sounds a bit cynical and over calculating, the album itself sounded anything but. It was a tremendous return to form, which dispelled any doubts created by the events of the previous couple of years. The new electronic keyboard sounds that featured so heavily on *A* were used more effectively within the traditional Tull elements of heavy rock and Celtic influences, and the result was a musical success on two counts. The media regarded *Broadsword* as the album that dragged Tull kicking and screaming into the 80's, and yet the band had achieved their goal of making what could be regarded as a classic, traditional Jethro Tull album.

Broadsword is still a favourite amongst the fans, yet ironically it was new boy Peter Vettese who was responsible for much of the excellent quality of the album. Although all the songs were written by Ian Anderson, as usual, the 'additional material by Peter Vettese' credit was more than just a sop to a few ideas. Clearly he had contributed a lot of wonderful instrumental passages, and some of the keyboard arrangements were on a par with the great work of David Palmer in his many years with the band. His arrival in the band, coinciding with Anderson hitting an incredibly rich songwriting vein, was the perfect combination of youth and experience required to put Tull back on the right track. And Tull fans were delighted to hear Martin Barre getting a chance to shine again on guitar, having been rather under used on the previous outing.

Another was the inspired choice of Paul Samwell-Smith as producer. It was the first time Tull had used an outside producer, and the experiment was a success. Well, it seemed that way to the listener, but Anderson has since been rather dismissive of the benefits:

"I did enjoy the feeling that it was not down to me all the way through. I spent most of the making of that album sat at the back of the control room, reading brochures of studio equipment while Paul was sitting at the desk. I wasn't having to play the role of 'our man in the studio', I didn't have to be on the ball to everybody. But I certainly didn't leave it all to Paul. He is a hell of a nice chap, and has some musical ability, a musical background, and he understands music. But basically he is someone who can coax another take out of someone, and he is an extra pair of hands on the mixing desk. I think he would be the first to admit that he wasn't the producer in the sense that he was terribly influential. He was instrumental in getting the final result maybe a little better than it might have been had he not been there, but he didn't really shape the feel of the music. That was all there before he came into it."

True to those sentiments, every Tull album since has been produced by Anderson.

As with the album, the live shows were a resounding success. Anderson and co. were attired in far more suitable minstrels garb, and the humour and visual jokes were back in force. It was not exactly a return to the rock theatre of the *Brick* and *Passion Play* era, but the shoestring budget effects like the giant broadsword that Anderson hauled across the stage, and the comically frightening "Beastie" (complete with glowing red eyes) on Anderson's back, were a welcome reminder of Tull shows of old. The most striking visual moment in the show came courtesy of more men in rabbit suits, another throwback to vintage Tull. During "Watching Me Watching You" a strobe light flashed continually as one roadie after another dressed in white coats walked onto and around the stage. It was a genuinely ludicrous and very funny spectacle, rounded off nicely with the arrival of the giant white rabbit at the end of the line!

The press (well, some of them!) were as enthusiastic as the paying punters for the rejuvenated live Tull. John Coldstream in *The Daily Telegraph* enthused that "It is an unconfined joy to report that this concert was the group's most rewarding and skilfully executed since an unforgettable stint at The Rainbow almost a decade ago". And Chris Welch in *Melody Maker* wrote:

"In an age when audiences start rushing down to the front, matches alight, even before the curtain has been raised, it's instructive to be reminded how the traditional rock concert is conducted. Jethro Tull reinforced some

103

basic lessons when they returned in triumph to London. Ian Anderson expects the audience to do some work. They have to listen, sometimes to new and unfamiliar material, and to tunes that don't have instant riot appeal. But gradually over two hours the pace hots up, the tension mounts, and you feel you've actually undergone a course of treatment instead of a quick energy fix. Ian Anderson's boundless energy after a dozen years of touring is quite astonishing. He twirled his flute and pranced a merry highland fling, and as he was chased around the stage by a large goose and men in white coats, the old Tull humour seemed just as manic."

In the break between the European and American legs of the tour, Gerry Conway was replaced by Paul Burgess, ex of 10cc. His first gig was at *The Theakston Music Festival* at Nostell Priory. It was and is rare to see Tull play a major festival in the UK, and it came about largely through Dave Pegg's relationship with the Theakston's brewery – both as a commercial and social acquaintance! The supporting bill was put together by Tull, and featured an up-and-coming band that had caught Anderson's ear, having sent in a demo tape and asking for his advice. Marillion, as they were known, were to repay the favour a few years later when they themselves were headlining a major UK festival, and tempted Tull out of a temporary enforced retirement to bolster the bill.

Before that festival, and the following US tour, Tull had been invited to play at the first Princes Trust concert in London, alongside the likes of Pete Townsend, Kate Bush, Madness and many more. Temporarily without a drummer, Tull played three songs with Phil Collins, two of which were included on the subsequent commercially available video. It was not a classic performance, but it's worth checking out if only to see Phil Collins struggling with material that he was clearly not over-familiar with.

It was perhaps surprising to see Tull included on a bill that included so many current pop and rock superstars, but Anderson sees it with his customary realism; "We were only asked to do it because David Bowie cancelled late on – and we never got asked back!" Anderson did, however, make something of an impression on Prince Charles, who later described him as "One of the most interesting and intelligent men in the music business."

Despite the greatness of the album, and the success of yet another sell-out tour, *Broadsword* was not the commercial success that it should have been. It did well in Europe, almost doubling the traditional Tull sales in Germany, their second biggest market, but in America it failed to sell in the quantities they had hoped for, and possibly even expected. Ian Anderson:

"I was very surprised that it sold very moderately in America. It didn't surprise me that *Under Wraps* later on didn't do terribly well, because it was definitely off on a different sort of tack, and I could see that could probably alienate a lot of people who thought they knew what they wanted to hear from Jethro Tull. But *Broadsword* was strange, I thought it would do well in America. I guess it was just the wrong time. Just another Tull album, just another tour. Nobody got terribly excited. People were still flirting with punk and the new-wave thing, and bands like us were definitely right out of fashion. We suffered also by not having a terribly convincing amount of radio play or promotion at that time. It's a shame, because it was a really good album. Certainly one of my favourites".

In 1983 Ian Anderson had another attempt at recording a solo album, and this time he succeeded. Or did he? 'Walk Into Light', released in November of that year, was at least credited to Ian Anderson rather than yet another 'new' Jethro Tull line-up, but in many ways he was less in control of the album than any Jethro Tull album before or since!

"I wanted to take the opportunity to experiment with something outside the Jethro Tull music of the time. I could have made an album of me singing and playing acoustic guitar and flute, but that just seemed too obvious. I wanted to get away from doing what I was known for, and do something more electronic. It was the beginning of the techno age, of sequencers and samplers, and back then it all seemed very exciting and interesting.

I guess I was interested in the idea of combining the songs that could have been Jethro Tull songs, with a more mechanical and disciplined arrangement that would come from computer driven music. It was in a way a direct precursor of the Tull album *Under Wraps* the following year. It is interesting that both albums were resoundingly unsuccessful commercially. And I can only assume that the two albums that marked a rather more experimental period with technology were not very successful because I wasn't very good at using that technology!"

That may or may not be the case, but certainly Peter Vettese was well acquainted with the keyboard technology, and he played a major role on the album. He was the only other musician on the album, and incredibly, co-wrote half of the tracks. The deep irony there is that Ian Anderson's percentage of writing credits on his solo album was far lower than on any Jethro Tull album! In fact, since *This Was* some fifteen years earlier, although there were sometimes acknowledgements of 'additional material written by....", only four Jethro Tull tracks had not been credited to Ian Anderson alone, and two of those were little more than live 'filler' instrumentals on *Bursting Out*. *Walk Into Light* boasted five co-credits for Vettese, and his influence, though impressive, was not what most Tull fans were looking for in an Ian Anderson solo album. Instead of the hoped-for acoustic collection, *Walk Into Light* was a very electronic, often cold and mechanical offering, with hardly a flute or acoustic guitar to be heard.

Of the major rock bands of the seventies which threw up a plethora of solo outings, Jethro Tull's leader had been the obvious contender to make a worthwhile solo album. After all, there had already been several solo offerings from Ian within the context of Jethro Tull albums. It was a major surprise to hear him forsaking his traditional sound, and a major disappointment to many fans. Was he deliberately trying to re-invent himself, and was he aware that it would come as a shock to Tull fans?

"It was just the realisation that there was something new out there. For the first time there was an alternative to the guitar, organ, piano and drum kit. Suddenly there were workable alternatives that gave you the opportunity to create more elaborate soundscapes, tonal tapestries, richer audio backgrounds to the rock or pop song. It was a question of biting the bullet and having a go, or simply turning away from it and confining myself to the old school of the traditional rock musician. And I guess we all have to at least have a go at something new.

Peter's input was quite a marked one. It went out as a solo album, but in many ways it was the most collaborative musical album that I've made, in the sense that there was definitely a work process every day that would utilise the efforts of other people. Peter is a live wire, a very bright and inventive musician, and never short of ideas.

I was quite pleased with the album at the time, though looking back on it now it could have been a lot better musically. It was a good experiment, but one that I enjoy in retrospect because of the songs more than the actual sound of the end result."

It was a resounding flop, commercially, possibly due in part to the low profile that Jethro Tull had in the media. It was often the case that a Tull fan would only discover a new Tull release by looking through the Jethro Tull section in record shops, so the likelihood of finding Ian Anderson under 'J' or 'T' was remote! There was also no tour to promote the album, and only a couple of TV appearances to promote the wonderful single "Fly By Night", one of the few bright (as in jolly) notes on an otherwise rather gloomy album. Anderson later joked, when Tull performed a couple of the songs in concert, that it had been released on the MI5 label, such had been the secrecy surrounding it!

One highlight of the year for onlookers, if not for Anderson himself, was his appearance on German TV, a special event organised by Ebehard Schoener. Jethro Tull played two tracks from *Walk Into Light*, with the 'assistance' of an orchestra. Or at least that was the way it had been planned, but Ian Anderson had other ideas:

"We did an amazing switch on the orchestra. They were a terrible orchestra; we had a run through in the afternoon and it was just abysmal. They were trying to play *Fly By Night*, and it was awful. Ebehard is a hell of a nice guy, but he's away with the fairies, he's just not with it. He's a lovely fella, but he thinks he's really arty, into rock & roll, the classics, and avant garde type things, but he is actually mildly crazy. I knew the orchestra might be terrible because I had seen a video of Ultravox the year before, and that was a total disaster. They were doing 'Vienna', and it was a nightmare, with the orchestra about half a bar out. I spoke to Midge Ure about it, and he confirmed it. So I took out two tapes for the show, one with just the drums on it and the other with the orchestral sounds.

David Palmer was out there to help with the score and so on, and he was in the control room for the live broadcast, and I got him to switch the tapes at the last minute, so he played the tape with the orchestra on it as well. I told him to kill the engineer if he had to, to make sure the orchestra faders were down on the live broadcast! And sure enough, as it went out there was a count in, and I knew as soon as he started to conduct he was half a bar out, and by the end the orchestra were a whole bar out, they'd actually lost a bit more on the way. Ebehard didn't suss it, and at the end came running over to hug and kiss me saying "Wonderful! Marvellous!", and so on. I couldn't say "Ebehard, you were bloody miles away but it doesn't matter because we switched the tapes on you" – I just couldn't bring myself to tell him. But it was wonderful!"

That was a treat, but even better was yet to come, as the viewers later saw an apparently bemused Ian Anderson stroll out, still assembling his flute, to jam with Fela Kuti and, seemingly, the entire population of the world. Anderson looked extremely uncomfortable, and in common with most of the other guest musicians didn't seem to know what was going on; after a few minutes of fairly aimless jamming he actually stopped playing and lit a cigarette! What the hell was going on?

"I was in the bar after doing my stuff. I was talking to Jack Bruce, who is one of my heroes, and I'd never met him before. I've always wanted to meet him, and here he was, so I was bending his ear at the bar. Suddenly these people came rushing in and said, 'Quick, you have to go on-stage'. I said, 'No, no, I've done my bit' but 'No, you must come and play with Fela Kuti, they are waiting for you'. I could hear this kind of jungle rhythm going on, and apparently they had actually announced that I was coming on to play. Once that commitment had been made for me without my knowledge I had no option but to leg it up there. My shoelace was un-done and I didn't even have my flute, it was in it's case back-stage. I had to run and get it and assemble it on-stage!

So there was this bunch of very untrained guys, all very rough and ready, and Fela Kuti, who was a total con man. He couldn't play at all, it was just musical bullshit which he passed off as avant garde playing. As far as I was concerned he just traded off being a black African militant, and all the critics were taken in by him. He didn't like me at all; to him I was 'Capitalist Whitey', but he was happy to get me up there promoting his career. Me and Jack Bruce and everybody else, we all got dragged up there, and it was chaos. It was just a rambling mess that went on and on until it ran out of steam.

The people in the audience weren't impressed, they knew it was dead boring, a total waste of time. But that's the sort of thing they do on German TV, they get these 'arty' ideas. The idea of people getting together and jamming, that it will somehow give rise to this remarkable spark of something wonderful happening – 9 times out of 10 it doesn't happen, unless everybody knows exactly what they are doing. Either you are working around the basic framework of blues or jazz, and everybody knows the rules, or you do something that looks like a jam but has in fact been properly rehearsed. As it was it was just a mess, but unfortunately it's one of those things I got dragged into."

If Tull fans had thought Anderson's solo outing had exorcised his new found fascination with electronic keyboards, they had another huge shock coming to them when Jethro Tull regrouped in the studio. This time forsaking a drummer altogether in favour of the dreaded drum machine, the four-piece came up with a startling and innovative masterpiece, *Under Wraps*. The gadgetry was still there up-front, but unlike the often sterile and unemotional Ian Anderson album, *Under Wraps* was bursting with energy and vitality. Vettese was magnificent throughout, and Martin Barre's guitar playing was a perfect foil to it. Anderson was singing with renewed vigour, stretching his vocal prowess to the limit – with very unfortunate repercussions, as it turned out.

Of the seventeen tracks on the longer CD and cassette version of the album, only three were written solely by Ian Anderson. Vettese was co-credited on the others, and even Martin Barre was credited on two tracks. The result, a more accessible and commercial sound, could have reaped great rewards had it been made by any other band. One reviewer wrote, "Take away Anderson's distinctive vocals and you could almost be listening to Ultravox". Had it actually been Ultravox of course it would have been a huge hit!

Under Wraps, more than any other Tull album, split Tull fans opinions right down the middle. To some it was an incredible, bold and exciting foray into a brilliant new direction. Others were simply horrified by what was happening to Tull. I recall when, in my role as editor of the Tull 'zine, I was collating the results of a poll to find the reader's favourite Tull album. Each album was graded, and although I was becoming accustomed to getting the 1/10 or even 0/10 votes for *Under Wraps*, I was amused to see one voter simply cross it out, writing "I refuse to accept this as a Jethro Tull album"! An extreme view perhaps, but it says a lot about the effect this album had on the fan base. And even the supporters of this new Tull were perturbed at the use of a drum machine on a Jethro Tull album! Nevertheless, even if the fans were unhappy, the band had enjoyed themselves. Martin Barre certainly had:

"It was a lot of fun to record. More than any of the other albums we had made, it seemed to be trouble free, and everything fell together so easily. It's one of my personal favourite Tull albums, even though now I can see that maybe it wasn't the right thing for us to do. When you are locked away in a studio for a year with only yourself to please, it is difficult to judge the results in an impartial way. We were making music to please ourselves, which is maybe a bit selfish. Music should be for everybody, not just for an elite bunch of people. Having said that though, nowadays it is one of the few Tull albums that I play to enjoy rather than for reference. Funnily enough, *A* is the other one that I think sounds really good. But *Under Wraps* is a great album."

Ian Anderson agrees:

"It really does have some great songs on it, and it was also the last time that I could sing really well. I think it was fun to make because we didn't record it in a commercial studio with tape ops and engineers. We were all in the room together, sat around the desk. We engineered and mixed the whole thing together. It was just us, the guys who made the music, with nobody else in the room. We didn't have an audience, so we could be a little braver in trying things out."

Dave Pegg was less happy with it. That was perhaps not surprising, given his background in folk and folk-rock music. He had, after all, joined Tull when they were almost looked upon as a folk-rock outfit themselves, only to find they had moved further from folk music than ever before on his arrival! *Under Wraps* was a great disappointment to Pegg – "The outtakes from *Broadsword* would have made a far better album" – but even he was outraged by the reaction the finished album evoked from Chrysalis Records, in the person of Terry Ellis. Ellis was brought to Ian's home, along with the rest of the band, to listen to the results of months of serious work in the studio.

As the whisky flowed, Ellis delivered his verdict; "If you think I'm going to release this fucking pile of crap on my label, you can think again! This isn't Jethro Tull. It's shit!" Coming from Ellis, that was damning indeed, for it was not the usual record company/artist relationship here. Terry Ellis had been there from the start, and had always been proud to be associated with Jethro Tull. It was Ellis who had greeted a Chrysalis employees convention by making them all stand, lift up their chairs, and read what was written underneath the seat. Underneath every chair was written, simply, "JETHRO TULL". He said "That band has given you your job. Now put your chair down, have a good lunch, and enjoy yourselves, but don't ever forget it!"

In spite of his…. err…. reservations, the album was released in September, as the band set out on another world tour, and it did in fact make number 18 in the UK album chart, their highest placing since *Bursting Out* in 1978. Actual sales however were less than spectacular, and the group were far from happy with the backing they were getting – or not getting – from Chrysalis. There were rumblings of discontent from some other big names on the label too, as Anderson remembers:

"The last couple of albums (*Walk Into Light* and *Under Wraps*) weren't great records, but they certainly should have done better than they did. Chrysalis just did an absolutely rotten job. They were in a terrible state at the time, with a lot of problems. We, along with Ultravox, Spandau Ballet and Pat Benatar were going to high-tail it out, to try to get away from Chrysalis because we really felt it was just not right. But I looked at the other record companies, and the dreadful reality was that we are up against an institution. I think, if anything, we would have been worse off had we left Chrysalis. At least there we had some people who had some sort of loyalty to Jethro Tull, and we could talk to them because we had known each other for some years. I don't think I could cope with some 25 year old A&R man being nice to us, all the while thinking 'God, we are stuck with this lot!' So we stayed, and fortunately they did eventually get their act together again."

For the live performances Doane Perry was enlisted on drums, the second American to join the band. He was an experienced session musician, having worked with major names ranging from Bette Midler, through Pat Benatar to Lou Reed, and had been a Tull fan since the first time he saw them in 1969. He was also a great friend of Mark Craney, and recalls his thrill when Mark got the gig back in 1980. "I was so excited, for him and me! Because he had got the gig, I almost felt like I had got it too. He was my friend, playing with the band I had loved for years!"

An advert in *Village Voice* in 1983 had prompted Doane to send in a tape, more in hope than expectation, but to his amazement he got the gig, and a few months later was part of the Jethro Tull live set up himself.

The *Under Wraps* tour was one of the most electrifying live sets that Tull have ever done, and one of the last times that they ever used anything even remotely approaching what could be described as stage props. The band members started the gigs, naturally, under wraps, and were joined at various points in the set by naked ladies and astronauts. It was an intense set, musically, and a punishing schedule which was due to finish with a tour of Australia. Tragically though the strain told on Ian's voice, as he developed serious throat problems as the tour wore on. By the time they got to Australia they had tried to minimise the problem by altering the set to make it less problematic for his voice, but just five shows into the Australian tour he had to admit defeat, and the rest of the shows were cancelled.

Some of the magic of the tour was captured for posterity when BBC Radio broadcast some of the Hammersmith gig on the Tommy Vance show. It was later released as an album by Strange Fruit, though unfortunately the need to limit the time for a vinyl release meant that only 40 minutes or so were made available to the fans.

On his return to England, Ian Anderson was ordered by doctors to rest his voice completely for a year. That meant no singing either live or in the studio. It was the start of the longest ever hiatus for Jethro Tull, which seemed for a while to mark the disintegration of the group.

Tull did play one gig in 1985 however. They were approached to perform in Berlin at a special evening to mark the 300th Anniversary of the birth of J.S.Bach. For this one-off concert, which was broadcast by German radio and TV, Eddie Jobson was reunited with Tull for a set that was remarkable for their tremendous rendition of Bach's Double Violin Concerto. It was a superb musical offering, and sadly this was the only performance. The other instrumental pieces played on the night were excellent too, but it was very obvious that Ian's vocal problems were far from over. Wisely, he decided that was it for the rest of the year, and devoted his time to his other interests, particularly the fish farms and factories in Scotland.

"I had already decided to slow down, to try to break the pattern of tour/record/tour/record. I had been doing that for almost twenty years, and it was time to live a slightly more normal life. It had been almost non-stop until about 1978 or '79, but we were able to take things a little easier in the 80's, with an album every couple of years instead of every year. But I did want a proper break for a while, and of course that decision was in a sense made for me when my throat problems developed. I had some kind of strain, an acquired muscular spasm, caused basically by singing.

When I started the tour in '84 I was fine, but when we were in America it started to get really tight and sore before the end of the show, and the only way to get the notes out was to sing even louder. It really was a problem, and it got steadily worse to the point that after just a couple of songs on stage my voice was almost gone. It was incredibly depressing. So when we got back from Australia I decided I would not sing a note for a few months, but after the Berlin gig, which was pretty wretched, it was very obvious that it was not something that would go away after just a couple of months rest, which was really very worrying. So quite a long time went by deliberately not doing anything, which coincided with me wanting to spend more time up North. By then we had quite a few people on the payroll, and 'commitment to bodies' transferred itself from people in the group to people on the fish farm side of things. I took a year off, and that year turned into almost two, so the break was rather longer than I'd intended. But it was a necessary break, and really it was the first time I'd been able to relax, and not worry about the other guys in the group.

Then it was really just me, Martin Barre and Dave Pegg in Jethro Tull. Martin and Dave are the kind of guys who are able to look after themselves, so I no longer felt that if I didn't organise a tour or an album that I was letting the guys down. Before there was the road crew, three of who were permanent employees, and five other people in the band. Eight people who were depending on me deciding to do something for their income. That's OK for a few years, but there comes a time when it's nice not to have that burden, not to have to consider other people's needs as much as you've had to from the start."

Martin Barre took the opportunity to start trying to write songs in earnest, and also set about the arduous and thoroughly unpleasant task of getting himself physically fit! Not only did he manage to shed the pounds, but he also eventually turned himself into a marathon runner of respectable times. He was unhappy with the long break though, missing the buzz of playing. He made a half-hearted attempt to get a deal for a solo album, but he was clearly not ready for such a step. "It was a bit unfortunate that I recorded a set of songs that were fairly dismal, and slung the tape around the record companies. They slung them back at me!"

Dave Pegg regrouped with his first musical love, Fairport Convention. A mixture of old and new members recorded *Glady's Leap*, a one-off comeback album. It was a great success, and Fairport were re-launched as a working unit once more. He subsequently split his time between both bands for many years, until ultimately the increasingly busy schedules of both could no longer be kept separate.

Peter Vettese rapidly became a sought after session musician, playing with the likes of Go West, Frankie Goes To Hollywood, and Simple Minds.

Chrysalis chose to fill the gap with their third 'Best Of' compilation. 'Original Masters' was released in October '85, and whilst it was a fair enough collection of some of Tull's better known songs, it was noticeable that the record company could find nothing more recent than 1977 to include as 'the best of'. The basic packaging did nothing to promote sales either, but at least this time around they resisted the temptation to include just one new track to prise the money from dedicated fans. The album did not chart, but maintained steady sales over a long period of time.

There was a very brief return to the studio for Tull, on the previously mentioned David Palmer projects. *A Classic Case – The London Symphony Orchestra Plays The Music Of Jethro Tull* was released in Europe and America, but not initially in the UK, by EMI as the first of a planned series from David Palmer. Previous classic/rock hybrids had failed miserably in artistic terms, although commercially they were hot stuff at the time. It was expected that David Palmer's attempt would be something rather different, given his credentials and experience in both fields, but sadly his first offering failed on the same terms. Ian Anderson, Martin Barre, Dave Pegg and Paul Burgess were all drafted in, obviously to enhance sales to Tull fans, but ironically it was their presence which proved to be the artistic downfall of the album.

The result was simply a rock band playing with an orchestra, rather than truly orchestral arrangements of Tull songs. There were some great moments, but too many poor moments to make it a worthwhile album. The one truly excellent track was Palmer's arrangement of 'Warchild', taken from the abandoned 1974 orchestral sound track. It was the one track which featured no rock musicians, and the one track which fulfilled the promise of the album. Ian Anderson himself was less than impressed with the album:

"The original idea as I understood it was that he was going to orchestrate those songs in a creative and totally different context, but all it turned out to be really was the same things. The same tempo with the wretched rock drumming and the orchestra just honking the tune. I thought it was very uninspired, and I felt that David was under a lot of pressure from the record company to do something that really was not adventurous. I had made a personal commitment to David to do it, so I felt obliged to do it.

His next one though, with Genesis music, on which I do play a very little bit of flute, sounds a lot better."

Far more artistically rewarding was Palmer's other major project at the time. The theme to *Blood Of The British*, called "Coronach", was eventually released as a single in June 1986, credited to 'Jethro Tull & David Palmer'. It did nothing chart-wise, but it really should have done. David Palmer is still aghast at the record company apathy that he believes doomed a wonderful record to obscurity.

"I had spoken to Chrysalis – to Chris Wright in fact – when I was first commissioned to write the music for the series. I told him that I was writing the title song for a prime time Channel 4 programme that would get a lot of viewers, and that we needed to get a record out. They did nothing. When the series started, every week the continuity announcer commented on how good the title music was, and Channel 4 were inundated with letters from people who wanted to buy it on record.

So one day I burst into Chris Wright's office and told him 'Look, we have got a song that people like, and they want to buy the record. I wrote it, Jethro Tull recorded it, Ian sings it. It is a Jethro Tull single. What are you gonna do?' But they wouldn't do anything until the series was repeated. Eventually it came out, but it had no major marketing effort behind it, and I think we missed slightly in the arrangement. We should have multi-tracked Ian's voice and gone for something like Clannad. If we'd done that we would have had a hit – it would have been just a fag paper away from Enya!"

Well, they didn't, and it wasn't. But at least the record was a sign that Jethro Tull were still alive and well, and very shortly afterwards more evidence came when they played a handful of festivals in Europe, thanks largely to the intervention of Marillion, now a hugely successful band.

They were headlining a festival at the Milton Keynes Bowl, and they really wanted Tull on the bill. Anderson agreed to do it, partly because he felt some sort of connection with them since inviting them to play at the Nostell Priory in '82, and partly because they offered 'a very substantial amount of money'! That covered the costs for all the rehearsals and preproduction required to get back on the road after the long break, thereby allowing Tull to put together a few more dates on the back of it. But it was not a good gig for Tull to play in terms of prestige. Although billed as "Very Special Guests" they were in effect third on the bill, playing before Gary Moore and Marillion. It was not where Jethro Tull were ever supposed to be on a festival bill. Remarkably, Anderson has apparently never been troubled by such ego trips, often preferring to play earlier in order to get away earlier, but Martin Barre was not happy with it.

> "I think it did us a lot of harm. It was still light when we came on. It was the first gig of the mini-tour, and it wasn't a great performance. You should never do your most important date on the first night of a tour, you should always play a low key warm up gig somewhere. We were supposed to be second on the bill, but it looked like we were third, and I think a lot of Tull fans felt it wasn't enough for them. It didn't look good, it wasn't us giving our best, and that should never happen."

No, it wasn't a great performance. The lay off did not seem to have done Anderson much good. His voice was still strained, and he looked and sounded very, very old. As he struggled with his voice, he actually began to perform the folk singer 'finger-in-the-ear' cliché, which is not the greatest image in the world to present to 15,000 rock fans! Although they went down really well (Tull fans seemed as plentiful as Marillion fans on the day) the rusty performance can not have impressed people catching them for the first time. To make matters worse, Tull's set at Milton Keynes was broadcast both on radio and on TV in the context of a documentary look at Ian Anderson, called *Fish'n'Sheep'n'Rock'n'Roll*. It was great for the fans to see them back on TV, but if only they had looked and sounded a bit better!

CHAPTER EIGHT
The Flute Is A Heavy, Metal Instrument

Jethro Tull were not seen or heard of again until August '87, when Ian Anderson and Martin Barre guested at Fairport Convention's annual Cropredy Festival, as organised by Dave Pegg and his wife Chris. They came on towards the climax of the Fairport set, and ran through a great forty-five minute set of Jethro Tull classics. It was a hugely successful return to the stage, and was greeted with rapture by the audience who had wondered just why Peggy had never got the guys along before. A highlight of the Cropredy Festival was always the amazing calibre of guests Fairport were able to bring out to do a few songs with, and as Pegg had been in both bands for seven years, Tull seemed the obvious choice for a guest slot.

Bizarrely, it was nothing more than a failure to communicate, and it only came about when it did as a result of separate conversations that I had with Anderson and Pegg whilst writing an issue of *A New Day*! Dave Pegg confessed that he was wary of asking Ian to join them in case he then felt pressured into saying yes, even if he didn't want to do it. Ian told me he would like to do it, but as he hadn't been asked, he didn't want to offer in case they didn't want him there! Don't these bloody rock stars ever talk to each other? Fortunately, in my role as go-between they finally came together, but clearly they didn't learn anything from it because exactly the same scenario was played out the following year. Jethro Tull were to play the Wembley Arena in July, and I suggested to Pegg that it would be a great opportunity to get Fairport on as the support. He agreed completely, but because Tull had not had a support band in the UK for ten years he didn't like to suggest it to Ian. When I mentioned it to Ian he said he had actually thought about asking Fairport to support Tull at the gig, but had not done so because they might have been reluctant to play such a big gig so close to their Cropredy Festival! As a result, Fairport played the Wembley gig.

Back to '87, and the Cropredy Festival. In addition to the live set, Tull fans also got their first opportunity to hear the new album, *Crest Of A Knave*, as it was played over the PA throughout the weekend. It was released the following month, exactly three years after *Under Wraps*.

Largely ignored on release by the press. *Q* dismissed it out of hand, assuming perhaps that nobody really cared anymore. Nevertheless *Crest Of A Knave* was exactly what was needed to haul Tull back from the brink of relegation and into the middle reaches of the Premier League. Peter Vettese having left the band after the Summer Festivals the year before, Ian Anderson decided to play what keyboards there were on the album himself. Therefore this was no keyboard-dominated album, with the flute, and acoustic and electric guitar returning to the foreground.

It was, with a few reservations, the Jethro Tull album the fans had been waiting for since *Broadsword*, and for once, the group knew what the fans thought of it before it came out. With obvious reference to the divided opinion on the album that preceded it, *Crest Of A Knave* was premiered, whilst still in preparation, to gatherings of Tull fans across America. Tracks intended for the album were played to them, and comments were invited and acted upon. It was a most unusual way to decide what to put on an album, and Anderson was accused of tailoring music to the audience, rather than creating music that he felt was artistically valid. He accepts that it might be perceived to be the case, but puts a completely different slant on the exercise.

"It wasn't a case of asking those fans what should be on the album. I knew what the album was going to be, and I knew people would like it. It was a very strong Jethro Tull album, with all the merits of what people perceive to be classic Tull. But the record company needed convincing, after the indifference that had met the previous album. It was they who wanted confirmation that we were doing what people liked to hear from us, and that it would be a commercial success. In those terms, it was a worthwhile exercise."

It was no accident that *Crest* was a return to 'classic' Jethro Tull music. Anderson had had plenty of time to reflect on the direction that Tull were to take, and had deliberately taken his time before making the album:

"After twenty years of playing under a certain identity it becomes important to you not to throw that away. Not to throw away something that in some ways represents a lot of time that I've not enjoyed, time that I might even think I've wasted. Like going off on certain musical tacks that were not all that great. There is a feeling that if you keep on at the same pace with the same total commitment to something, sooner or later it will just completely run out of steam. We had stopped, taken stock, and made a really good album.

We didn't want to make another album that was going to be dominated by keyboards, and certainly not something that sounded like we were trying to update ourselves. That's why Peter Vettese is not on the album. He was never going to be a full time member of the band, not least because when he joined us it was a stepping stone for him towards making a living this end of the country. Jethro Tull was always going to be something he could come in and out of as required. And it had got to the stage where, unless he had a great deal of involvement in the writing, or at least a lot of input into the music, he felt very frustrated. The rest of us felt we didn't want to follow the direction of the previous album, and we wanted to get back to a more guitar driven sound".

The resulting album was a masterpiece, and although good reviews were thin on the ground, it was a great commercial success, shipping huge quantities, particularly in America where it spent more than half a year in the Billboard 100, peaking at number 28. It even earned Tull a Grammy, as winner of the first award in the 'Best Heavy Metal/Rock Album' category. For most bands such an accolade is greeted with at least respect, if not enthusiasm, by fellow artists and the media. In Tull's case though it was quite the opposite. As far as everybody had been concerned before the awards ceremony, Metallica had won it, with the other nominees there simply to make up the numbers. Ian Anderson himself had accepted that as a fact, but had offered to play at the awards, as a 'Thank You' gesture for the nomination. The record company dissuaded him - 'Metallica are playing, they have won the award. There's really no point in you being there". Consequently when Jethro Tull were announced as the winners, there was nobody from the band to collect it. Perhaps if they had been, it might have deterred the morons amongst the audience from booing the award, dismayed that a classic rock band had robbed Metallica of their heavy metal crown.

That reaction, and the fawning press reaction that followed, certainly took the shine off a deserved award, but Chrysalis responded with a tongue-in-cheek full page advert in the US trade papers. 'THE FLUTE IS A HEAVY, METAL INSTRUMENT' was all it said, with no mention of Jethro Tull anywhere. Ian Anderson took it all with resigned amusement, but defended Jethro Tull's right to the Grammy.

> "The award is not for a Heavy Metal album. It is for best Metal OR Rock album, and *Crest Of A Knave* is a rock album. Jethro Tull is a rock band. It is not even a soft rock band, it is a heavy rock band. Bruce Hornsby and The Range we are not! But I don't see it as an award for this one album anyway. It's simply a recognition of the fact that we've been around for ever, sold millions of albums, and put a lot of bums on seats. *Crest Of A Knave* is a good excuse to give us an award, just for hanging in there for so long!"

The album was very soon, and still is, a firm favourite with the fans. A year after it's release, "Budapest" toppled "Aqualung" in the *A New Day* readers poll as favourite track. That was something of a surprise, although "Budapest" certainly bore all the hallmarks of Tull's traditional classic style. The ten minute epic was a wonderful collage of vocal and brilliant instrumental passages, and we can only wonder what the original twenty minute version would have sounded like. It was originally going to spread over one entire side of the vinyl album.

But for all the euphoria amongst the relieved fans, there was no little concern at the similarity in sound to that of Dire Straits. It is undeniable that there are echoes of Mark Knopfler on several tracks; parts of "Budapest" are ringers for "Private Investigations", and "Said She Was A Dancer" is even more reminiscent of them. One review of the track, which was released as a single, even offered the opinion that it was "Not the most obvious track for a single, but Mark Knopfler as guest guitarist makes it the most commercial!" In fact it was their 'biggest hit' for years, peaking at the dizzy heights of number 55 in the UK chart.

Perhaps there was some subconscious influence there – Anderson has always admired Mark Knopfler's playing – but the reasons for the sound were more a mixture of practicalities and coincidence than straightforward plagiarism. Before the album had even been released, Anderson had spoken to me about the vocal styling, and the reasons behind it:

"I have made a deliberate attempt, as far as the vocals are concerned, not to invite a repeat problem with my voice when we tour again. I've deliberately tried to pitch the songs a tone lower than I would normally sing them. Although actually in the studio I have had no problems at all and I could be singing them a tone higher, but from past experience I know that if I do that I would be struggling half way through a tour. The vocals would sound better, a bit more gutsy, if they were pitched a bit higher, but it is better to be safe than sorry. Better to be able to do those songs at the end of a six week tour rather than to have to ditch them half way through because I couldn't cope with it".

Well OK, that explains the vocals. But how about the 'Knopfleresque' guitar playing of Martin Barre:

"It's just a style of music. You can hear a hundred heavy metal guitarists, and they all sound the same. It is as relevant to me as saying they all sound like whoever it was that started that style of playing. That's just faceless playing, no matter how good it is, because it could be anybody playing it. And there are a lot of people who play with the percussive Strat sound that Mark Knopfler has made famous, but it's not necessarily his sound. I hadn't suddenly started playing it; I think I started playing a Strat around 1982, or maybe before that. It's the best sound you can get on a Strat, and I did it to get some different sounds on the album. I'm always looking for new ideas and sounds, as every guitarist is."

Further evidence for the defence is offered by Ian Anderson, who is delighted to relate the tale of how Mark Knopfler had apparently called Hamer guitars some time earlier and asked them to build him a guitar that would give him, "the sound that Martin Barre of Jethro Tull gets". Chicken and egg, anyone?

Anderson properly put the whole thing into perspective during a press conference in Italy. Asked about the apparent Dire Straits influence, he replied, "That's OK. If you're gonna sound like anyone, Dire Straits is not bad. But if you'd said we sounded like The Pet Shop Boys I would have jumped over this table and punched you on the nose!"

For once, Chrysalis Records made a valiant effort to get Jethro Tull back into the singles charts, selecting not one but two album cuts as singles. "Steel Monkey", and then "Said She Was A Dancer" both got the multi-format treatment, and both entered the top 75. British radio was having none of it though, and yet again Tull were denied the exposure they might have expected in the UK. Alan 'Fluff' Freeman remained a supporter however, citing *Crest Of A Knave* as "The most complete album of 1987".

With their best album in years under their belts, and after three long years without a real tour, Jethro Tull were ready to return to touring with a vengeance. On the album Doane Perry and Gerry Conway had shared percussive duties, but it was Doane who got the live gig. He was delighted, and confessed at the time that he had been hurt by the proclamation on the sleeve of *Crest Of A Knave* that "Jethro Tull are: Ian Anderson, Martin Barre and Dave Pegg."

"I was surprised, and very disappointed when I saw that. Having done the record initially, it went through a couple of changes with Gerry on drums. But I definitely felt very much a part of the band, not just a sideman. I'd contributed a lot to the live show, and it was a little distressing to be seen as a session player on the album. Obviously that's something I hope will change in the future."

Indeed it did change, and Doane has been a member of Jethro Tull ever since, although there have been occasions when a stand-in has been used for practical reasons. He was in fact supposed to have played on all the tracks on the album, but during rehearsals his mother was taken ill, and sadly died. The band were supportive, telling him to come back when he was ready to finish the album, but he was unable to complete all the tracks to his, or their, satisfaction in the short time available.

Peter Vettese was invited to rejoin the band for the tour, but was unavailable due to his many other commitments. After a series of auditions the keyboards slot was filled by Don Airey, who had previously played with heavy weight names like Black Sabbath, Cozy Powell, Gary Moore, Whitesnake and Rainbow. He remembers his audition well, since he made the almost fatal error of underestimating the task that faced him:

> "I told them I wasn't familiar with their music, so they sent me a tape. I didn't have time to listen to it, and I didn't play it until the evening before the audition. When I played it I thought 'Oh shit!', I just hadn't realised the complexity of it. I had to write it all down and tried to learn it through the night. It was great stuff. "Budapest", "Hunting Girl", and "Songs From The Wood" – that is a work of genius.
>
> In fact I had heard a lot of Tull's music before, but it was through hotel walls when I was in Rainbow, because Ritchie Blackmore is such a big Tull fan! He phoned me once when we were in America and ordered me to go and see Jethro Tull at the Nassau Coliseum. I asked him 'is it compulsory?' and he said yes, it was! 'Go and see Jethro Tull – that's how it should be done". And they were good. I was knocked out. I remember thinking it was the best out-front sound I'd ever heard."

The *Crest* tour started in Scotland in October, and finished in America mid-December with three nights at the L.A. Ampitheatre. It had been a major success, and although Anderson's voice was nothing like it had been before his problems, and there had been a few nights when it was really quite poor, at least he had made it through an arduous tour undamaged. And although the sold-out gigs were still in the huge venues that Tull were accustomed to playing, there was a noticeable shift away from theatricals. The humour was still there – the sight of a dozen or so roadies in white coats playing cardboard guitars to the heavy metal reprise of

"Jump Start" will live in the memory forever! – but the emphasis was clearly on the music itself.

On the European and American legs of the tour, Fairport Convention were the support band, as they took the rare opportunity to promote their new album "In Real Time" in the States. Although it made it a very long night's work for Dave Pegg, who was in effect supporting himself, it helped Fairport to sell out their album in America. It also brought about further connections between the two groups, with the Fairporters joining Tull on-stage each night for a rousing version of "Skating Away On The Thin Ice Of The New Day". They also got the opportunity for a thrash about on heavy metal cardboard guitars on "Jump Start"! Jethro Tull must have felt like home from home for Fairport fiddler Ric Sanders, who had also played violin on two tracks on *Crest*.

The dividing line between Fairport and Jethro Tull became even more blurred the following year, when Tull went back on the road to celebrate their 20th Anniversary. Don Airey, although a very fine player, had looked and sounded out of place in Tull. His experience of playing almost exclusively with heavy metal bands had perhaps numbed his senses to the self-deprecating humour that surrounded Tull's forays into that genre. His solo during the live shows, complete with air-raid and police sirens, was not the standard fare at a Tull gig.

Worse still were the sequenced parts; most of the fans didn't mind the use of sequencers and samplers, but did wonder why he felt the need to pretend to be actually playing them. And Airey himself did not seem overly pleased with the situation after the final UK show in London, during which Anderson had introduced him as Doane Airey! He and Tull parted company at the end of the tour.

The choice of new keyboard player was a surprising one, to say the least, as Anderson asked Dave Pegg to sound out fellow Fairporter Martin Allcock for the job. Allcock was and is a masterful musician, who could play expertly almost any instrument you care to give him. He was, first and foremost, a bass player, but as Dave Pegg was the bassist with Fairport when he joined them he was working as the lead guitarist, to great effect. As Ric Sanders would say when introducing him on-stage, he was "possessed by the dual spirits of Cecil Sharpe and Jimi Hendrix!", and had brought a distinct and very welcome heavy rock feel to much of the Fairport set. He was also no mean mandolin and bouzouki player.

He did not, however, play keyboards, and was naturally shocked to be offered the role with Tull. But, he was a fan, and Tull was a wonderful opportunity, so he quickly taught himself to play keyboards and landed the gig! Admittedly, Tull were not looking for another keyboard wizard like Peter Vettese or Don Airey, and a keyboard player who could also play guitar was a bonus. But the choice of Martin Allcock was further evidence that Jethro Tull – or, more to the point, Ian Anderson – still placed more importance on personality than musical prowess when choosing who he would have in the band.

And Martin, or Maart, to give him his customary moniker (No, it's not Dutch, that's just the way he, and now everybody else, pronounces it) was certainly a personality. His arrival within the Tull camp not only doubled the Fairport Convention representation in the band, but it also, by definition, doubled the alcohol consumption on tour! During the tour of '88, it was clear that Jethro Tull was a happy camp, even though the personality differences could not be more marked. Doane Perry was the ultra-serious drummer who would happily sound check all day, and analyse the entire gig afterwards, but would not be deflected by anything from his apres-gig dinner.

Martin Barre was the runner, taking every opportunity to run for miles for no apparent reason. Ian Anderson, as ever, had his business head on, having every aspect of the tour to consider as they went through it. And then there was Maart and Peggy, the people's friends. Having come from Fairport, a band that has always made a point of mingling with the punters rather than hiding from them, they saw no reason to change their ways when they were with Tull. In their selfless dedication to customer relations, deigning to 'have a drink' with fans in every town in the world, they went a long way in breaking down the barriers that had existed between 'them and us' until then. And it rubbed off on Ian eventually, who gradually became visibly more at ease with fans than before. It was amusing to hear him say, on the 20th Anniversary video that year, that now he felt

"Very happy to talk to fans, and have a beer with them. Providing they are buying of course!"

1988 was a year of celebration, with an abundance of recorded material being made available to mark the 20th Anniversary. Ian Anderson was not particularly interested in the landmark, preferring as always to look forwards rather than backwards. "And anyway, surely the 25th Anniversary is more suitable for a celebration?" And although initially Chrysalis had no intention of doing anything substantial, they had to think again when they were inundated by letters from fans demanding that they mark the occasion in style. Faced with such a display of force, and of course clear evidence of an audience willing to part with cash, Chrysalis eventually came up with the goods – and then some!

Nowadays, everybody has a box-set out, but in '88 it was an honour reserved for a few major names. Chrysalis decided that Tull were prime candidates, and keen to make sure it would be what Tull fans wanted, they wisely decided to involve some fans in the compilation right from the outset. They asked the world's 'two most knowledgeable Jethro Tull fans' to meet with them to come up with the definitive boxed set. Unfortunately all they got was Martin Webb and myself. That was not such a bad deal, as it turns out, because between us we had the ideal credentials. As editor of the Tull magazine I had feedback from fans all over the world, and consequently had a good idea of what the fans wanted and, just as importantly, what they didn't want. And Webb was a civil servant, which at least meant he had very little to do, and was able to devote his time to the Tull project!

The initial meeting was a revelation. Chrysalis had been criticised heavily over the years for their half-hearted promotion and apparent indifference to Jethro Tull, and we really expected to have a battle on our hands to get a half-decent package from them. So we were stunned when they presented us with their proposed project, which was more than we had dared hope for. A five album boxed set, another double album, a video, a TV special and a radio series were all in the early stages of planning, even before we had got our proposals to them. And, radio series apart, that's exactly what eventually came out. The BBC and Independent Radio

Network were not interested in a 'Story Of Jethro Tull' series, which was slightly disappointing. They had, after all, recently broadcast a series detailing the careers of those perennial rock giants Stock, Aitken and Waterman!

The video was commissioned, and made by a new company formed by Philip Goodhand-Tait, once a successful musician himself, with strong connections to Chrysalis. He set about the project with great enthusiasm, but the end result was very disappointing. It seemed little effort had gone into digging up some of the many real gems that exist somewhere on film, and it had been put together very sloppily, with little or no regard to continuity. It was a good collection of (mostly recent) Tull videos, but the title of 'The First Twenty Years' was very misleading. A 60 minute version of the 80 minute video was sold to TV companies, and most of the UK Independents did broadcast it.... at 3 in the morning!

The double album was a straightforward affair; basically a sampler of the full 5-album boxed-set, concentrating on the better known tracks. But the boxed-set was the jewel in the crown; we were able to convince Chrysalis that most people buying the box would already have all the albums, so it should concentrate on otherwise unavailable music. After much persuasion we came up with a 65 track collection, of which only eleven had been on albums before in the same form. Early radio sessions, singles and B-sides, unreleased masters and live versions of classic tracks formed the bulk of the collection, and it was a huge success. 4 star reviews in *Kerraang* and *Q*, a rave review in *Sounds*, and sales that were "far better than anybody had expected" at Chrysalis. And the highly respected *Record Collector* magazine devoted three pages to their review, concluding that "This collection sets the standard that future boxed sets must try to follow".

A two month tour to promote the box-set followed, which took Tull to Brazil for the first time. Again, only one gig in England, but who could complain after such bounty earlier in the year? With no new album to promote, it was very much a greatest hits live package, and Anderson was at his jocular best. With reference to the undeniable encroachment of middle age, Tull stole a march on the ageist critics by laughing at themselves, as a wheelchair bound Anderson was pushed on-stage, accompanied by a 'doctor' and a pretty nurse, volunteers selected from the audience each night.

To neatly book-end the old age joke, Anderson, Barre and Pegg would collapse at the end of the show, to be helped off stage by means of a stretcher, crutches and the wheelchair! Maart Allcock joined in the on-stage fun, taking to running to the front of the stage to deliver a blistering "Aqualung" solo on a broom-handle. Even the tour banner, proudly proclaiming "20 years of Jethro Tull", had been customised with the usual Tull humour. Spray painted across the top was the additional wording "Oh no! Not Another...."

The only blight on the year came during some of the gigs, where Ian Anderson's vocals were quite wretched. Strangely though it was not a consistent problem. One night his voice was fine, the next he might not be able to hit a note. It was a terrible and frightening realisation to face: his throat problems were still with him four years on, and they were not, ever, going to go away completely. It has been something of a running sore ever since, and a constant talking point amongst fans and critics.

The following year it was business as usual, with a new studio album and three months touring through the UK, Europe and America. *Crest Of A Knave* and the *20 Years Of* box set were hard acts to follow, and *Rock Island*, released September '89, did not quite match the standard. It was an immediately impressive album, but most fans agree that Tull albums can only be truly judged some time after the event. The classic ones lose nothing with the passing of time, weaker albums fade from the memory. It was a valiant effort though, with the emphasis firmly on hard rock, and Martin Barre's superb guitar playing shining throughout. It was however a bit too 'rock'n'roll' for some; "Budapest" on *Crest Of A Knave* had worried some sensitive souls, concerned by Anderson's lecherous lyrics, and they found further evidence of his degeneration into a dirty old man on *Rock Island*, with the deeply unsubtle "Kissing Willie" coming in for major flack for its "outrageously sexist lyrics". Well, yeah, can't argue with that one, but at least the video was funny, in a *Carry On* kind of way!

While songs like "Rock Island", "Ears Of Tin" and "The Whaler's Dues" could stand alongside their best work, others were sub-standard, almost filler tracks by Tull's lofty principles. The reviews were not bad though, particularly with regard to the treatment normally handed out to Tull. Mark Putterford in *Raw* wrote "In their 21 years, Tull have rarely made a bad album. In fact their last effort was their best for years, and Tullites will be pleased to know that *Rock Island* jigs around in similar fashion." Roy Wilkinson in *Sounds* – "*Rock Island* opens with a tousle-haired, firm buttocked rocker which signals that Tull are BACK FOR THE ATTACK. Watch out, Metallica!" And *Q*, after their savaging of *Crest*, gave it a 4 star review written by Rob Beattie – "Favourite Tull themes emerge blinking into the sunset again, with Martin Barre's electric guitar and Ian Anderson's hustle-bustle flute well to the fore. The crowds are going to eat this up."

Ian Anderson produced and wrote all the songs on *Rock Island*, and again played keyboards on some of the tracks. Maart Allcock played keyboards on a couple, and Peter Vettese returned to play on four tracks. Allcock had in fact played on three tracks, but at the eleventh hour one of them, "Hardliner", was dropped from the album and replaced by "Rattlesnake Trail". John Evans, a Tull hero from the past, had been invited to play on the album, but flatly refused to be involved. Not only did he have no desire to play music again, he had even sold all of his equipment.

Maart was on keyboards for the tour, which was one of the most ingenious sets Tull had ever put together, even though it was hardly lavish.

Inverness was the unusual setting for the opening night, as Tull played a benefit gig for a local good cause. It was strange to see Anderson draw a raffle halfway through the concert!

The 'special effects' were primitive, but very effective. Images were projected onto two large screens either side of the stage, with a pointed jab at some well known figures during *Thick As A Brick*, who were shown with bricks substituted for heads. Thatcher and Bush were easy and obvious targets, but the sight of Metallica, still whinging about 'their' Grammy, as brick-heads raised a few chuckles.

Maart Allcock's custom built steam driven keyboards broke down during the opening to 'Budapest', and a roadie ran on with more coal to get it fired up again. And, again laughing at themselves, Jethro Tull's version of the cliché heavy metal laser shows was provided by more roadies in white coats, white masks and miners helmets, who walked onto the stage throughout the show to project synchronised light shows via the lights in their hats! It was funny at first, but as it went on it simply became puzzling.

All was explained with the brilliant finale; on previous tours Ian Anderson had tricked audiences with a silhouetted figure, perceived to be him, singing the last few lines at the end of the show, whereupon he would miraculously appear on the opposite side of the stage. *Rock Island* was finishing the same way, as the silhouette sang stage left while the men in white gathered round a huge balloon stage centre. But we all knew Ian was going to magically appear behind the balloon.... how could they possibly attempt the same trick again? But no, the balloon burst, revealing nothing. The 'roadies' shrugged their shoulders, and started to shuffle offstage. Then they turned to the audience, removed their masks, and revealed themselves as Messrs. Anderson, Barre, Pegg, Perry and Allcock.

Critics heaped praise upon the inspired shows; perhaps the unlikeliest accolade came in the pages of *The Sun*, courtesy of the music industry's most annoying genius, Jonathan King, who wrote:

"I was astonished by how good Jethro Tull were when I saw them at the Hammersmith Odeon in London. Every line of every song had been thought through visually. The effects were clever, the performance was superb, the chat witty and the sound balance simply the best I've ever heard at a concert. Excellent stuff!"

Will Jackson in the *Portland Express*, with a dig at the heavy metal Grammy moaners wrote: "Mixing in material old and new, electric and acoustic, this merry band of over 40's rockers showed more energy and creativity than 50 average 'heavy rock' groups".

"Jethro Tull Returns To Rock'n'roll's Fore-front" screamed the *Worcester (USA) Enterprise*. Peter Feasby in *The Newcastle Chronicle* – "The audience was spellbound and Anderson, the chief sorcerer, and his band at their brilliant best". Paul Taylor in *The Guardian* put it simply: "Jethro Tull have been dismissed as horrendously unfashionable for what seems like a lifetime now, and yet can still pack the Manchester Apollo two nights running, offering tremendous entertainment value. There's a moral in that somewhere."

CHAPTER NINE
Back To The Roots

Jethro Tull had no plans to release any records, old or new, in 1990, but nevertheless they decided to embark upon yet another UK tour. Perhaps for other bands in Tull's position it would have been just another way of raking in the cash in between records, but clearly that was not the case here. It was deliberately restricted to smaller venues, with minimal advertising restricted to the local press. Anderson explained the apparently backward step:

"We have been talking about doing a proper tour for ever, and this time we've decided to go for it. We've got nothing to sell, no new album or single or video. We just want to get out and about, and go back to some of the places that we've maybe neglected for ten or fifteen years, or perhaps have never played before. We are going out on a very low key level, with less crew and equipment obviously because the venues are smaller. We need to sell out every venue, even on this smaller scale, otherwise it is a goodwill gesture that will cost us a packet!

We did three shows in London last year, and they have a catchment area for miles around, so this time we are skipping London and going instead to the surrounding areas. We are taking the music to the people, rather than them having to drive through the night to see us. And we will only advertise locally, so people in Birmingham will be able to go to the show in their town without Londoners snapping up all the tickets first! Unfortunately there are still loads and loads of places that we've had to leave out, because the venues just aren't available."

It was an unusually noble gesture from a high profile band, but whilst it delighted those fans who had not seen Tull play live before, it was a worrying development in the eyes of some. Although it was a conscious decision to play smaller venues, would not the cynics declare that Jethro Tull had been reduced from playing Wembley Arena to the Livingstone Forum?

"I don't care what they think. There are lots of people who will say that, but we did play three nights at the Hammersmith Odeon last year. That's 15,000 people, or a Wembley and-a-half!"

The wonderfully relaxed atmosphere on the tour, engendered by the intimate surroundings and the freedom to select a set that was not largely dictated by new product for sale, made for one of the most fondly remembered Tull tours. Ian Anderson had (almost) always enriched a Tull concert with his great wit and well rehearsed comic 'asides', but this time out his genuinely friendly onstage patter was extended almost to the realms of stand-up comedian.

Later in the year Tull played a handful of festivals in Germany and Brazil, sandwiching a less than glorious return to London, as the special guests of Fleetwood Mac at Wembley Stadium. Although they produced a magnificent performance which had the immediate audience in raptures, they were badly let down by the equipment. The sound was far too slight for such a massive venue, and the huge video screens either side of the stage remained defiantly blank throughout their performance. Mysteriously, both sound and vision were perfectly restored as soon as Tull departed and Fleetwood Mac hit the stage.....

Ian Anderson was particularly unhappy at the way they had been treated at Wembley:

"I think we all hated it really, because the atmosphere was terrible, it was a very uncomfortable thing. The members of Fleetwood Mac didn't arrive in separate limos, they all arrived in separate buses with their entourage! As far as they were concerned it was their gig, end of story. They even cordoned off certain areas of the stage that I wasn't allowed to use. I couldn't believe how petty it all was. I mean, they asked us to do the gig, it wasn't something we had asked for. We were asked to help out because it was selling so badly to begin with. I'm not saying that we made that much difference, but we were certainly responsible for some of the ticket sales.

The thing that totally threw me, which I was only made aware of 20 minutes before we went onstage, was that they were using the old fashioned video screens that only work when it's dark. We couldn't use them, because they are totally useless during daylight. Had I known they weren't using star vision screens I would not have played the gig. I accept these things will happen when we play in Czechoslovakia or Turkey and so on, but the fans over there don't expect things like that. They are just happy that there's a good gig they can go to. But at Wembley Stadium it should be rather better than that."

One other truly memorable event that year, for those who were lucky enough to be there, was the Jethro Tull Convention organised by a group of dedicated fans. The inauspicious surroundings of the Woughton Centre in Milton Keynes was the scene of a remarkable and impromptu set by what was very nearly the original 1968 Tull line-up. Ian Anderson, Mick Abrahams and Clive Bunker were joined by Maart Allcock for three songs, in what was the first in a series of amazing performances by various Tull members at subsequent Tull Conventions. The musicians seemed to enjoy it as much as the audience, and Anderson freely admitted that the experience reminded him of how nice it was to play in a really small and intimate venue. It was one of the catalysts for a remarkable semi-acoustic tour a couple of years later.

To round the year off in typically eclectic style, Anderson made his most bizarre musical collaboration to date, when he was invited to play flute on an album by a thrash metal/hardcore band from New York, called The Six and Violence. They were all Tull fans, and had met Ian originally when they organised a gig in New York specifically to coincide with his arrival there. Having been invited, he decided to attend at least for a few minutes, to be polite. He was knocked out by what he saw and heard, and was genuinely excited to be involved with their album.

"It's unbelievable stuff! They do make a racket, it's crazy stuff, but it's wonderful. It's Captain Beefheart meets The Zorg People! Everything is incredibly fast, the songs are never more than about two minutes long, but they are about real things. These are out of work, young kids in New York, who know they are never going to make it but do it because they have to. I'm not like them, I don't come from their sort of background, and I don't really understand what they are doing, but I treated it in the spirit in which I think they were intending it. I just went for it!"

And yes, he certainly did go for it, fitting in superbly well on an album that would otherwise appear to be the very opposite of what Tull stand for. Or is it? Kurt Stenzel, the frontman of The Six and Violence, eloquently outlined the appeal of Jethro Tull, the archetypal English progressive/classic rock band, to a gang of anarchist punk rockers in New York thus:

"The fact is, had we not sat around listening to as much Jethro Tull at a tender young age as we did, we may never have been inspired or driven to play music. We might instead have grown up and got REAL JOBS! Although Ian probably wouldn't want to take responsibility, a lot of our musical mayhem came from the Jethro Tull spirit that music should be fun, and that the music that you play should sound like no-one else's. The influence is not all that incongruous for us – Jethro Tull is it's own genre, and that is what we're all trying to be. Just how many bands want to play music for it's own sake, to defy fashion, the critics and record labels, and then fall by the wayside when they cash their first cheque? Very few play on their own terms, fewer still play well, and so few do it on such a grand underground scale as Jethro Tull. Theirs is a fine instrument, the Six and Violence a blunt one, but both are an attempt at honesty."

There was in fact a 'new' album from Tull in 1990, although for the first time ever it came out on a different label. Strange Fruit, the label set up by Clive Selwood to release archive BBC recordings, finally got around to Tull with an album recorded at Hammersmith in 1984 on the *Under Wraps* tour. Sadly, due to the limitations of vinyl, only 40 minutes of the original 60 minute broadcast were used, but nevertheless it was a very welcome bonus, and a reminder of just how good those shows had been.

The new year began with Jethro Tull once more ensconced in the studio, with yet more personnel changes. The Jethro Tull nucleus of Anderson, Barre, Pegg and Perry was still intact, but no less than three keyboard players were involved in the sessions (or four, including Ian Anderson) – with a notable absentee being Maart Allcock, Tull's keyboard player for the last few tours. Perhaps the most peculiar aspect was that Allcock was retained in the band for the subsequent tour!

The assortment of keyboard players had arisen due to a number of reasons. Anderson wanted to move completely away from synthesised sounds, to get back to the more organic sound of piano and Hammond organ. "John Evans would have been a choice" says Ian, "but he had stated quite clearly a couple of years before that he just wasn't interested. It would have been nice had he done it, because he is a really good player. Peter Vettese would have been another choice, but a lot of those guys are just never available".

They opted initially for John 'Rabbit' Bundrick, of Free and The Who to name but a couple of legendary rock outfits:

"He was a good player and slipped right into it. It was really good stuff, but he is a fighting man, and nice chap though he is, he gets a bit crazy when he gets a drink inside him! It wasn't going to work out, so that relationship was severed after quite a lot of work was done. Only one of those tracks made it onto the album. Another guy was Foss Paterson, who was highly recommended by Peter Vettese. He did one track on the album."

Andy Giddings was the third man, playing on three tracks. His entrance to the band was via a more complicated route. During the course of the recording sessions Ian Anderson had placed an advertisement in his local press looking for musicians to join him in a 'low-key' band, a project not associated with Jethro Tull.... allegedly. It read – "Long standing front man of international rock band seeks musicians for band/solo projects. Blues/rock style". Anderson explained the move thus:

"I would like to be able to just go out and play some very low-key gigs, perhaps at very short notice. I was looking for local musicians who would be available to play pubs or clubs, just for the enjoyment of playing. It seemed like a good idea, in these menopausal years, to find a way of playing to people in very informal surroundings, like the guys in Fairport do from time to time. Unfortunately it came to nothing in the end."

That may well have been the intent, but at the time it looked like he was planning another major reshuffle in the Tull ranks – and one year on, for a while at least, that's exactly what happened.

One direct result of those adverts was the recruitment of Andy Giddings, albeit in an indirect way. Steve Jackson, the drummer with Cornish legends The Mechanics, was one of many who sent in tapes for Ian's perusal. Although he had nothing suitable by The Mechanics on tape, he sent in some material by his other band, The Chase. Ironically, it was the keyboards of fellow Chase-man Andy Giddings that caught the ear, and after a further audition the pleasantly surprised Giddings was in the studio with Tull. "I can't thank Steve enough for that" enthused Giddings some time after the event. "I had no idea he'd sent Ian a tape, and I was completely gob-smacked when they got in touch with me. Without Steve Jackson it would never have happened". Jackson was understandably beset by mixed feelings after he had accidentally helped Andy towards his biggest break, but had the good humour to joke that, "I'm delighted for him of course. But the tight-fisted sod still hasn't bought me a bloody drink!". Well, I think he was joking!

Another debutante in the Tull line-up was bassist Matt Pegg, deputising on three tracks for father Dave when he was otherwise involved with Fairport Convention. Yet another new name was Scott Hunter, drummer with The Larry Miller Band. He had answered the advert, and played on two tracks, one of which made it onto the album. Scott was thrilled, because not only was he playing on record with one of the country's foremost rock groups, but he had always been a huge Tull fan. But to his dismay due to an error in the sleeve production, he is not credited as playing on the album.

The album that emerged from the sessions, *Catfish Rising*, was the most earthy and organic sounding music that Tull had produced since the very early days, and was met with mixed reactions from the fans. To some it was like a breath of fresh air, a welcome return to their roots that was rampant with energy and enthusiasm, and the sheer joy of playing music. Others bemoaned the retrograde step by the grand daddies of progressive rock, or the heavy metal folk-rockers, depending on their initial view! The chart compilers certainly were not sure, as *Catfish* was listed on release in the top 10 heavy rock chart and the folk/roots chart!

Reviewers were divided too. Heavy metal mag *Riff-Raff* liked it a lot, as did *Vox*, but Rob Beattie in *Q*, normally as close as the band gets to a Tull-friendly critic, dismissed it as merely "Jethro Tull mucking about". Personally, I could not understand what he meant at the time, as it struck me as being a perfectly rounded album, with some brilliant playing and at times quite astonishing vocals from Anderson. He was singing as if in defiance of the vocal problems that still plagued him at times in live performance. He seemed to be saying, "Look, this is what I can still do in the studio, I still have a great voice!" However, as I said earlier, Tull albums are best judged with hindsight, and now I can see what Rob Beattie was getting at. The material on *Catfish* still sounds good, the music and singing still wonderful, but there is little on the album that bears the hallmarks of classic Tull. They weren't just 'mucking about', but this was no *Passion Play* after all. It was fun though, and Anderson agreed:

> "I love doing acoustic music that's got an attack to it, and that's what I tried to do on Catfish. To make basically acoustic songs, but a bit more aggressive and pushy. Most of the songs were written on open tuning mandolins, so therefore they have a kind of bluesy feel about them, although they are not 'the blues' as such. I've taken those ideas and feelings and tried to go somewhere else with it, both musically and lyrically. I've made it a bit less Louisiana, and a bit more Surrey!"

Catfish Rising was released in September 1991, charting at a lowly number 27. A delicious irony was enacted at the press launch for the album, held in a barn near Anderson's Berkshire estate. Bizarrely, Tull did not perform and the album was not played, but Fairport played an acoustic set to enliven the proceedings, featuring a guest drummer – Chris Welch, the *Melody Maker* journalist who had slaughtered *A Passion Play* back in '73, almost leading to the demise of the band itself!

Chrysalis made a valiant attempt to push the album, releasing two multi-format singles. The heavy rocker "This Is Not Love" made a very slight dent in the top 100, but the more commercial "Rocks On The Road" looked in danger of actually being a hit, entering the chart at number 47. Radio ignored it though, maintaining the status quo!

Before the album was released Tull did another short tour through seldom visited parts of Europe, playing a similar set to the earlier UK tour, after which the trio of Anderson, Barre and Pegg undertook a two week promotional tour of America, playing a host of live acoustic sessions for radio stations. The last ten weeks of the year were spent touring *Catfish* through the UK, Europe and America. That would have been enough for most bands – particularly those that had been in existence for 25 years – but in 1992 Ian Anderson went completely overboard, hauling 'The Jolly Jethros" out for no less than three separate tours!

The third leg of the *Catfish Rising* tour, which was another month in Europe and the UK, was puzzling to the UK fans who were amazed and disappointed to find Tull playing the same set they'd had the year before, but with a different line-up! Andy Giddings had replaced Maart Allcock, and more surprisingly, Fairport Convention's drummer Dave Mattacks had replaced Doane Perry. It had come as something of a surprise to Maart Allcock too:

"Ian didn't tell me face to face that I was out of the band. I just got a letter, from his secretary I think, telling me that Ian wanted to experiment with different players, so my services were no longer required. He congratulated me on the improvement in my keyboard playing while I'd been in the band, and offered me a reference should I need it to find further work! I was really hurt. I didn't mind that he wanted to use somebody else, it's his band and I respect that, obviously. But it would have been nicer to hear it from him personally."

Oh dear – déjà vu. Obviously the experience of 1980 and the subsequent recriminations had done nothing for man-management practices. Allcock bounced back almost immediately however, continuing his work with Fairport Convention and a host of sessions, along with an improbable stint with Goth rockers The Mission. He subsequently left Fairport in 1997 to form his own band, Waz, with Pete Zorn and Dave Whetstone.

Doane Perry's departure was less dramatic, as he was committed to other projects at the time, and Dave Mattacks had been drafted in as a temporary replacement. Mattacks was still there just a few weeks later when Tull set out on the second tour of the year, but Giddings was not. The long awaited 'acoustic' Tull tour was under way, with a stripped-to-the-bones line up and stage set. Or was it?

No, not really. Billed as *A Little Light Music*, it actually fell confusingly between two stools. It was largely an acoustic set, but still included heavy rockers like "Aqualung", featuring Martin Barre's electric guitar. Ian Anderson sought to justify the inclusion of those songs with the reasoning that there will always be people who expect to hear them at a Tull gig. That is undeniably true, but here was one occasion to go out on a limb and experiment with a set built around the acoustic traditions of Jethro Tull. When everybody and his dog are appearing 'unplugged' on MTV, the one major rock band that had always played a lot of acoustic music were entitled to a one-off acoustic tour.

Evidently, right from the start there were problems with how to bill and promote the tour. In the event they came up with the catchy hook "A Little Light Music Featuring The Songs Of Jethro Tull: A More Or Less Acoustic Performance By Ian Anderson, Martin Barre, Dave Pegg and Dave Mattacks"! Ignoring the fact that it's a bit of a mouthful, to those who think Jethro Tull is the one-legged man with flute, it looked like four blokes playing Tull songs.

The *Light Music* tour started with a frankly shambolic performance in Guildford, with a seemingly very nervous band making more mistakes than I can ever remember at a Tull gig. Things improved dramatically though for the only other UK gig the following night, at the rather more prestigious Wembley Conference Centre. It was far from sold out, possibly due to the dubious billing, but with first night nerves behind them, the unusual set proved to be a rather wonderful experience, despite the previously mentioned acoustic-heavy metal anomalies. Live rarities such as "From A Dead Beat to an Old Greaser", "Look Into The Sun" and "Life Is A Long Song" were the kind of things that the 'acoustic' tag had promised, and the majority of the audience were well satisfied.

There were some disappointed punters though, as had been inevitable from the outset. It was too electric to be regarded as a special acoustic show, and there was too much acoustic material for a regular Tull show! Another worrying aspect, yet again, was the voice of Ian Anderson. Some nights it was fine, other nights it was awful, and this time it was harder to disguise the vocals with electric bombast from the rest of the band.

As the tour continued through often tiny venues in Germany, Austria, Czechoslovakia, Greece, Israel and Turkey, the billing became more direct and less accurate: "An Acoustic Jethro Tull Concert" was the straightforward half-truth on the posters.

After Guildford each concert had been recorded, and in September a double album was released with tracks taken from each gig. During one of the two shows in Athens, Tull had been joined onstage by Greek superstar George Dalares, who sang "John Barleycorn" and "Ruby Tuesday" with them. The choice of those songs was due to an agreement that they should not perform Jethro Tull songs or George Dalares songs together, so they picked a couple that they both liked, and of course, knew! They had been listed in the tour programme as possibilities for inclusion in the set, but that one night in Athens was the only performance of those songs on the entire tour, and only "John Barleycorn" made it onto the live album.

Collectors and completists should note that whilst Ian Anderson overdubbed the vocals on that track for general release, in Greece and Israel the duet was included. Apparently the record company's reasoning was that Dalares "means nothing to most people outside of Greece", but it seemed to be a rather ungracious gesture to remove him from the album in the rest of the world, not to mention an expensive one for the fans who simply had to have both versions. And subsequent sell-out performances at Wembley by George Dalares would seem to negate the reasoning altogether! Having said that, the version with just Ian singing is vastly superior, the pairing of Anderson and Dalares hardly being a musical delight.

The album was a great souvenir of the concerts, and although the quality of Ian's singing on record would indicate that he may have overdubbed a lot of the other vocals, he insists that overdubs were kept to a bare minimum. "One guitar part on 'John Barleycorn' and a couple of added percussion parts. No other vocals." If that's the case, he obviously had more good nights than bad!

By the time the tour hit America in October some of the anomalies had been ironed out, and the self-explanatory *Light and Dark* tour was presented to the punters. Andy Giddings was brought back to beef up the sound, and though it was basically the same set as before, the songs were split into two distinct sets, with the quieter, acoustic songs largely in the first half, the heavy rockers in the second. The one real surprise in the set was the inclusion of an instrumental passage from *A Passion Play*. It wasn't particularly great, but it was the first time Tull had played anything from that album since 1975, and those many fans eager for more representation of the classic album in concert were given a glimmer of hope for the future. Sadly, at least to date, it was false hope. *A Passion Play* remains the one album that is completely overlooked whenever a Tull set is put together.

In the break between the two tours, the UK Tull Convention had been treated to a rare performance by 'The Summer Band', an infrequent combo assembled by Martin Barre to play the odd gig in – you've guessed it – the summer. The concert was recorded to DAT, and the following year after much arm twisting from *A New Day* a limited edition CD was released, available only by mail order through the magazine. It came out as *Martin Barre – A Summer Band*, and is sometimes mistakenly perceived as Martin's eagerly awaited first solo album, but it was in truth merely a chance for fans to hear Martin and chums playing a set of rock and blues covers. His first real album did not appear until 1994, but *A Summer Band* is now a highly sought after collectors item.

CHAPTER TEN
Living In The Past?

After five tours in two years, surely it was time for Jethro Tull to come off the road and get to work on a now overdue new album? Perhaps in any other year that might have been the case, but 1993 was another major landmark, being the 25th anniversary of the group. Once again Ian Anderson, against his better instincts, gave way to pressure from fans and the record company, and became heavily involved in putting together a major body of work to celebrate the occasion. If the 20th anniversary box set had been a wonderful surprise for Tull fans, the 25th series of releases was even more of a shock, for a number of reasons.

Although the anniversary was important to a lot of people, Ian Anderson was not one of those. He genuinely prefers always to look forward, to work on new projects and new music, rather than wallow in nostalgia. He had done the decent thing by the fans in '88, and I personally did not hold out much hope for a repeat just five years later. I knew Chrysalis wanted to do something, but they were looking at a simple *Best Of* album (again!) and perhaps a new video.

Martin Webb and I were again involved in the planning and compiling of the albums, but unlike the 'first round' in '88 we were miles apart from Chrysalis in our initial thinking. After much badgering a 4-CD box-set was proposed, plus the double CD *Best Of*. After more badgering directed at Ian Anderson personally, *two* 4-CD box-sets were planned!

The first instalment came in April '93. Something of a mixed bag, it included two CDs of live recordings, a CD of remixed classics, and another CD of newly recorded classics. The remixes and re-recordings were interesting, but hardly essential, and the 'Pot Pourri' live compilation was rather disjointed, with a disappointing emphasis on fairly recent recordings. The real gem in the box was the almost complete recording of Tull's gig at the Carnegie Hall in 1970. A tremendous record of the raw power and energy of early Tull, it beggars belief that it had remained in the vaults for over 20 years. The one disappointment was that the opportunity to re-unite the two previously released tracks (on *Living In The Past* in 1972) with the rest of the set was wasted, even though they could have been accommodated within the CD running time.

The general feeling was that it fell a long way short of the excellence of the 20th box, but the promise of another box set later in the year was great consolation.

Two months later *The Anniversary Collection* was released. The definitive Jethro Tull best of, the well presented double CD was a great summary of, and introduction to Jethro Tull for those who were wary of shelling out big bucks for an expensive box set.

To tie in with the album, Chrysalis had another attempt at getting Jethro Tull back into the singles charts, with multiple format releases of "Living In The Past". Two CD-singles, a 12" and 7" vinyl, each with new exclusive tracks, and even a club remix 12" single, much to the horror of some loyal fans! It very nearly worked too. The single entered the chart at number 47, rising to number 32 the following week. Frustratingly, that was just one placing too low to secure a video slot on *Top Of The Pops*, and without the essential push from TV or radio it slipped down to number 50 the following week. Nice try though! They did however secure an unlikely hit in the dance chart with the remix 12", helped by a club DJ only promo, "Living In The Dub"! Purists were alarmed by such sacrilege. Realists were amused by the wheeze!

To tie in with the anniversary, Jethro Tull embarked on a massive world tour. Starting with a couple of dates in England mid-May, the first leg of the tour went right through to mid-November, taking in most of Europe, Canada, the USA and South America – and that was just the start! It seemed that Tull in the 90's were trying to gig as much as Tull in the 60's, and Ian Anderson was looking to more and more exotic and unusual places to play. Was it simply a commendable desire to perform to an audience, or a straightforward celebration of 25 years of Jethro Tull - or was it a final, world-wide 'Goodbye' tour? Well, it turned out to be anything but a farewell tour, and it certainly wasn't an anniversary celebration for Anderson, as he told a press conference in South America mid tour:

> "I am not celebrating the 25th anniversary of Jethro Tull. I hate the 25th anniversary of Jethro Tull! The 24th anniversary was OK, and the 26th anniversary will probably be quite fun too. 25 years is one of those important birthdays that attractive ladies and middle aged men like to forget. But Chrysalis and EMI are definitely celebrating 25 years of Jethro Tull, and the least we could do was come out and celebrate it with our friends".

As the tour rolled on, Chrysalis came up with the next instalment of the archive releases, but it was not quite what had been promised. The planned second box-set was to have included three CDs of vintage live material and an album of unreleased studio masters. In the event the box set was scrapped and replaced by *Nightcap*, a double CD of studio recordings. It was certainly a case of quality over quantity, for although it still left a big gap in the Jethro Tull 'live' catalogue, the treasure trove of unreleased studio material was manna from heaven for the fans.

The second CD in the set, christened "Your Round" by Ian Anderson, gathered up unreleased gems from 1974 to 1988, plus the *Rock Island* and *Catfish* session tracks that had appeared on the "Living In The Past" singles earlier in the year. The inclusion of the latter annoyed some fans who had already laid out for all the single formats, but it was really a case of "as well as" rather than "instead of". It was decided they should be included for the benefit of overseas fans who would not have been able to buy the singles, and even had they not been included there were no other tracks that would have taken their place.

But it was the first CD, "My Round", that caused the most excitement. During exhaustive searches through hundreds of old studio tapes, Ian Anderson had unearthed the missing parts of the legendary Chateau D'Herouville (Chateau D'Isaster) sessions, and with the unhappy memories of those times now confined to the past, he realised that they were not too bad after all! Although some of it was unfinished, he set to work in the studio to present it almost as it was originally intended. A lot of the flute playing on the tracks is therefore of recent pedigree, but he decided against recording the missing vocal parts.

> "It's OK to add flute to something 20 years after the rest of it was recorded, because it would have sounded the same had I done it 20 years ago. Vocals are a different matter though: I was a young man then, with a much better voice and a different way of singing things, and it would sound decidedly odd should I try to sing those songs now. It's better to leave them as they are."

He was probably right, but the absence of vocals in some sections is the one flaw in an otherwise faultless album. The Chateau D'Isaster Tapes are the Tull equivalent of The Beach Boys' *Smile*, and a dream come true for fans of the 'progressive' era Tull, none of whom ever really expected to hear these tapes. The blueprint for *A Passion Play* was there, with much additional music never heard before. Sadly, it was still not quite the whole work. Thankfully the three segments already available on the 20th box set were included, as was "Solitaire" from the *Warchild* album, but there were a few pieces that Anderson refused to include, claiming they were "Simply wretched!" It is a great pity, because they were actually very good, and it would also have been nice after so many years to hear where "Skating Away On The Thin Ice Of The New Day" was placed on the original album as was the case with "Solitaire".

But who could complain, with such a feast of 'new' Tull material to enjoy? It was a neatly packaged collection, released on Anderson's insistence at low price, with his royalties going to charity. His sleeve notes neatly outlined the motives behind the release, obviously aware of the possibility of being accused of scraping the bottom of the out-takes barrel:

> "This collection of hitherto unreleased recordings is now available at the request of the many hard-core Tull fans who have learned, over the years, of the existence of the material. Most of the sessions for past studio albums have produced an extra song or two surplus to requirements. Sometimes these pieces failed to make it onto a record because they were too

similar to one of their brothers or sisters: sometimes, as the ear may just detect, because they were too different!

The infamous 1973 recording sessions at the Chateau D'Herouville, near Paris, were never completed due to ill-health, technical and production problems, and the sudden decision of the band to return to the UK from temporary and ill-advised tax exile. Rather than continue with the Chateau Tapes, we decided to begin again with a virtually new work which quickly became the more down-beat and controversial *A Passion Play*. So, here we have it. Not a cup of tea for everyone, but a slightly dizzy night cap for old friends in need of that last dram before laying down their heads to dream of what might have been.

Lest anyone feel (though understandably) that this bottom drawer collection is merely the exploitation of warty rejects to earn another miserable buck, I wish it to be known that we have fought hard to keep the price of this set to lowest possible levels and that I am donating all song writing royalties accruing to me from this material to (Listed) charities".

The final part of the celebrations, as far as Chrysalis were concerned, came in the shape of Tull's third video release. The snazzily named *25th Anniversary Video* featured some great live footage and promos, built around new interviews with Tull members past and present. They had been reunited for the video in a pub in London early in the year, and a combination of booze, fading memories and possibly sharp editing effectively glossed over any sharp edges of bitterness that might still lurk within some ex-Tullies.

The assorted musos come across as one big happy family, and, after all these years, why the hell shouldn't they? As Mick Abrahams so eloquently puts it: "I had the hump with Ian many times, and Glenn (Cornick) and I hated each other at times, but it was all a long time ago. Life is too short to hold grudges against anybody. And looking back on it all, whatever arguments we had were all about nothing really". Bridges were mended and hatchets were buried even further on the tour, when Mick, along with Clive Bunker and Gerry Conway, joined Tull on-stage in London.

The 25th Anniversary tour continued unabated as Tull entered their 26th year, with gigs in India, New Zealand, Australia, USA, Canada and

Europe, and then back to England for their second tour in eight months. The idea was to hit places not visited on the previous UK tour, but of course many of the same fans saw the gigs and were rather disappointed to find Tull still knocking out basically the same set. The fans wondered when and if the tour might ever end, and even some of the group members obviously found it all too much. When even more dates were added in June and July, Dave Pegg was forced to declare himself unavailable due to recording and live commitments with Fairport. His place was again taken by his son Matt, who had played on *Catfish* and was familiar with most of the material already. Doane Perry too had to pull out of some of the European festivals, and Marc Parnell, from Martin Barre's band, sat in for a week. This switch was not so successful, and the gigs with Marc were roundly hammered for uncharacteristic sloppiness and a perceived lack of rehearsal. Martin Barre saw the reasoning behind it, but had to agree that it had been a mistake:

> "It was considered impractical to get Doane over for just those few gigs, and the idea was that it would be nice to have somebody in England that we could call on in an emergency, like a short notice TV show or something. But it just didn't work out. Marc is a great player, and the stuff he has done with me is wonderful. He played stuff on my first album that other people can't play, but it sometimes works like that. I can't play what Mick Abrahams or Al Hodge can play, that's just how some people are. Some musicians, like Steve Bailey (who played on *Roots To Branches*), can play anything, but they are few and far between."

It was clear to some, though evidently not to Ian Anderson, that in trying to play to absolutely everybody, Jethro Tull were losing a degree of quality control, and the apparent ease with which Anderson was prepared to use 'temps' was worrying.

There was however the bonus of a unique gig from Tull at the Clapham Grand in August, when 'Jethro Tull & Friends' played a benefit for Friends Of The Earth. The Friends of Jethro Tull on this occasion were The Martin Barre Band, Mick Abrahams, Roy Harper and Gary Brooker, who played in various combinations throughout the evening. It was a memorable concert indeed, even down to Anderson's characteristic mocking of the beneficiaries of his nights' work. "We are trying to raise money for Friends of The Earth", he announced – "Bunch of bastards that they are! But somebody has to point the finger!" It was possibly a reference to having been pestered by them for months to play a benefit. "I thought I'd better do it just to shut them up!"

Dave Pegg was still absent, busy preparing for the Cropredy Festival a few days later. Tull flew out to Budapest to headline the 'Euro-Woodstock' festival over there, and the night after Tull played Ian Anderson joined an all-star band assembled by Leslie Mandoki for the festival. Bobby Kimball, David Clayton-Thomas, Bill Evans, Tony Jackson and many more legendary musos made up Mandoki's band, and they have also recorded three albums together on which Anderson plays flute and sings on several tracks. I still haven't worked out quite how Mandoki, a moderately talented drummer, manages to assemble such a heavyweight band, but they do make a pretty good sound when they come together.

It had been (for the most part) a great tour, but it had been a long time since anything really new had come from Tull. Since *Catfish Rising* in '91 there had been no less than nine CDs of archive material released and endless 'greatest hits' tours, and understandably there was a growing perception that Tull, or rather Ian Anderson, had dried up creatively. The tour had to end, and Tull had to return to the studio. At last, with seven gigs in South Africa in October '94, the mammoth tour came to an end, and work commenced shortly after on a new studio work. But even then it was not, as had been expected, an immediate return to the studio for Jethro Tull, as Ian Anderson set about recording his second solo album.

Meanwhile, Martin Barre had at last released his first solo album, *A Trick Of Memory*, on ZYX, a German label. Backing him on his highly impressive debut were the nucleus of his 'Summer Band', which included Matt Pegg on bass, as well as Fairport's Ric Sanders and Maart Allcock, Mel Collins, and Tull's Andy Giddings. Having taken so much time and trouble to record the album and find the right outlet, Barre's initial jubilation quickly turned to frustration as the record company seemed incapable of promoting his album. At each town or city on subsequent Jethro Tull tours he took to checking out all the local record shops, only to find that nobody appeared to be stocking his album. To say he was disappointed would be something of an understatement:

"Disappointed is putting it very, very mildly. I could swear for two full minutes, without repeating one swear word, to describe my thoughts on the promotion the record company gave it. It was really upsetting. In Britain it was pathetic, and even worse in America. The trouble is they don't care, because they make millions from dance records, which is what they specialise in. I think they took mine as a token rock album, and then found they really weren't geared up to handle it."

So Martin Barre's first stab at a solo career was not quite the huge commercial success it might have been, but artistically he was very pleased with it (as were the lucky few who managed to find the album), and quickly set about recording the follow up during gaps in the Tull calendar.

Almost at the same time as Ian Anderson's new solo offering there was another live Jethro Tull album release, courtesy of Windsong. *In Concert* was an hour long BBC radio recording of Tull's 1991 London *Catfish Rising* show, and helped satisfy fans demand for Jethro Tull product for a while on it's release in May '95, although the timing of the release, so close to both Anderson's solo and the new Tull album, could have been better. Thankfully it concentrated on more recent material rather than earlier classics, but of course it was no substitute for *new* material. It had been a long time coming, but it proved to be well worth the wait. The quality of the new CDs on offer after a four year break was breathtaking.

CHAPTER ELEVEN
"In The Grip Of Stronger Stuff"

Ian Anderson's *Divinities: Twelve Dances With God* was released for Easter '95. Although it was actually another 'solo' album from Ian Anderson, once again it was a far cry from what might have been expected of him. Unlike his earlier album, *Walk Into Light*, it was a very acoustic sounding album, but it certainly wasn't the simple acoustic guitar, flute and vocals set that the fans still cried out for. "Music For Flute and Orchestra performed by Ian Anderson and Andrew Giddings" was printed on the outer back cover of the CD to emphasise that it was in fact aimed more at the classical music lovers than at traditional Tull fans. It also emphasised that the "orchestra" was within the wonderfully gifted fingertips of Andy Giddings and his array of keyboard gadgetry. It had in fact been commissioned by the classical division of EMI Records, but it was not a case of Ian Anderson "doing a Thijs Van Leer" and running through the classics on his trusty flute, as Andy Giddings was at pains to stress:

> "Roger Lewis, head of EMI Classical, approached Ian and they discussed the fact that, for whatever reason, you couldn't buy any classical music that wasn't already the heavy, established classical stuff or the traditional modern composers that everybody knew about. He wanted somebody to come up with something new, a different slant on classical music. So that's what we tried to do, but really we only called it 'classical' as a convenience; I don't know that it really is classical music. A lot of people would find that term a bit frightening, or perhaps boring. It is classical in

the sense that it has orchestral instruments and orchestral sounds. It is a mixture of real instruments and synthesised sounds, almost by accident.

Ian and I recorded it over several months, with him giving me his ideas and melodies that I would develop and play using the sound of an orchestra. The idea was to demo everything that way and then to recreate it with an orchestra or quartet depending on what was required, but we found that much of it was OK as it was. I hope and think that it's hard to tell which is real and which is "Memorex!" We aren't trying to trick people though. The real musicians are all very good players, from the Royal Philharmonic Orchestra, but they might be accompanying synthesised sounds. We think it works really well".

It certainly does! The twelve instrumental pieces are a showcase for the wonderful talents of Ian Anderson, flautist, perhaps celebrating the fact that he had only very recently discovered that he had been "playing the flute the wrong way all these years"! Although his unique style was a large part of the appeal of Jethro Tull, having been pointed in the direction of correct fingering of his famous silver instrument he became an almost born-again musician, eager to improve as much as possible. The result was quite remarkable, and *Divinities* was rightly hailed by many as a masterpiece. Actual sales however did not quite match the quality of the album, due in no small part to confusion on the part of retailers. This time it was not merely a question of should it be under Jethro Tull or Ian Anderson, but should it be in the 'rock', 'pop', 'folk' or 'classical' section? It did score something of a hit in America though, which gave Ian more material for his 'stand-up' routine on later tours when introducing a piece from the album. "This gave us a number 1 hit in America.... in the Billboard Classical Crossover Chart. Whatever the fuck that is!"

The double-barrelled title was a compromise between artist and record company. Anderson wanted simply 'Divinities'. EMI wanted 'Twelve Dances With God'. Either way, why the religious overtones. Was this Ian Anderson getting all religious on us? No, thank God, as Andy Giddings explained:

"It isn't a celebration of Ian's religious beliefs, but it's an acknowledgement of all the religions that are around. It's not aimed at religious people or at any particular religion, it's just a theme for the album. Different religions tend to stem from different countries and continents, and those people all have their own kind of music. It was the musical element that was important to us, in as much as it gives us twelve different styles of music that we could work from, and then develop it in our own way."

Ian Anderson has always stressed that his music is not complete until it has been performed live, and true to form he assembled a band to play 18 concerts in Europe, USA and Canada in May and June. Doane Perry, who had played on *Divinities*, joined Tull-mates Anderson and Giddings on the tour, but for the first time since his arrival at the end of '68 Martin Barre was not part of Ian Anderson's group. It was not an unexpected omission, because *Divinities* did not involve a guitarist, but it was strange to see Anderson on-stage without his long-standing friend and colleague.

The Tull trio was augmented on tour by Chris Leslie, an outstanding violinist who had previously been a member of Whippersnapper and Fairport Convention, and a young bassist called John Noyce who came with a very different pedigree. There was something of a Jethro Tull connection, as Noyce was a member of the rock group section of David Palmers orchestral rock entourage, but his CV also included stints with such "rock luminaries" as Sister Sledge, Diana Ross, Lisa Stansfield and... Take That! Even Ian Anderson's kids were impressed that their Dad was working with somebody who had worked with Take That! And maybe the famous five themselves were impressed by Noyce's new role, having been bold enough once to admit to being Jethro Tull fans on Children's BBC? But how had the bassist with the nation's children's fave pop group become involved with a bunch of old geezers like Tull? John Noyce:

"I met David Palmer while I was a student at the Royal Academy of Music in London. He hired me for his orchestral projects, which is where I met Mark Parnell. Mark was playing on Martin Barre's solo album, so when Martin was looking for a bass player Mark put my name forward, and Martin asked me to do his album. Subsequently when Ian Anderson was looking for somebody to do the *Divinities* tour Martin Barre recommended me. So the Jethro Tull network contrived to get me in the band; it was simply a case of very good luck, being in the right place at the right time."

It was Tull's usual bassist Dave Pegg who recommended Chris Leslie, as Anderson was keen to find a skilled violinist who could also handle a midi system.

The short tour proved to be a musical treat of the highest order, as Anderson's new ensemble not only performed remarkably authentic live renditions of the whole of the *Divinities* album, but also served up some brave new interpretations of several Jethro Tull classics. Although most of the 'Tull' set was the acoustic material that often features in their traditional set, the inclusion of the heavy rockers like "Aqualung" and "Locomotive Breath" was a surprise, but as it turned out, a very welcome one. Wisely there was no attempt to play them as rockers without Martin Barre, but they were miraculously transformed into mini orchestral suites. It was an absolute triumph for the musicians and yet more confirmation of the genius of Ian Anderson. Sadly Martin Barre himself did not get to see first hand what the guys had managed to do with his personal live tour-de-force, "Aqualung":

"I was supposed to go to the London gig, but I couldn't make it in the end. Well, actually I didn't feel comfortable about going. It would have been nice to be there, and I should have been there, but I really didn't want to see them up on the stage playing 'Aqualung' without me. It seems silly, but after all this time it would have felt terrible."

It was of course only a temporary parting of the ways, as Barre and Tull were reunited for the next Jethro Tull album and tour. But for Dave Pegg, the time had finally come when he felt he had to leave the group.

The new Tull album had been recorded before the *Divinities* tour, and Ian Anderson had felt it necessary to start the recording whilst Pegg was on tour with Fairport Convention, despite the fact that Fairport were always on tour at that time of the year. Consequently Dave Pegg only played on three of the tracks, with legendary American session player Steve Bailey on the others. It was the last straw for an increasingly disillusioned Pegg. Already critical of Ian Anderson's recent policy of almost never ending touring of almost the same set, the decision to record most of the album without him did nothing to boost his morale. More importantly, he found that he did not actually like the new album, and the thought of having to learn it all to play live did not fill him with joy. All of this, coupled with his ever increasing commitments to Fairport, convinced him that he had to go.

"It wasn't really a snap decision. I'd been thinking about it for a couple of years. I had a great time with the band, and I was really honoured to be a part of it. When I joined Tull it was fantastic, but during the last couple of years, doing all the other things that I'm involved with, it was always a juggling act. Ian made many allowances for me. He has to do his thing when he wants to do it, but he knew there were times when I wasn't available, and Matt would dep for me.

Ian was very understanding about it, but in the last year it just got too difficult to juggle stuff around. Fairport always tour at the beginning of the year, and we have the Cropredy Festival in August. We need that to keep us going, and all of the guys in Fairport rely on it. I could never jeopardise Cropredy, but there were a couple of years where it was a very close thing. Tull were playing more gigs, and even though Fairport actually cropped a couple of tours so that I could tie in with Tull it still wasn't working.

Ultimately, the way the last Tull album was recorded meant that I was hardly involved in it, because I was busy with Fairport. Ian and Martin were very understanding about it, but I felt I didn't have any involvement anymore, and my input was getting less and less. Anybody could do what I did, and if you are not 100% committed, and it doesn't make you happy, there is little point doing it. So that's why I left Tull. I had too many other things going on that were important to me, and I was no longer giving 100% to Jethro Tull.

The older you get the more valuable your time becomes. I got out when I did because nothing was happening with Tull, so it didn't cause too much upheaval. John Noyce knew a lot of the material anyway because of his involvement in the Divinities tour, so I didn't drop anybody in it. Ian was very good about it. He suggested I take a year out and then maybe rejoin the band, but it was time for a clean break."

His decision shocked Tull fans, who had taken 'Peggy' to their hearts over his 15 years with the band. And yes, Jethro Tull had become 'a band' again as opposed to Ian Anderson's backing group, with the enduring core of Anderson, Barre, Pegg and Perry. But Dave Pegg had never really seen it like that:

"It isn't really a band. It's Ian's thing and it always has been. You don't have much of a say in it, not that it bothered me. For most of my time with Tull it was great to have somebody telling me what to do, because it was the complete opposite from Fairport where I have to do much of what Ian does for Tull, although on a much smaller scale. He has had that incredible pressure since the start of Tull, so obviously he has to do things his way. Making allowances for somebody like me so many times is something in principle that you can do without, and the longer it went on the more distant he became from me. There were a couple of tours where he never spoke to anybody. That's not a problem, because you get used to things like that on the road, but it all became a bit too much.

I wasn't really doing anything within the band, I didn't have anything to play during the stage show. The little bits I used to do, as we all did, got whittled down to nothing. And the music we were playing changed so much. When we did all that box set stuff, re-recording old songs and so on, it was the first time I felt the band was going in the wrong direction. It upset me to be doing it, and I felt there were some bad decisions being made.

The 25th Anniversary tour went on far too long, and too many of the gigs were not as good as they should have been. If your voice is giving you problems you shouldn't go out and do thirty gigs. I don't understand why Ian feels obliged to carry on playing so often if it's causing him problems. Every time you play a bad gig, or every night Ian's voice lets him down badly, you are going to disappoint and possibly alienate a lot of fans. And there were some nights when his voice was really bad. He doesn't need to work like that. He doesn't need to keep finding newer and weirder places to play.

He is a workaholic, and he does feel responsible for the livelihood of lots of other people, but he should not push himself so hard all the time.

He is still a great singer in the studio, and he doesn't do anybody any favours by putting so much strain on his voice by gigging so often."

The sadness amongst the fans at Dave Pegg's departure was tempered by the widely held view that the album which had contributed to his decision, *Roots To Branches*, was a magnificent return by any standards. Not as accessible or immediately commercial as much of their earlier work, it was nevertheless a brilliant and inspired body of work that dispelled any doubts as to the creative spark within Ian Anderson. There were hints of much of Tull's greatest previous offerings, yet it sounded unlike anything they had done before. Coming hot on the heels of *Divinities*, another creative masterpiece, it seemed Jethro Tull were hitting yet another fertile musical peak. And of course, yet another huge tour was lined up to promote the album, running initially from September through November, in the UK, Europe and the USA. One of the UK shows was recorded by the BBC for a 60-minute broadcast the following month on Radio 2 as that station at last made some attempt to cater for 'mature' rock fans who could no longer listen to Radio 1.

During a break in the tour a remarkable event took place in a tiny studio in Buckingham. Original Tull guitarist Mick Abrahams, taking a break from Blodwyn Pig, had been recording a solo acoustic album, and he invited Ian to play on a few tracks. Thus in early December '95 Ian Anderson and Mick Abrahams recorded four tracks together, marking the first time the erstwhile colleagues had recorded together since the debut Tull album in 1968.

The album, *One*, was released the following year, just as Martin Barre released his second solo album, *The Meeting*. Thankfully free from his deal with ZYX, he decided to release it initially on his own Presshouse label via *A New Day* magazine. Just 1,000 were sold through that outlet before Imago Records in America took it on. Collectors should note that the Imago CD features a change of singer on one track!

In March '96, Jethro Tull embarked on the second leg of the mammoth *Roots To Branches* tour. Colin Harper, writing in *A New Day* magazine, asked the questions: Would Ian Anderson ever slow down? Just why did he still work so hard?

"I'm sure it's the same for Bob Dylan, Van Morrison and so on – people who have real artistic credibility, who are tortured, tormented, desperate and, I'm told, particularly unpleasant souls! I'm sure their motivation is the same as mine, except that I'm willing to talk about it. It's the feeling that perhaps, to many people, your best work and heyday is long since past, but there's this desperate need to go out and somehow try to push something onto a different level. Trying to prove to yourself that you still have a place in the musical firmament. It's not about making money, it's about making better music – which is why I don't understand somebody like Phil Collins doing what he does again and again and again. 'Musician as tortured artist' is not something we would normally attribute to him! He is a great pop singer and a great writer of pop music, but musicality is not what that's about."

And when would it finally be time to start winding down the Jethro Tull machine?

"Well, plotting the failure curve – in terms of 'systems failure' – it's not a smooth curve. It's more of a parabolic rather than a straight line. We are a lot luckier than tennis players or footballers, but there comes a point when it goes downhill very quickly in a physical sense, and those of us who do have physically demanding performances have to face facts. It's not simply that I move about a lot on-stage, the actual tasks of singing and playing flute, using different sets of muscles, are very fatiguing. And it's not like we are 20 year olds going on to do a 30 minute support slot. We are 50+, playing a two hour-plus show, which people rightfully expect. It is important that you carry with you this sense of preparation.... preparation for death! You know that there is going to be an end to it, but you don't know when it's going to be, and you don't want to know.

I don't want to know when the end comes for me as a musician and/or for Jethro Tull. But I do know that it's not that far away, and I know that when it happens it happens – there ain't no coming back. I'm not going to be one of those people who announces retirement and then pops up a couple of years later, or every time the money runs out."

Although Anderson's "preparation for death" was intended as a humorous reference, it was very soon to take on a horrifying new aspect, as the rolling Tull tour was beset first by misfortune and subsequently by near tragedy.

In March '96 Tull started a tour of South America, completing a successful series of gigs in Chile, Argentina, Uruguay and Brazil. Two weeks into the tour however Anderson fell badly on an uneven stage in Peru, severely injuring his knee. It was towards the end of the show, and after a short break, always the true professional, he managed to finish the show in a chair. The rest of the tour, mainly in America, was completed with Ian performing in a wheelchair, which caused much puzzlement within the audiences. Remember, Ian had appeared on-stage wheelchair bound before on the 20th Anniversary tour as a jokey reference to impending middle age. It took a while for the punters to realise that this time round it was for real!

The other band members and entourage did not fare much better, as they were without exception struck down with various illnesses, most notably food poisoning, in South America. One member of the road crew was taken so seriously ill that at one point they genuinely feared for his life.

The US tour finished early in April, and Ian returned to England for surgery on his knee. Jethro Tull had been scheduled to start a tour of Australia and New Zealand on 11th May, and naturally the promoter over there started proceedings to cancel the tour. But Ian Anderson was determined to go ahead with the tour, and made it clear that Tull would make themselves available for the tour even though he would be in a wheelchair. It was a decision that underlined his aversion to cancelling any gig if it was at all possible to play, but ultimately it proved to be a foolhardy decision.

They flew to Australia, and almost immediately he suffered great discomfort in his injured knee. By the time they played the fourth gig of the tour he was in such pain he could not continue with the tour, and was subsequently admitted to hospital with a potentially life threatening thrombosis. Naturally the Australian tour and the following six week European tour were cancelled immediately, and the world's press ran "Jethro Tull Star Fights For His Life" horror stories. These were Dark Ages indeed, as

fans and well-wishers prayed for his recovery and reflected on the unthinkable prospect that his desire to play to people at every opportunity
might well have taken him from them forever.

After a tense couple of weeks of conflicting reports came the confirmation that yes, it had been a very serious injury, but he was on the way to a
complete recovery and would fly back to England as soon as he was fit to
travel. With the scare diminished, he confirmed the previously arranged
UK tour, and lined up a huge American tour for the summer, whilst going
about a daily routine of specific physiotherapy exercises to repair the dam-
age to his knee. Ironically one of the exercises involved him "bobbing up
and down standing on one leg while carefully maintaining my balance!"
All those years of practise finally paid off then!

The American tour, from August to the end of September, saw Tull
selling out 10-15,000 seaters yet again, helped no doubt by the presence of
another musical legend from the 70's, the newly reformed Emerson, Lake
and Palmer. Martin Barre had suffered problems with his arm, causing
him to stop playing guitar for a while – and "more seriously, I can't play
tennis either!" - and Keith Emerson was also recovering from a serious injury to his arm, causing Ian to dub the tour a "greatest crocks tour". But it
went extremely well, as Anderson eased himself back into performance
mode.

"The best physiotherapy I've had seems to have been simply being on
tour. Walking through airports, miles every day, seems to have done some
good. I still have to be careful, and I will never completely recover, but
it's getting better all the time. Clearly there is an impediment in the performances that I've done hitherto, and I would doubt whether realistically
I will get back into that particular set of moves. Running and jumping
around the stage at the moment is not a feasible option, but it was interesting to note that none of the recent reviews made any reference to my
being less animated on-stage. I expected to get comments like, 'Poor old
Ian Anderson, dragging himself around the stage', but it seemed to have
escaped people's attention…. which is a bit of a back-handed compliment
in a way. I'm relieved that nobody is saying I'm giving a second rate per-

formance, but on the other hand it makes me wonder if what I was doing before was at all important or meaningful anyway if people didn't miss it!

It's nice to know that maybe I don't have to be quite so energetic on-stage. It has always been a bit of an obligation, pressure to fulfil people's expectations. Once you start doing it and people write and talk about you as if you are some sort of cross between Rudolf Nurejev and Little Rich-ard it becomes rather 'show-biz', something that you are expected to do. It is nice to be able to do it, but it's also nice not to have to.

The tour has been very useful to me in that sense, as it was to Keith Emerson. It was really for him to find out if he could manage to play for an hour or so every night. I personally thought they (ELP) should have played a bit longer, because they started the tour doing just 50 minutes and no encore. It must have looked to their fans like Jethro Tull would not let them play any more than that, and it didn't do us or them any favours. I managed to persuade their manager to get them to play an encore, even if it meant taking 15 minutes out of our set, but they still only played for barely an hour. But they were in a difficult situation, and they did well and went down really well.

ELP fans got a 'greatest hits' show, and Tull fans got a good introduc-tion to ELP. They got through the tour OK, and they were still talking to each other at the end so it was a success in that respect. The ELP thing used to be in their notorious days in the '70's that they never spoke to each other. They travelled in separate limos and even their equipment travelled in separate trucks! I never saw them then, I didn't know them, and all I remember is the folk-lore of them being this really over-the-top, big rock'n'roll star band.

The last time I saw them at an airport there were limos outside, which we assumed were for them. We thought about telling the drivers we were ELP and stealing their limos for a laugh, but decided against it. But we waited in our cabs for ELP to get into their limos, until we realised that they too were waiting for a taxi. I thought 'poor old sods – they haven't got their limos anymore', so I sent somebody out to get three Dinky toy super-stretch limos, which we autographed and left for them in three real limos that we hired to take them from their hotel to the airport at the end of the tour. The beauty of it was that the airport was very close to the ho-tel so they only got to ride in them for three minutes. I hope their sense of

humour encompassed all of this in the spirit in which it was intended....
but they might have been really pissed off about it!"

In 1995 Ian Anderson had contributed a track to a Peter Green tribute
album. Although he had always viewed such albums with suspicion, he
was more than happy to make an exception for Green, whom he had always admired, and his version of "Man Of The World" was one of the
highlights of the set, which also included a track from Mick Abrahams.
The tables were turned in '96, when Magna Carta records in America
compiled *To Cry You A Song - A Collection Of Tull Tales*, a tribute to
Jethro Tull. There was a heavy Tull presence on the album, with Glenn
Cornick, Mick Abrahams and Clive Bunker (75% of the original line-up)
providing the backing for four of the tracks, and Dave and Matt Pegg performing a poignant version of "Life Is A Long Song". Roy Harper, John
Wetton, Keith Emerson, Glenn Hughes and Charlie Musselwhite were
some of the bigger names involved, but Magellan were the stars of the
show with their magnificent version of "Aqualung". The album did nothing to change Ian Anderson's views on tributes however:

"I really liked some of the tracks, particularly Roy Harper's 'Up The
Pool' and Robert Berry's 'Minstrel In The Gallery'. But there were three
or four tracks that I thought were terrible, absolute stiffs. It really let it
down badly which is a shame, because the blokes who really did a good
job were up against things that were, at the worst extremes, crudely ama-
teurish. I would rather hear The Six and Violence doing Tull songs than
some of the people who were on that album, because it's reckless. They
mean it as a mark of respect in the same way a tomcat will spray on your
favourite rose bush! But I hear they actually tried to get current members
of Jethro Tull to play on their own tribute album, which is where you really have to start questioning things. If you can't round up enough mar-
ketable names then you have to ask 'A tribute to what?' I mean, I didn't
notice David Bowie doing a track, or Elton John or Phil Collins or whoever. Tribute albums are incredibly difficult things to put together and,
with just a few exceptions, I don't think they are usually a good idea. But
it had its moments, and if nothing else it got us playing 'Up The Pool'

live, and reminded me of how, on a good night, something like 'Minstrel In The Gallery' can sound."

Ironically, not only were Tull inspired to include "Up The Pool" in the live set for the first time, but they performed a version as modified by Roy Harper on the tribute album. What finer example of a mutual appreciation society could there be?

There was a six month break from touring, purportedly for writing and recording of the next Jethro Tull album, but Martin Barre managed to find a few weeks between Tull commitments to record a remarkable album with an old friend and musical partner from pre-Tull days. Way back in 1965 Martin had been in a band called The Moonrakers, with a singer called John Carter. Although they had lost contact soon after Barre joined Tull, they met up again in the mid 70's and had stayed in touch ever since. Although Carter was no longer professionally involved in the music business, he was a keen songwriter, and the two had often discussed the possibility of making an album together. When Carter finally sent Barre a tape of his songs he was so impressed he decided they had to make the album.

A monster band was assembled for the sessions, including Tull associates John Noyce, Dave Pegg, Chris Leslie and Paul Burgess, and the album was recorded at Martin Barre's studio in Devon. Although it was originally intended as a John Carter album, Martin Barre's involvement as both musician and producer was so great that it eventually came out co-credited to him.

The Carter/Barre album, *Spirit Flying Free*, was released on the very day that Ian Anderson and chums served up another great treat for UK fans. Another fans' convention had been arranged in the rock'n'roll hot spot that is Gravesend, with profits going to Lupus UK, a charity set up to fight that horrific disease. It was in response to a plea from David Palmer who had recently lost his wife after she had suffered with the disease for many years. Consequently David Palmer had offered to perform at the convention, and John Evans had also agreed to come along. Clive Bunker was there with his new band Solstice, and Glenn Cornick was scheduled to appear with the newly reformed Wild Turkey. Mick Abrahams, a regular supporter of the Tull convention was again bringing his Blodwyn Pig along for the day.

The amazing line up of ex-Tull members was boosted to staggering proportions with the arrival of Ian Anderson, John Noyce and Andy Giddings. Martin Barre was unfortunately absent, giving his reason (as announced on-stage by Ian Anderson) as "No bastard asked him to come!" Not true obviously, and the truth of the matter was more likely that nobody could seriously really want to spend the day in what David Palmer was to describe as "the God-forsaken hole" that is Gravesend!

Ian Anderson guested with Solstice, David Palmer and Blodwyn Pig, and also delivered a fine mini Tull set with Andy, John and Mick Abrahams on guitar. It was an incredible event, and was just a whisper away from reuniting the four original members for the first time since 1968. Sadly though Glenn Cornick was forced to pull out after undergoing heart surgery just weeks earlier. He was thankfully well on the way to a complete recovery, but was naturally not able to travel from his home in America for the gig, although Wild Turkey went ahead without him.

Cornick was back with Wild Turkey a few months later when they played at the German Tull Convention, along with Vikki Clayton, Solstice and Fairport Convention. Clive Bunker, a permanent member of Solstice, sat in with the drummerless Vikki Clayton for the show, and was so impressed with the music he volunteered to join her band whenever she needed him. He is now a member of both bands! One week after the Convention Glenn Cornick made it to England for a highly unlikely reunion. *A New Day* Records hosted a gig at the 100 Club in London featuring three of their signings. Vikki Clayton opened the show with a band that again included Clive Bunker, Maart Allcock and special guest Martin Barre. Solstice were second on the bill, with Blodwyn Pig headlining. Glenn Cornick, having called a truce in the hostilities between him and Mick Abrahams, jumped up to jam on a couple of songs during the Pig set. Musically it was a mess, but it was a rare sight indeed to see the old adversaries at last publicly burying the hatchet.

The Jethro Tull tour rolled on through most of 1997, as the band seemed to be repeating the dubious policy of playing live as though there was no tomorrow. Bearing in mind that it had almost literally been the case just a couple of years before it mystified the fans who had assured themselves that Ian Anderson would surely be mindful of the need to take things just a bit easier. And as the tour expanded ever further, so the long awaited new album seemed less and less likely, even though Ian and Andy Giddings had been talking about 'the new recordings' for well over a year.

Anderson would surely be mindful of the need to take things just a bit easier. And as the tour expanded ever further, so the long awaited new album seemed less and less likely, even though Ian and Andy Giddings had been talking about 'the new recordings' for well over a year. EMI again chose to fill the gap with yet another 'Best Of' in the shape of *Through The Years,* but at least this time it was a nicely presented collection at a price low enough to tempt the casual buyer into sampling the music of a band that perhaps they had heard a lot about, but never heard the music.

Tull took the unusual step of playing two major festivals in the UK in the summer of '97. The first was the Pentrich Rock & Blues Festival, which is basically a bikers' rally with music. Tull went down a storm with the record 20,000 revellers, but the band were surprised to find they were sharing the bill with tribute bands and strippers! And Anderson was less than impressed when the generator that powered the stage equipment ran out of fuel, causing a 20 minute break in the set. Nevertheless it was an impressive performance, which was matched the following day when they topped the bill at the increasingly important Guildford Festival. There had been rumblings of discontent throughout the three days of the festival because the huge marquee for the main stage, apparently erected solely on the insistence of Jethro Tull, prevented those outside the tent from seeing the groups on-stage. Tull's actions were fully justified however when the heavens opened on the final day, and a miserable wash-out was averted. There was more controversy when the festival security firm, who had done an admirable job all weekend, were grounded by Tull with the curt announcement that "Jethro Tull will be responsible for security whilst they are on-stage". Consequently all children were removed from their closely guarded vantage points at the front of the stage, for safety reasons. Perhaps it was a wise precaution, in case of a crush at the front, but still there was great anger and disappointment amongst those fans that had secured their positions at the start of the day in order to catch a close up view of their heroes. A stage rush was an unlikely scenario anyway from the Tull audience at the Guildford Festival, which is as close in spirit to the always friendly Cropredy Festival as it is possible to get, but it is just possible that visions of the previous nights biker crowd influenced the decision!

On a brighter note, it was a blinding set from the band, and halfway through, Ian Anderson took time out to give a huge plug to "Dave Pegg's wonderful Cropredy Festival next week", clearly demonstrating that Peggy's departure from the band had caused no bad feeling between the two.

In the middle of the umpteenth leg of the American tour Jethro Tull performed a special set at another Tull convention, in Burlington, Vermont. It was the first time the whole band had played at such an event, and it seemed to cement the growing affinity between this remarkable band and the army of intensely loyal fans. Tull collectively played a selection of acoustic material, interspersed with solo 'party pieces' from each individual member, before reeling off the traditional heavy numbers at the end. "Locomotive Breath" proved to be the surprise of the day, when Anderson invited a member of the audience to join the band on-stage to sing the song with them. It was, of course, musically awful, but it was powerful evidence of the latterly relaxed Ian Anderson. For all the stories of his lofty arrogance, the accusations of delusions of grandeur and swipes at pretentious progressive/classical concept albums etc. etc., there is the reality of Jethro Tull playing an afternoon set in a cider mill to a few hundred devotees, answering even the most banal audience questions with great humour in a 'question and answer session', giving out the raffle prizes and finally enlisting one of the fans as guest singer. Jethro Tull - the people's band! There was even a repeat performance at the hastily arranged German Tull Convention in April '98, (but this time without the guest singer!) when Tull flew out to play a full set to just 700 fans, even though it was in complete isolation from any tour. It was another goodwill gesture to the fans, although Ian Anderson had one eye on promoting Martin Barre's tour of Germany the following month.

One slight difference in the set was the inclusion of a new tune, the title track from Anderson's next solo album *Boris Dancing* (so called after Ian saw film of Boris Yeltsin dancing). It was the first confirmation that there is to be another Ian Anderson solo offering, for throughout the months and possibly years of recording new material nobody has really been sure what it was for - including Ian Anderson.

"I have been working on three separate musical projects in the last couple of years. Some of the music is purely acoustic, some of it is heavy rock. It may come out as a Jethro Tull album, or it may be an Ian Anderson album, or both. Or a combination of the two!" Confused? You will be!

The downside to all this on-the-road activity is that there has still to date been no sign of the new Jethro Tull album or the Ian Anderson solo album, even though the first half of 1998 saw Tull taking a complete break from touring and recording. The only group activity had been the German Convention and a three song set for an Austrian TV special in March, which was notable mainly for the inclusion of yet another drummer in the line up. Tull were not playing 'live', so rather than fly Doane Perry in from America, Ian's son James sat in for the evening. Remarkably, until the last minute Jeffrey Hammond was going to join the band for the show, but had to cry off when his wife was taken ill.

In an almost perverse twist it seems that Ian Anderson has decided to 'celebrate' the 30th Anniversary of Jethro Tull with no group album and (by Tull's standards) only a few concerts. Three mini tours of America have been lined up for the latter half of 1998, to cover parts of that country "that will not be touched by the major world tour scheduled for 1999". The word is that Ian's solo album will be out in October '98, with a new group album in April '99, marking a worrying break of almost four years since the last Tull album. Fans will no doubt be encouraged however by the long term plans and ambitions still being formulated by Anderson, with not a hint of impending retirement in sight.

In recent times, despite a paucity of Tull recordings, there have been plenty of outlets for Ian Anderson's talents on other people's albums. Although he has never been one of those guys who seems to turn up on everybody's album as a special guest, he has boosted his 'session man' CV considerably in the last year. He can be heard playing flute on one track on the latest Ritchie Blackmore album *(Blackmore's Night)*, and plays flute and harmonica on two tracks on *Pin-board Wizards*, the first studio album from the legendary rocker Jackie Lynton for 15 years. Ex-Savoy Brown frontman Lynton also enlisted the services of Martin Barre, Mick Abrahams and Clive Bunker, along with other legendary players like Big Jim Sullivan, Rick Parfitt, Mick Moody and Al Hodge. Incidentally, it is the only time Tull guitarists Barre and Abrahams have ever appeared on record together.

Anderson also makes an appearance on Clive Bunker's new album *Awakening* (along with Martin Barre), and Roy Harper's new CD *The Dream Society* features Anderson on the 15 minute epic "These Fifty Years".

The rest of Jethro Tull have been busy too, having gone out as The Martin Barre Band on a tour of Germany in May '98, playing tracks from Barre's two solo albums, as well as a brilliant new version of the Tull classic 'To Cry You A Song'. Incredibly though, even though it was the complete Tull line-up minus Ian Anderson, playing in Jethro Tull heartland, the concerts were very poorly attended. It seems that even in Germany Jethro Tull is Ian Anderson, period. And yet, as the relatively low sales of Anderson's solo albums indicate, the reverse is not true - Ian Anderson is not Jethro Tull.

Barre has played a lot of sessions too, featuring on recent albums by Jackie Lynton, Vikki Clayton, and Spirit Of The West, and even featured as flute player on a world-wide dance hit single!

His future projects include the possibility of another album with John Carter, and he has recently upgraded his Presshouse studio with a view to becoming more involved with production and promotion of other artists.

Doane Perry has formed a band with Vince DiCola and Ellis Hall, called Thread, who released an eponymous album in '96. He has also been heavily involved in raising funds to help ex-Tull drummer Mark Craney, who suffered a serious set-back after appearing to be making a full recovery from his previous health problems. One of the fund raising projects was a CD featuring many of the artists that Craney has worked with, including Jethro Tull who contributed two exclusive tracks. One is a live recording of 'Black Sunday', the other - actually credited to Ian Anderson but also featuring Martin Barre and Andy Giddings - is a great new studio recording of 'A Song For Jeffrey'.

So that is, or if you prefer, this was, the first thirty years of Jethro Tull. Three decades during which a remarkably gifted band of minstrels, guided by one of the true musical geniuses of our time, have created a unique brand of music. You can't dance to it, many simply can't listen to it, but to the millions of delighted record buyers and concert goers that discovered the special sound of Jethro Tull at various points on the epic journey, there is nothing quite like it. The sound is still indefinable, yet instantly recognisable. Jethro Tull have drawn on influences from all types of music and entwined them with classic British rock, adding the essential ingredient of Ian Anderson's masterly lyrical prose. There may have been one or two slight hiccups along the way, an own goal here and there which momentarily threatened their position at the top of 'division one', but even then it has been a case of an experiment that failed. Jethro Tull have rarely stood still and basked in the glory of earlier successes, and it is that very determination to move onwards and upwards that has, at times, led them up the wrong path.

Jethro Tull do not need to make any more records, or play any more gigs. 50 million albums sold brings a lot of financial security, and in Ian Anderson's case his other business interests help to make him a permanent fixture in the annual published 'rich lists'. So just why does one of the wealthiest men in Britain still choose to play tiny theatres in Turkey and Israel for example, when he could be at home enjoying his luxurious surroundings? Why does he turn up in places like Gravesend on a miserable grey November morning to play, for nothing, to a few hundred punters? It can only be that he loves to play, with a passion for performance that is undiminished even after thirty-plus years.

And why do the fans still turn up in their thousands? There are hundreds of reasons, of course, but if one word has to be highlighted to explain the enduring appeal, then let it be INTEGRITY. Throughout the long and illustrious career, the works, ideas and ambitions of Ian Anderson's

Jethro Tull have been governed by integrity. Ian Anderson has a lot of admirers, but he has his critics too within the music business who are quick to describe him as, to put it bluntly, 'an awkward bugger'. That is to say of course, that whatever he does, he wants to do it right. If whatever he is doing involves other people, he wants them to do it right also. To less dedicated people that is a failing, but to a real professional, it is integrity. Away from music, he has gone about his other duties with the same level of integrity, transforming a remote, barren wasteland into a thriving industrial community, bringing employment where before there was nothing, and achieving the prestigious accolade of Scots Businessman Of The Year along the way.

Returning to his music, the desire to play the best possible concert, and to make the best possible album, is the key to the huge success that Tull have enjoyed. And though the album sales have decreased in recent years, and the concert venues may be smaller, the values remain the same. Jethro Tull will always be a premier league team in terms of attitude to the paying fans and dedication to delivering value for their money.

Some years ago Ian Anderson stated that Jethro Tull would continue "until the year 2001". I don't know why he chose that particular year, and at the time it really didn't matter, but now as it rapidly approaches it is reassuring to find that he has modified that particular prediction. In a recent interview in *Progression* magazine he envisaged that "Jethro Tull would continue for a few more years yet", and talked of yet more musical projects away from the confines of the rock band environment.

There is clearly plenty more to come from Anderson & Co, and on past achievements alone who can say that Jethro Tull will not again come up with an album that captures the imagination of the public at large, gaining a whole new audience? If anybody can do it, Ian Anderson can. So let's raise a glass and toast the last, glorious thirty years, and look forward with gleeful anticipation to the next.... 'few years' of Jethro Tull!

Appendix 1
MICK ABRAHAMS & BLODWYN PIG

Of all the many musicians that have passed through the ranks of Jethro Tull, Mick Abrahams is perhaps more deserving of special mention than anyone else. Although his tour of duty was brief, and few would argue with the fact that Martin Barre is *the* guitarist in Jethro Tull, it is also undeniable that big Mick Abrahams was a major factor in Jethro Tull's spectacular rise to prominence in 1968. Back then Jethro Tull was not Ian Anderson's band, it was a four-piece unit with two incredible front men. Many were drawn to the live performances by Anderson's wild antics, but others were there to see and hear Abrahams, rightly regarded as one of the premier guitarists in the country. No less an authority than Martin Barre himself first went to see Tull because he was such an admirer of Mick Abrahams' guitar playing, and Barre is still the first to stress the importance of Abrahams to the Jethro Tull success story. In '68 Tull were a truly unique musical experience, with two sure-to-become megastars at the helm. Ian Anderson is still there, and true to expectations, is categorically one of the most noteworthy figures in the history of rock music. And Mick Abrahams? Well…. What went wrong?

With hindsight it is easy to say that it was doomed from the start. Two such strong personalities, apparently pulling in different musical directions, was always a recipe for ultimate collapse. Abrahams, the established rock star (albeit still on a small scale) was a blues player first and foremost, and although he clearly loved the life of a musician he had no desire to play seven nights a week. Anderson on the other hand was already moving away from the blues music of early Tull, with a vision and ambition far beyond the average musician, and was willing and determined to do whatever was required to attain the success awaiting him. One of them had to go, and Ian Anderson made sure it was not him. Mick was partly pushed, and he partly jumped, but it largely boils down to the same thing; throughout Abrahams' stop-start career he has been felled at several hurdles by his own in-built self-destruct button that has caused him to make, frankly, strange decisions. At best they have done his musical career no good, at worst they have been disastrous.

At the beginning, it was the best thing that could have happened. Jethro Tull was a great blues band in '68, but there were a lot of those about. They were always different, but just how different only really became apparent once Anderson alone was at the helm. Had Abrahams remained with Tull, with the inevitable compromise to Ian's creative genius, then truly great works like *Thick As A Brick* and *Passion Play* would surely never have been born. How long would Tull have lasted without the singular drive and determination of Ian Anderson, undiluted by others who might have seen other directions for the music? Perhaps as long as Blodwyn Pig, the band formed by Mick on his departure from Tull.

Mick's new band was christened Blodwyn Pig in typically surreal fashion:

"A lunatic gave us the name! We were in the rehearsal studio when this fella called Graham came in. He had just come home after spending four years as a Buddhist monk. Really! He was one of the best jazz keyboard players I've ever heard, but he just went potty, took too much LSD, shaved his head - he couldn't become a Christian because they are too pious, so he became a Buddhist which was the more acceptable, hippy version of religion. He left because the monks would not let him have Kelloggs corn flakes! Anyway, we asked him if he had a name for the band and he came straight back with Blodwyn Pig, so we took it."

Ironically, *Ahead Rings Out*, the first album from Blodwyn Pig, was in many ways more of a follow-up to *This Was* than was *Stand Up*. The music was very much in the same style as early Tull, even down to the excellent flute playing of Jack Lancaster. One of the tracks on the album even appeared later on Tull bootlegs credited as "Unreleased Instrumental", so similar was the sound to early Tull. Lancaster brought jazz into the equation as well, and the new band found immediate success, with *Ahead Rings Out* charting at Number 9 in the UK. Two tours of America also helped the Pig to great success on the other side of the Atlantic. The album is remembered as much for the cover as the music, with the striking and bizarre pig's head complete with headphones, shades and fag in mouth! Incredibly gross and tasteless certainly, but an unforgettable image and a great cover nevertheless!

Getting To This continued the success story, charting at number 8 in the UK. Blodwyn Pig even managed an appearance on *Top Of The Pops*, although Abrahams upset the powers that be by refusing to play the song they wanted, opting instead for "Slow Down", a Larry Williams song that was a permanent fixture in the Blods live set and the B-side to their "Same Old Story" single.

Everything pointed to a rosy future for Mick and the Pig, when suddenly they parted company. Bizarrely, Abrahams suffered the indignity of being kicked out of his own band! "It was disappointing that the original Blodwyn Pig didn't fulfil it's true potential, and the way it ended was a shame too. I just wasn't doing it their way and they booted me out". Mick has never elaborated on the actual circumstances of the split, and anyway, it's all rather academic. Blodwyn Pig was, whatever Pyle, Berg and Lancaster might have believed, Mick Abrahams' band, so although they tried to soldier on with Peter Banks replacing Mick, the band soon folded.

Undeterred, Mick formed a new band with Ritchie Dharma (ex of The John Evan Band), Pete Fensome and John Darnborough on violin. "He was a great lad" recalls Mick, "but as soon as we went onstage he would forget everything we had done in rehearsals and just go wild. One of the hardest things I ever had to do was fire him". That band – the curiously named Wommet – did not make any records even though they landed a BBC Radio 1 'In Concert' broadcast.

In 1971, after the rapid disintegration of Wommet, Mick formed yet another band, this time with the infinitely more self-explanatory name of The Mick Abrahams Band. Ritchie Dharma remained on drums, with

Walt Monaghan (bass) and Bob Sargeant (keyboards, vocals) making up the four piece.

The first album – either called simply *Mick Abrahams* or 'A Musical Evening With The Mick Abrahams Band', depending on how you interpret the cover! – was something of a disappointment after the promise of Blodwyn Pig. Mick's guitar playing can't be faulted of course, and there are some great moments on the album, but overall the progressive blues of the Pig gave way to a sometimes tepid country blues. One other noticeable missing ingredient was the wonderful sax playing of the hugely talented Jack Lancaster. That fault was rectified when he was enlisted to the band for their second album, *At Last*. Better than the first, but still a rather patchy affair, the album is remembered mostly for the elaborate cover – a circular sleeve that folded outwards with two 'wings' attached by an inch or so of card, which naturally fell to pieces after just a few outings! A good idea, but perhaps requiring a few refinements!

Once again the band secured a Radio 1 "In Concert" and a John Peel session, and even made it onto *Top Of The Pops* again in their short lived experimental album track slot, but album sales failed to match those of the Blodwyn Pig albums, with neither of the Mick Abrahams Band albums making the chart. Disillusioned, Abrahams folded the band and hung up his guitar in late '72.

Two years later Mick was back with a revamped Blodwyn Pig. Andy Pyle and Jack Lancaster were back again, with Clive Bunker on drums. It was a very short lived reincarnation, but remarkably one of the four gigs the band played was for Radio 1 "In Concert", and they played another Radio 1 session. It could have been another new start for the band, but tragically their manager June Whyton killed herself, and again the band disintegrated. Mick quit the music business, "found religion in a big way", and took a series of 'proper jobs', confining his role in music to very occasional gigs for charity. It was one of those gigs that accidentally re-launched Blodwyn Pig in 1988.

Mick had been asked to put together a band to play at the opening of a new leisure centre in his home town of Luton. He joked that "for an extra £50 I'll get The Blods back together!", but it became a reality after the idea was eagerly encouraged by anyone that heard it. Mick assembled a formidable band to carry the Blodwyn Pig moniker, although at the time it was still intended to be a one-off gig. Andy Pyle and Clive Bunker from earlier Blods line-ups were willing volunteers, and Bruce Boardman (keyboards) and Bernie Hetherington (sax) from Mick's occasional pub band joined the line-up. Mick had gone to find Boardman playing at a local gig to ask him if he was up for it, and was amazed to find the legendary sax-man Dick Heckstall-Smith playing the gig with him. Heckstall-Smith was amazed too: "Wow! It's Mick Abrahams.... and he's still alive!" was his greeting. Not wishing to waste the opportunity, Mick invited them both to join the band, and consequently he got the line-up that he had wanted from the outset.

> "I'd played with him a couple of times before. Once when I was with John Mayall, and I sat in with Coliseum after I left Tull. I always thought Dick would have been great with Blodwyn Pig. I loved the stuff he did with Graham Bond, which was what really got me into music in the first place, so it was fantastic to finally get him into the band".

That 'one-off' gig was such a success that the band decided to remain together, and have another go at establishing Blodwyn Pig as the ongoing success it always should have been. Plans were made to record an album, and an ambitious tour was talked about.... but failed to materialise. Once again Mick seemed to snatch defeat from the jaws of victory, with a policy of playing 'too small, too long'. The initial warm up gigs in pubs and clubs were rightly seen as a necessary build up to the half-way circuit, with plans to break into the 100 Club, Marquee and University circuit when the time came. But it never came, as the band wasted the initial flurry of interest by playing the wrong venues for too long. The opportunity for a return 'with a bang' had gone, and the Blodwyn Pig reunion became a permanently low-key affair. The perennial "musical differences" set in and group members came and went, including Dick Heckstall-Smith and eventually Clive Bunker.

A very limited edition cassette was released to promote the band in 1989, but it was not until 1991 that a new album was released. And although it had been recorded by Blodwyn Pig it actually came out credited as a Mick Abrahams solo album, *All Said And Done*. It was a fine album that deserved to do well, but despite record company hopes of huge sales it did not exactly set the charts alight.

Nevertheless, it meant that Mick Abrahams was back, and this time, for good. And at last, after some twenty years, all four of Mick and Pig's previous albums were available again, re-issued on CD.

In 1993, after countless personnel changes, Blodwyn Pig returned to the studio to make the superb *Lies*, and Mick set about looking for a meaningful deal to do justice to a great album. Incredibly there were no takers until I persuaded him to make it available to readers of *A New Day*. Consequently in November '93 the Tull magazine released its second CD, in the hope that a 'proper' record company would be moved to follow it up with a large scale release. It has subsequently appeared on at least three other labels to my knowledge!

The following year Mick made another of his famous bad decisions when he allowed Indigo Records to release *All Tore Down – Live*. True, the Blods are a great live band, and the playing on the album is quite wonderful, but it was not the greatest representation of the live experience due to the less than perfect recording quality. It is taken from a sound board recording, with the completely over-the-top audience noises added, rather unconvincingly it must be said. At the time it was very welcome, being the first ever live Blodwyn Pig album, but with hindsight it was no great shakes, to put it mildly. And to a certain extent the album came at the wrong time, when The Pig were on the verge of getting stuck in a rut, trotting out an identical set to the same punters for months, even years, on end.

Quality control was regained the following year when Mick decided to record an album of basically acoustic music. He had earlier guested on *A New Day*'s album by veteran rocker Jackie Lynton, who he knew well from their days on the circuit when Lynton was fronting Savoy Brown. By this time *A New Day* was itself almost a proper record company, and delighted to welcome Mick to the roster of artists – even more so when Ian Anderson agreed to play on the album! It was the first time the two had recorded together since the acrimonious Tull split in 1968, although they had played live a few times in recent years. Apart from the Tull Convention reunions, Mick had joined Tull onstage during the 25th anniversary tour, and Ian Anderson had appeared as special surprise guest at Blodwyn Pig's Christmas Bash in London in 1993.

The album, *One*, was released in March 1996 and met with favourable reviews from fans and critics alike, all pleased to see another album from Mick after so long. They didn't have to wait too long for the next one though, as *Mick's Back*, an album of mostly blues/rock covers from Mick and a backing band appeared just a few months later, and that itself was followed in December '96 by a new Blodwyn Pig album, *Pig In The Middle*. Recorded and produced by long time Tull associate Robin Black at his studio in Ripley, it was by far the best work that Mick had produced since the beginnings of Blodwyn Pig, and the superb production showed the way forward for the ever improving Pig, with the now well established nucleus of Mick on guitar and vocals, Mike Summerland on bass, and Graham Walker on drums. But, even though they were all completely different albums showcasing different aspects of Mick Abrahams' talent, three new albums in just one year was perhaps pushing it a bit! It was all good stuff admittedly, but it seemed that the flood of new material might turn into a torrent, with the subsequent drop in quality that would inevitably follow. If that was the worry, the reality was even worse.

In 1997 Mick, with an eye on his wallet and a finger on the old 'self-destruct' button, allowed Indigo Records to release not one but two highly suspect 'live' albums from the 70's. Although the recordings were not too bad, they were not too good either, yet the CDs were presented in such a way that gave no indication whatsoever that the sound quality was less than perfect. Indeed one of them, *Blodwyn Pig – The Modern Alchemist* does not even mention the fact that it's a live recording anywhere in the CD inlay, inside or out. Naturally some fans were less than pleased to find they were buying what was not much more than a good quality bootleg masquerading as a properly recorded album, and the reputation of Mick Abrahams and Blodwyn Pig was tarnished. Matters got even worse with the release of a third 'dodgy' recording *Live At Lafeyette* in 1998, although the limited edition *The Full Porky* in May '98 was an altogether better affair.

The avalanche of indifferent quality live albums has diluted the quality of Mick's catalogue, and one can only wonder what the future holds. After the quality of *Pig In The Middle* it would be a tragedy if he did not follow it up with more of the same, but will record companies be willing to invest big money in new material when the public have indicated that they would rather have vintage recordings, regardless of sound quality? It is a problem that faces other bands that are regarded as 70's relics, but that is a tag that Mick Abrahams certainly doesn't deserve. After over 30 years in the rock business Abrahams still puts heart and soul into every performance, and no matter how many times I see him play I still come away amazed. Good guitarists are ten-a-penny. Great guitarists are few and far between, and Mick Abrahams definitely falls into the latter category. Whilst far lesser talents reap the rewards and accolades brought about by familiarity rather than raw talent, Mick Abrahams has still not received the plaudits or success that he deserves. Yes it's true, when he reflects on it, that he himself has been responsible in part for his failure to fulfil his real potential, but it is also true that it's because he is fundamentally true to his art. With the talent he has at his fingertips it would perhaps have been easy to find stardom by way of compromise, but he has always chosen, come what may, to follow his heart rather than his head. A major irony is reflected in the huge success in recent years of his contemporaries like Eric Clapton and Gary Moore with their rediscovery of the blues. Whilst Clapton was shifting millions of units of an album full of the music that Abrahams has played all his life, Mick was writing and recording his own material with his thoughts focused on the future.

But then into 1998, and possibly the strangest twist yet in the Blods story. Although the band has now been together again for ten years, albeit with many different line-ups, there has been a consistent policy of looking ahead rather than backwards. The live set always includes a few blues classics, as well as "Cat's Squirrel" from the Tull days, but the 70's Blodwyn Pig material has been almost completely ignored despite demand from the audiences for classics like "See My Way". He was even asked to re-record that song again for a German record company but he turned them down, for some reason. With that in mind, his new project comes as a major surprise.

Mick has always been fiercely proud of 'This Was', the only Jethro Tull album that he was involved with, and has often been tempted to include a track or two from it in the Blods set. The temptation was ignored, but late in '97 he came up with the idea of getting a band together to take *This Was* on the road, as '98 marks the 30th anniversary of the album as well as Jethro Tull. He invited Clive Bunker to join the band, which would of course have meant that half the original band would be playing their album, but Clive refused point blank to take part, saying it was a terrible idea. Undeterred, Mick called Steve Dundon, the talented singer and flautist with respected Tull cover band Seismic Ring, who joined with Blodwyn Pig for the project.

After just a couple of rehearsals the band were to premiere the new set at the 100 Club in London, but a few days before the gig drummer Graham Walker had to pull out due to a crisis at home. Mick turned again to his old friend, and Clive Bunker agreed to sit in 'just this once'. It was a tremendous gig, and the audience were in raptures as Blodwyn Pig ripped through the set that Tull might well have been playing back in '68. More tellingly perhaps, the previously sceptical Bunker thought it was great too, and gladly volunteered his services should the need arise again. It seemed that this time Mick had hit on the right idea, and a lengthy tour was set up for later in the year. Remarkably, reports soon started to come in of sell outs for gigs some six months in advance, something that Blodwyn Pig were not used to!

Around the same time I, as editor of the Jethro Tull magazine, started getting letters from people who had bought tickets for "the Tull gig in Hastings Town Hall in October", or who were "delighted to see on the internet that Tull are playing Glasgow in October – what are the other tour dates?" Well OK, the Internet always gets it wrong, but how, I wondered, has somebody bought a ticket for a gig that just isn't going to happen? Smiling cruelly, I figured it was yet another case of confusion between Jethro Tull, ace rock band, and Jethro, crap Cornish comedian. It is a strange fact that since the rise of the aforementioned comic there have been several mix-ups with venues selling tickets for Jethro Tull to people expecting the comedian – just ask the coach load of little old ladies who actually sat through the first half of Tull's set at the Brighton Dome a couple of years back! Unfortunately though it soon became clear that it was not a Cornish caper that was to blame, but somebody in the Mick Abrahams promotion team who was at best, naïve, at worst, pulling a fast one!

Although the new Blodwyn Pig 'Tull' set was an incredible experience and fully deserving of sell out crowds, it now seemed that the advance sell-outs might have something to do with the rather imprecise billing and creative typography on the posters that the promoter had used to publicise the tour dates. JETHRO TULL was easy to read. Not so easy to see was the much smaller 'as performed by original guitarist Mick Abrahams' way down in the corner.

Apparently Abrahams was not aware of the poster design before they went out, and when he discovered what had happened he called Ian Anderson to apologise. Anderson, more than most, knows how these things can happen and accepted Mick's innocence in the affair, and happily they remain on speaking terms – Ian even hinted that he might 'jump up' at one or two of the gigs if he got the chance. There is the distinct possibility however that some of the punters might not be quite so understanding when they turn up to see Rock Monsters Jethro Tull playing in their local club, only to find Blodwyn Pig +1. If they stay for the gig they'll enjoy it anyway I'm sure (unless of course they are there to see Cornish Jethro!), but there will always be some disgruntled customers who will feel they've been misled. Once again it's a case of a silly mistake damaging the name of Mick Abrahams, and unnecessarily bringing controversy to what began as a bloody good idea. A shame, because Mick had actually agonised long and hard and discussed it with all interested parties before going ahead with it. The reservations that Clive Bunker had were always in his thoughts, but he was persuaded to go ahead with it by simple logic. Tribute bands are everywhere these days, seemingly outnumbering original bands on the club circuit. There are half a dozen bands around the world that make their money playing nothing but Tull music, and Mick was concerned that he would be seen to be jumping on that band wagon until it was pointed out to him that he was a major part of the band. By sticking to *This Was* he would only be playing the music that he had a hand in creating, which gave him as much right as Jethro Tull to play it, and more right than anybody else. With that in mind he scrapped his original idea of including "Living In The Past" and a couple of classics from *Stand Up* in the set. Everything was above board, and ethically sound.... and then came those posters!

This book will be out by the time 'Blodwyn Tull' discover the extent of the possible wrath engendered by the dubious billing, but I sincerely hope it goes well for them – they, and specifically Mick Abrahams, deserve a break. There is only one thing that could possibly turn the project into a humiliating cash-in, and that would be if Mick took up one of the offers he has recently had to go into the studio to re-record *This Was* with his current band.

Nah, he wouldn't do it. Would he?

Appendix 2

JETHRO TULL (and related) ALBUM DISCOGRAPHY

Listed are all Jethro Tull albums released in the UK, and selected Tull-associated albums. With so many ex-members it would require a whole other book to include everything that every member has been involved in, so I have used the following criteria for inclusion:

The four original members are covered, of course, as well as those members who could be considered to be of most importance within the Jethro Tull story. Therefore Ian Anderson, Mick Abrahams, and Martin Barre are covered in full, with Clive Bunker's current recordings. Glenn Cornick's albums with Wild Turkey are here because that's what he did after leaving Tull, and Doane Perry is included because he is still a member of Tull. Much of Dave Pegg's work is omitted simply because he has played on literally hundreds of albums, including dozens with Fairport Convention, and is well served by other books.

At the time of writing, all Jethro Tull albums are still available on CD, except the 20th Anniversary Box Set. However Chrysalis are currently employing a policy of deletions and re-issues, and it looks likely that the 'special edition' releases will continue as the relevant anniversaries arise.

Some time in 1998 EMI plan to issue an audio documentary CD called "In Profile", featuring interviews, narration and music from 30 years of Jethro Tull, but details are not available at press time.

There is also a "30 Years Live" CD in the schedule for late 1998, but again, no details are available.

JETHRO TULL

THIS WAS October 1968

Ian Anderson Mick Abrahams Clive Bunker Glenn Cornick
Produced by Terry Ellis and Jethro Tull
Original LP - ISLAND RECORDS ILP 985 (mono) or ILP 985S (stereo)
Tracks
1] My Sunday Feeling (Anderson) 3.38
2] Some Day The Sun Won't Shine For You (Anderson) 2.42
3] Beggars Farm (Abrahams / Anderson) 4.19
4] Move On Alone (Abrahams) 2.00
5] Serenade To A Cuckoo (Kirk) 6.01
6] Dharma For One (Anderson / Bunker) 4.11
7] It's Breaking Me Up (Anderson) 4.56
8] Cat's Squirrel (Trad. arr. Abrahams) 5.36
9] A Song For Jeffrey (Anderson) 3.18
10] Round (Anderson / Abrahams / Bunker / Cornick / Ellis) 0.50
22 weeks in UK album chart, reaching # 10. #62 in USA
Went Gold in the UK.
Initially released in mono. The stereo album released soon after is a slightly different mix.
Re-issued in 1997 boxed with Stand Up and Benefit in 3CD set "The Originals". Each CD came in a miniature reproduction of the original LP sleeve.

STAND UP July 1969

Ian Anderson Martin Barre Clive Bunker Glenn Cornick
Produced by Terry Ellis and Ian Anderson
All songs written by Ian Anderson
Original LP – ISLAND RECORDS ILPS 9103
Tracks
1] A New Day Yesterday 4.11
2] Jeffrey Goes To Leicester Square 2.10
3] Bouree (J.S.Bach – arr. Anderson) 3.44
4] Back To The Family 3.50
5] Look Into The Sun 4.20
6] Nothing Is Easy 4.24
7] Fat Man 2.50
8] We Used To Know 4.00
9] Reasons For Waiting 4.04
10] For A Thousand Mothers 4.14
29 weeks in UK album chart. Entered chart at # 1. #18 in USA
Went Gold in UK and USA.
Re-issued in 1997 boxed with This Was and Benefit in 3CD set "The Originals". Each CD came in a miniature reproduction of the original LP sleeve.
Also issued on 24 kt gold plated CD by Mobile Fidelity Sound Lab in USA.
Issued on high grade audiophile vinyl in 1997.

BENEFIT April 1970

Ian Anderson Martin Barre Clive Bunker Glenn Cornick John Evans
Produced by Ian Anderson
All songs written by Ian Anderson
Original LP – ISLAND RECORDS ILPS 9123
Tracks
1] With You There To Help Me 6.20
2] Nothing To Say 5.15
3] Alive And Well And Living In 2.49
4] Son 2.52
5] For Michael Collins, Jeffrey And Me 3.49
6] To Cry You A Song 6.17
7] A Time For Everything? 2.45
8] Inside 3.50
9] Play In Time 3.50
10] Sossity; You're A Woman 4.33
13 weeks in UK album chart, reaching # 4. # 10 in US chart.
Went Gold in UK. Platinum in USA.
Re-issued in 1997 boxed with Stand Up and This Was in 3CD set "The Originals". Each CD came in a miniature reproduction of the original LP sleeve.

AQUALUNG March 1971

Ian Anderson Martin Barre Clive Bunker Jeffrey Hammond Hammond John Evans
Produced by Ian Anderson and Terry Ellis
All songs written by Ian Anderson except where indicated
Original LP – ISLAND RECORDS ILPS 9145
Tracks
1] Aqualung (Ian Anderson / Jennie Anderson) 6.37
2] Cross Eyed Mary 4.09
3] Cheap Day Return 1.23
4] Mother Goose 3.53
5] Wond'ring Aloud 1.55
6] Up To Me 3.14
7] My God 7.12
8] Hymn 43 3.19
9] Slipstream 1.13
10] Locomotive Breath 4.26
11] Wind Up 6.07
12] Lick Your Fingers Clean 2.46
13] Wind Up (Quad Version) 5.23
14] Interview with Ian Anderson 13.58
15] A Song For Jeffrey (BBC Version) 2.51
16] Fat Man (BBC Version) 2.56
17] Bouree (BBC Version) 3.58
21 weeks in the UK album chart, reaching # 4. #7 in USA.
Went Platinum in the UK, Australia, Canada, New Zealand and Switzerland. Triple Platinum in USA. Gold in Austria, France, Germany, Holland, Italy, Spain and South Africa.
In 1974 a quad version was released, accidentally including a different version of 'Wind Up'. First CD release in America missed 30 seconds from the end of 'Wind Up'! Has been re-issued, revamped and reinvented many times recently. 'Special Edition' Chrysalis CD in blue case and long box should be avoided. 24kt gold CD from DCC in USA is remastered from original tapes. 25th Anniversary Edition from Chrysalis in 1996 includes extra tracks, listed in italics above, including the quad 'Wind Up'. 'Lick Your Fingers Clean' was recorded during the Aqualung sessions and scheduled for release as a single, but did not appear. It was however included on the 20th Anniversary box set in 1988, as were the three BBC session tracks.

THICK AS A BRICK February 1972

Ian Anderson Martin Barre Barrie Barlow Jeffrey Hammond Hammond John Evans
Produced by Ian Anderson
Written by Ian Anderson (Gerald Bostock)
Original LP – CHRYSALIS RECORDS CHR 1003
Tracks
1] Thick As A Brick pt.1 22.45
2] Thick As A Brick pt.2 21.05
3] Thick As A Brick (live) 11.48
4] Interview with Ian Anderson, Martin Barre and Jeffrey Hammond 16.28
14 weeks in the UK chart, reaching # 5. 3 weeks at # 1 in America.
Went Gold in the UK, Italy and Spain. Platinum in USA, Australia, Canada, Holland and New Zealand
Issued as a 24kt Gold CD by Mobile Fidelity Sound Lab in America. Repackaged in 1997 by Chrysalis EMI for the 25th Anniversary edition, with extra tracks as listed in italics above, and including a reproduction of the original spoof newspaper cover.
Issued on high grade audiophile vinyl in 1997.

LIVING IN THE PAST June 1972

Produced by Ian Anderson and Terry Ellis
All songs written by Ian Anderson except where indicated
Compilation double album of classic, rare and unreleased tracks.
Original LP – CHRYSALIS RECORDS CJT 1
The original albums had slight differences in the UK and USA. Subsequent CD versions, both as single and double CDs, complicated matters even further. In 1998 however, Mobile Fidelity Sound Lab in America issued the definitive, remastered 24kt Gold CD set, including

full original artwork and all the tracks from the different album and CD releases. The following track listing is from that double CD.

DISC ONE
1] Song For Jeffrey 3.20 (from This Was)
2] Love Story 3.02 (A-side, 1968)
3] Christmas Song 3.05 (B-side, 1968)
4] Living In The Past 3.20 (A-side, 1969)
5] Driving Song 2.39 (B-side, 1969)
6] Bouree (J.S.Bach – arr. Anderson) 3.43 (from Stand Up)
7] Sweet Dream 4.02 (A-side, 1969)
8] Singing All Day 3.03 (previously unreleased)
9] Teacher 4.08 (from US version of Benefit. Teacher had been a UK B-side, but this was a different mix, with more flute.
10] Witch's Promise 3.49 (A-side, 1970)
11] Inside 3.45 (from Benefit)
12] Alive And Well And Living In 2.45 (from the UK version of Benefit)
13] Just Trying To Be 1.36 (previously unreleased)

DISC TWO
1] By Kind Permission Of (Evans) 10.11 (Live at Carnegie Hall 1970. Previously unreleased)
2] Dharma For One (Anderson / Bunker) 9.58 (Live at Carnegie Hall 1970. Previously unreleased)
3] Wond'ring Again 4.12 (previously unreleased)
4] Hymn 43 3.17 (from Aqualung)
5] Locomotive Breath 4.24 (from Aqualung)
6] Life Is A Long Song 3.18 (1971 ep track)
7] Up The 'Pool 3.10 (1971 ep track)
8] Dr. Bogenbroom 2.59 (1971 ep track)
9] For Later (From Later, depending on which credit you believe!) 2.06 (1971 ep track)
10] Nursie 1.36 (1971 ep track)
11 weeks in the UK album chart, reaching # 8. #3 in USA.
Went Gold in the UK, Australia, Canada and New Zealand. Platinum in USA.

A PASSION PLAY July 1973
Ian Anderson Martin Barre Barrie Barlow Jeffrey Hammond Hammond John Evans
Produced by Ian Anderson
Written by Ian Anderson except where indicated
Original LP – CHRYSALIS RECORDS CHR 1040
Until March 1998 'A Passion Play' has consisted of the title track and the interlude, 'The Story Of The Hare Who Lost His Spectacles'. Yet again though, those wonderful chaps at MFSL have issued a superb 24kt Gold CD of Tull's masterpiece, and mysteriously each segment of music now has its' own title. We must assume that they did not simply make them up, and that Ian Anderson must have given details of individual track titles, as listed below.
1] Lifebeats 1.14
2] Prelude 2.14
3] The Silver Cord 4.29
4] Re-Assuring Tune 1.11
5] Memory Bank 4.20
6] Best Friends 1.58
7] Critique Oblique 4.38
8] Forest Dance #1 1.35
9] The Story Of The Hare Who Lost His Spectacles (Hammond Hammond / Evans /Anderson) 4.18
10] Forest Dance #2 1.12
11] The Foot Of Our Stairs 4.18
12] Overseer Overture 4.00
13] Flight From Lucifer 3.58
14] 10.08 To Paddington 1.04
15] Magus Perde 3.55
16] Epilogue 0.43
8 weeks in the UK chart, reaching # 13. #1 in America. Went Gold in the UK, USA and Canada.

WARCHILD October 1974
Ian Anderson Martin Barre Barrie Barlow Jeffrey Hammond Hammond John Evans
Produced by Ian Anderson

All songs written by Ian Anderson
Original LP – CHRYSALIS RECORDS CHR 1067
Tracks
1] Warchild 4.36
2] Queen and Country 3.00
3] Ladies 3.18
4] Back-door Angels 5.29
5] Sea Lion 3.37
6] Skating Away On The Thin Ice Of The New Day 3.58
7] Bungle In The Jungle 3.37
8] Only Solitaire 1.39
9] The Third Hoorah 4.50
10] Two Fingers 5.11
4 weeks in the UK chart, reaching #14. #2 in USA.
Went Gold in the UK, USA, Canada and Australia
A quadrophonic version of the LP was released in America at the same time as the standard version.

MINSTREL IN THE GALLERY September 1975
Ian Anderson Martin Barre Barrie Barlow Jeffrey Hammond Hammond John Evans
Produced by Ian Anderson
All songs written by Ian Anderson
Original LP – CHRYSALIS RECORDS CHR 1082
Tracks
1] Minstrel In The Gallery 8.17
2] Cold Wind To Valhalla 4.19
3] Black Satin Dancer 6.52
4] Requiem 3.45
5] One White Duck / 0^{10} = Nothing At All 4.38
6] Baker St. Muse 16.42
  including Pig – Me and the Whore, Nice Little Tune, Crash Barrier Waltzer, Mother England Reverie
7] Grace 0.37
6 weeks in the UK chart, reaching #20. #7 in USA.
Went Gold in the UK, USA and Canada.

M.U. – THE BEST OF JETHRO TULL January 1976
Original LP – CHRYSALIS RECORDS CHR 1078
Tracks
1] Teacher 4.07 (from Living In The Past)
2] Aqualung 6.34 (from Aqualung) [Different Mix]
3] Thick As A Brick Edit #1 3.01 (from Thick As A Brick)
4] Bungle In The Jungle 3.34 (from Warchild)
5] Locomotive Breath 4.23 (from Aqualung)
6] Fat Man 2.50 (from Stand Up)
7] Living In The Past 3.18 (from Living In The Past)
8] A Passion Play Edit #8 3.28 (from A Passion Play)
9] Skating Away On The Thin Ice Of The New Day 4.02 (from Warchild)
10] Rainbow Blues 3.37 (previously unreleased)
11] Nothing Is Easy 4.23 (from Stand Up)
5 weeks in the UK chart, reaching # 44. #13 in USA.
Went Gold in the UK, Australia and New Zealand. Platinum in the USA and Canada.

TOO OLD TO ROCK'N'ROLL:TOO YOUNG TO DIE! April 1976
Ian Anderson Martin Barre Barrie Barlow John Glascock John Evans
With David Palmer (sax), Maddy Prior & Angela Allen (backing vocals)
Produced by Ian Anderson
All songs written by Ian Anderson
Original LP – CHRYSALIS RECORDS CHR 1111
Tracks
1] Quizz Kid 5.11
2] Crazed Institution 4.48
3] Salamander 2.52
4] Taxi Grab 3.55
5] From A Deadbeat To An Old Greaser 4.12
6] Bad-Eyed and Loveless 2.12
7] Big Dipper 3.38
8] Too Old To Rock'n'Roll: Too Young to Die 5.43

9] Pied Piper 4.35
10] The Chequered Flag (Dead Or Alive) 5.24
10 weeks on the UK chart, reaching # 25. #14 in USA.
Went Gold in the UK.

SONGS FROM THE WOOD January 1977
Ian Anderson Martin Barre Barrie Barlow John Glascock John Evans
David Palmer
Produced by Ian Anderson
All songs written by Ian Anderson, with additional material by David Palmer and Martin Barre
Original LP – CHRYSALIS RECORDS CHR 1132
Tracks
1] Songs From The Wood 4.56
2] Jack-In-The-Green 2.31
3] Cup Of Wonder 4.34
4] Hunting Girl 5.13
5] Ring Out, Solstice Bells 3.46
6] Velvet Green 6.04
7] The Whistler 3.31
8] Pibroch (Cap In Hand) 8.37
9] Fires At Midnight 2.27
12 weeks in the UK chart, reaching # 13. #8 in USA.
Went Gold in the UK, USA, Canada and Australia

REPEAT – THE BEST OF JETHRO TULL VOL II October 1977
Original LP – CHRYSALIS RECORDS CHR 1135
Tracks
1] Minstrel In The Gallery 4.12 (from Minstrel In The Gallery)
2] Cross–Eyed Mary 4.06 (from Aqualung)
3] A New Day Yesterday 4.08 (from Stand Up)
4] Bouree (J.S.Bach – arr. Anderson) 3.40 (from Stand Up)
5] Thick As A Brick Edit #4 3.25 (from Thick As A Brick)
6] Warchild 4.33 (from Warchild)
7] A Passion Play Edit #9 3.29 (from A Passion Play)
8] To Cry You A Song 6.09 (from Benefit)
9] Too Old To Rock'n'Roll: Too Young To Die 5.39 (from Too Old To Rock'n'Roll)
10] Glory Row 3.34 (previously unreleased)
The first Jethro Tull album to fail to make the UK chart. #94 in USA.

HEAVY HORSES April 1978
Ian Anderson Martin Barre Barrie Barlow John Glascock John Evans
David Palmer
With Darryl Way on violin
Produced by Ian Anderson
All songs written by Ian Anderson, with additional material by David Palmer and Martin Barre
Original LP – CHRYSALIS RECORDS CHR 1175
Tracks
1] ....And The Mouse Police Never Sleeps 3.14
2] Acres Wild 3.25
3] No Lullaby 7.55
4] Moths 3.27
5] Journeyman 3.57
6] Rover 4.16
7] One Brown Mouse 3.23
8] Heavy Horses 8.59
9] Weathercock 4.02
10 weeks on the UK chart, reaching #20. #19 in USA.
Went Gold in the UK and USA

LIVE – BURSTING OUT September 1978
Ian Anderson Martin Barre Barrie Barlow John Glascock John Evans
David Palmer
Recorded live in Europe 1978
Produced by Ian Anderson
All songs written by Ian Anderson except where indicated.
Original LP – CHRYSALIS RECORDS CJT 4
Disc One

1] No Lullaby 5.54
2] Sweet Dream 4.27
3] Skating Away On The Thin Ice Of The New Day 3.22
4] Jack In The Green 2.35
5] One Brown Mouse 3.43
6] A New Day Yesterday 2.49
7] Flute Solo Improvisation / God Rest Ye Merry Gentlemen / Bouree 5.41
8] Songs From The Wood 2.29
9] Thick As A Brick 12.27
Disc Two
1] Hunting Girl 5.17
2] Too Old To Rock'n'Roll: Too Young To Die 3.54
3] Conundrum (Martin Barre / Barrie Barlow) 6.47
4] Minstrel In The Gallery 5.44
5] Cross-eyed Mary 3.38
6] Quatrain (Martin Barre) 1.32
7] Aqualung (Ian & Jennie Anderson) 8.33
8] Locomotive Breath 6.37
9] The Dambusters March / Medley (Eric Coates / Ian Anderson)
8 weeks on the UK chart, reaching # 17. #21 in USA.
Went Gold in the USA and Canada. Silver in the UK.
A double LP, it was edited when first issued on CD in America, with Sweet Dream, Conundrum and Quatrain cut out. When it was issued as a double CD, with the three missing tracks restored, Quatrain was put back in the wrong place! The correct (vinyl) version has Ian Anderson saying goodbye after Cross Eyed Mary, followed by the encore of Quatrain which leads directly into Aqualung, with no break. On the double CD Anderson says goodbye after Quatrain. Aqualung then starts with the last note of Quatrain. Nice one Chrysalis!

STORMWATCH September 1979
Ian Anderson Martin Barre Barrie Barlow John Glascock John Evans
David Palmer
Produced by Ian Anderson
All songs written by Ian Anderson except where indicated
Original LP – CHRYSALIS RECORDS CDL 1238
Tracks
1] North Sea Oil 3.08
2] Orion 3.55
3] Home 2.44
4] Dark Ages 9.07
5] Warm Sporran 3.31
6] Something's On The Move 4.24
7] Old Ghosts 4.20
8] Dun Ringill 2.37
9] Flying Dutchman 7.42
10] Elegy (David Palmer) 3.30
4 weeks on the UK chart, reaching # 27. #22 in USA.
Went Gold in the USA and Canada

A August 1980
Ian Anderson Martin Barre Dave Pegg Eddie Jobson Mark Craney
Produced by Ian Anderson and Robin Black
All songs written by Ian Anderson, with additional material by Eddie Jobson
Original LP – CHRYSALIS RECORDS CDL 1301
Tracks
1] Crossfire 3.51
2] Fylingdale Flyer 4.27
3] Working John – Working Joe 5.01
4] Black Sunday 6.33
5] Protect And Survive 3.32
6] Batteries Not Included 3.47
7] Uniform 3.30
8] 4.W.D. (Low Ratio) 3.37
9] The Pine Marten's Jig 3.23
10] And Further On 4.19
5 weeks on the UK chart, reaching # 25. #30 in USA.

THE BROADSWORD AND THE BEAST April 1982

Ian Anderson Martin Barre Dave Pegg Peter-John Vettese Gerry Conway
Produced by Paul Samwell-Smith
All songs written by Ian Anderson with additional material by Peter-John Vettese
Original LP CHRYSALIS RECORDS CDL 1380
Tracks
1] Beastie 3.57
2] Clasp 4.11
3] Fallen On Hard Times 3.12
4] Flying Colours 4.39
5] Slow Marching Band 3.38
6] Broadsword 4.50
7] Pussy Willow 3.53
8] Watching Me Watching You 3.40
9] Seal Driver 5.10
10] Cheerio 1.00
19 weeks in the UK chart, reaching #27. #19 in USA.
Went Silver in the UK
The original cassette version came in a limited edition 'deluxe' outer case.

UNDER WRAPS September 1984

Ian Anderson Martin Barre Dave Pegg Peter-John Vettese
Produced by Ian Anderson
Original LP CHRYSALIS CDL 1461
Tracks
1] Lap Of Luxury (Anderson) 3.35
2] Under Wraps #1 (Anderson) 4.02
3] European Legacy (Anderson) 3.22
4] Later, That Same Evening (Anderson / Vettese) 3.52
5] Saboteur (Anderson / Vettese) 3.32
6] Radio Free Moscow (Anderson / Vettese) 3.41
7] Astronomy (Anderson / Vettese) 3.37
8] Tundra (Anderson / Vettese) 3.39
9] Nobody's Car (Anderson / Barre / Vettese) 4.07
10] Heat (Anderson / Vettese) 5.37
11] Under Wraps #2 (Anderson) 2.14
12] Paparazzi (Anderson / Barre / Vettese) 3.47
13] Apogee (Anderson / Vettese) 5.29
14] Automotive Engineering (Anderson / Vettese) 4.05
15] General Crossing (Anderson / Vettese) 4.03
5 weeks on the UK chart, reaching # 18. #76 in USA.
Tracks 7,8,14 and 15 are on CD and cassette versions only.
A vinyl picture disc is also available (CDLP 1461).

ORIGINAL MASTERS October 1985

Another 'Best Of'. Original LP – JTTV 1
Tracks
1] Living In The Past
2] Aqualung
3] Too Old To Rock'n'Roll: Too Young To Die
4] Locomotive Breath
5] Skating Away On The Thin Ice Of The New Day
6] Bungle In The Jungle
7] Sweet Dream
8] Songs From The Wood
9] Witches Promise
10] Thick As A Brick
11] Minstrel In The Gallery
12] Life's A Long Song
3 weeks on UK chart, reaching #63.
Went Gold in the UK.

CREST OF A KNAVE September 1987

Ian Anderson Martin Barre Dave Pegg
With Doane Perry (drums), Gerry Conway (drums) and Ric Sanders (violin)
Produced by Ian Anderson
All songs written by Ian Anderson

Original LP – CHRYSALIS RECORDS CDL 1590
Tracks
1] Steel Monkey 3.40
2] Farm On The Freeway 6.31
3] Jump Start 4.55
4] Said She Was A Dancer 3.43
5] Dogs In The Midwinter 4.37
6] Budapest 10.05
7] Mountain Men 6.20
8] The Waking Edge 4.49
9] Raising Steam 4.06
10 weeks on UK chart, reaching # 19. 28 weeks on US chart, reaching #33.
Went Gold in the USA, Silver in the UK.
Tracks 5 and 8 are on CD and cassette versions only.

20 YEARS OF JETHRO TULL 5 LP (3CD) BOX SET

with 24pp booklet July 1988. All songs written by Ian Anderson except where indicated.
CHRYSALIS TBOX 1
ALBUM 1 – The Radio Archives
1] Song For Jeffrey 2.47 BBC Session 1968 (previously unreleased)
2] Love Story 2.43 BBC Session 1968 (previously unreleased)
3] Fat Man 2.55 BBC Session 1969 (previously unreleased)
4] Bouree (J.S.Bach - arr. Anderson) 4.04 BBC Session 1969 (previously unreleased)
5] Stormy Monday Blues (Ecstine/Crowder/Hines) 4.05 BBC Session 1968 (previously unreleased)
6] A New Day Yesterday 4.19 BBC Session 1969 (previously unreleased)
7] Cold Wind To Valhalla 1.32 BBC Session 1975 (previously unreleased)
8] Minstrel In The Gallery 2.08 BBC Session 1975 (previously unreleased)
9] Velvet Green 5.52 BBC In Concert 1977 (previously unreleased)
10] Grace 0.33 BBC Session 1975 (previously unreleased)
11] The Clasp 3.30 Live in Hamburg 1982 (previously unreleased)
12] Pibroch / Black Satin Dancer (instrumental) 4.00 Live in Hamburg 1982 (previously unreleased)
13] Fallen On Hard Times 3.59 Live in Hamburg 1982 (previously unreleased)
ALBUM 2 – The Rare Tracks (Released But Only Just)
1] Jack Frost And The Hooded Crow 3.20 1986 b-side. Recorded 1981
2] I'm Your Gun 3.18 1987 b-side. Recorded 1981
3] Down At The End Of Your Road 3.30 1987 b-side. Recorded 1981
4] Coronach (David Palmer) 3.52 1986 a-side.
5] Summerday Sands 3.45 1975 b-side.
6] Too Many Too 3.27 1987 b-side. Recorded 1981
7] March The Mad Scientist 1.47 1976 b-side. Recorded 1974.
8] Pan Dance 3.24 1976 b-side. Recorded 1974
9] Strip Cartoon 3.16 1977 b-side. Recorded 1976
10] King Henry's Madrigal (trad. arr. David Palmer) 2.58 1979 b-side.
11] A Stitch In Time 3.38 1978 a-side.
12] 17 3.07 1969 b-side. [Fades out halfway through the original 6 minute track]
13] One For John Gee (Mick Abrahams) 2.04 1968 b-side.
14] Aeroplane (Ian Anderson / Glenn Barnard [Cornick]) 2.16 1968 a-side
15] Sunshine Day (Mick Abrahams) 2.26 1968 b-side
ALBUM 3 – Flawed Gems (Dusted Down)
1] Lick Your Fingers Clean 2.47 (previously unreleased) Recorded 1970
2] The Chateau D'Isaster Tapes 11.09 (previously unreleased) Recorded 1972
Scenario
Audition
No Rehearsal
3] Beltane 5.17 (previously unreleased) Recorded 1977
4] Crossword 3.34 (previously unreleased) Recorded 1979
5] Saturation 4.23 (previously unreleased) Recorded 1974
6] Jack-a-Lynn 4.41 (previously unreleased) Recorded 1981
7] Motoreyes 3.39 (previously unreleased) Recorded 1982
8] Blues Instrumental 5.15 (previously unreleased) Recorded circa 1978

9] Rhythm In Gold 3.04 (previously unreleased) Recorded 1981
ALBUM 4 – The Other Sides Of Tull
1] Part Of The Machine 6.54 (previously unreleased) Recorded 1988
2] Mayhem, Maybe 3.04 (previously unreleased) Recorded 1981, vocals, flute & whistles added 1988
3] Overhang 4.27 (previously unreleased) Recorded 1981
4] Kelpie 3.32 (previously unreleased) Recorded 1979
5] Living In These Hard Times 3.09 (previously unreleased) Recorded 1978
6] Under Wraps #2 2.14 (from Under Wraps)
7] Only Solitaire 1.28 (from Warchild)
8] Cheap Day Return 1.22 (from Aqualung)
9] Wond'ring Aloud 1.58 Live in London 1987 (previously unreleased)
10] Dun Ringill 3.00 Live in London 1987 (previously unreleased)
11] Salamander 2.49 (from Too Old To Rock'n'Roll: Too Young To Die)
12] Moths 3.24 (from Heavy Horses) [different mix]
13] Nursie 1.32 (from Living In The Past)
14] Life's A Long Song 3.17 (from Living In The Past)
15] One White Duck ' 0^{10} = Nothing At All 4.37 (from Minstrel In The Gallery)
ALBUM 5 – The Essential Tull
1] Songs From The Wood 4.29 Live in London 1987 (previously unreleased)
2] Living In The Past 4.07 Live in Philadelphia 1987 (previously unreleased)
3] Teacher 4.43 1970 b-side
4] Aqualung 7.43 Live in Hamburg 1982 (previously unreleased)
5] Locomotive Breath 6.00 Live in Hamburg 1982 (previously unreleased)
6] Witches Promise 3.50 (from Living In The Past)
7] Bungle In The Jungle 3.33 (from Warchild)
8] Farm On The Freeway 6.33 Live in Philadelphia 1987 (previously unreleased)
9] Thick As A Brick 6.32 Live in London 1987 (previously unreleased)
10] Sweet Dream 4.32 Live in Hamburg 1982 (previously unreleased)
One week at #78 in UK chart

20 YEARS OF JETHRO TULL Double LP / Single CD August 1988

CHRYSALIS CJT 7
A selection of tracks from the box set
1] Stormy Monday Blues
2] Love Story
3] A New Day Yesterday
4] Summerday Sands
5] Coronach [not on CD version]
6] March The Mad Scientist
7] Pibroch / Black Satin Dancer [not on CD version]
8] Lick Your Fingers Clean
9] Overhang
10] Crossword
11] Saturation [not on CD version]
12] Jack-a-Lynn
13] Motoreyes [not on CD version]
14] Part Of The Machine
15] Mayhem, Maybe
16] Kelpie
17] Under Wraps #2 [not on CD version]
18] Wond'ring Aloud
19] Dun Ringill
20] Life's A Long Song
21] Nursie
22] Grace
23] Witch's Promise
24] Teacher [not on CD version]
25] Living In The Past
26] Aqualung
27] Locomotive Breath

ROCK ISLAND September 1989

Ian Anderson Martin Barre Dave Pegg Doane Perry

With Maart Allcock (keyboards) and Peter-John Vettese (keyboards)
Produced by Ian Anderson
All songs written by Ian Anderson
CHRYSALIS CHR 1708
Tracks
1] Kissing Willie 3.32
2] The Rattlesnake Trail 3.59
3] Ears Of Tin 4.53
4] Undressed To Kill 5.24
5] Rock Island 6.52
6] Heavy Water 4.12
7] Another Christmas Song 3.30
8] The Whalers Dues 7.53
9] Big Riff And Mando 5.57
10] Strange Avenues 4.09
6 weeks on UK chart, reaching #18. 18 weeks on US chart, reaching #56.
Went Silver in the UK.
A vinyl picture disc is also available (CHRP 1708).

LIVE AT HAMMERSMITH '84 – The Friday Rock Show Sessions November 1990

Ian Anderson Martin Barre Dave Pegg Peter-John Vettese Doane Perry
Produced by Tony Wilson and Dale Griffin
Recorded at the Hammersmith Odeon, London 9th September 1984 for the BBC
Tracks
1] Locomotive Breath (instrumental) 2.36
2] Hunting Girl 4.56
3] Under Wraps 4.30
4] Later That Same Evening 4.03
5] Pussy Willow 4.44
6] Living In The Past 4.29
7] Locomotive Breath 7.43
8] Too Old To Rock'n'Roll: Too Young To Die 9.08

CATFISH RISING September 1991

Ian Anderson Martin Barre Dave Pegg Doane Perry
With Andy Giddings (keyboards), Foss Paterson (keyboards), John 'Rabbit' Bundrick (keyboards)
Matt Pegg (bass) and Scott Hunter (drums – not credited)
Produced by Ian Anderson
All songs written by Ian Anderson
CHRYSALIS DCHR 1886
Tracks
1] This Is Not Love 3.56
2] Occasional Demons 3.48
3] Roll Yer Own 4.25
4] Rocks On The Road 5.30
5] Sparrow On The Schoolyard Wall 5.21
6] Thinking Round Corners 3.31
7] Still Loving You Tonight 4.30
8] Doctor To My Disease 4.34
9] Like A Tall Thin Girl 3.36
10] White Innocence 7.43
11] Sleeping With The Dog 4.24
12] Gold Tipped Boots, Black Jacket & Tie 3.38
13] When Jesus Came To Play 5.03
14] Night In The Wilderness (On Japanese CD only) 4.00
3 weeks on the UK chart, reaching # 27. #88 in USA.
Vinyl album included only ten tracks but first pressing came with a 12" single with the missing three tracks.

A LITTLE LIGHT MUSIC September 1992

Ian Anderson Martin Barre Dave Pegg Dave Mattacks
Double LP / Single CD recorded in various places in Europe, and Israel May 1992
Produced by Ian Anderson
All songs written by Ian Anderson except where indicated
CHRYSALIS CHR 1954
Tracks

1] Someday The Sun Won't Shine For You 3.59
2] Living In The Past 5.07
3] Life Is A Long Song 3.37
4] Under Wraps 2.30
5] Rocks On The Road 7.03
6] Nursie 2.27
7] Too Old To Rock'n'Roll: Too Young To Die 4.43
8] One White Duck 3.15
9] A New Day Yesterday 7.33
10] John Barleycorn (Trad. – arr. Anderson) 6.34
11] Look Into The Sun 3.45
12] A Christmas Song 3.45
13] From A Dead Beat To An Old Greaser 3.51
14] This Is Not Love 3.53
15] Bouree (J.S.Bach – arr. Anderson) 6.06
16] Pussy Willow 3.31
17] Locomotive Breath 5.51
The version released in Greece features George Dalares duetting with
Ian Anderson on John Barleycorn. Standard version has overdubbed vocals by Anderson throughout the song.
Did not chart in UK. #150 in USA.

25th ANNIVERSARY BOX SET – 4 CDs with booklet
April 1993
CHRYSALIS CDCHR 60044 (CD only)
CD 1 "REMIXED – CLASSIC SONGS"
1] My Sunday Feeling 3.40
2] A Song For Jeffrey 3.20
3] Living In The Past 3.23
4] Teacher 4.05
5] Sweet Dream 3.58
6] Cross Eyed Mary 4.06
7] The Witch's Promise 3.49
8] Life Is A Long Song 3.17
9] Bungle In The Jungle 3.38
10] Minstrel In The Gallery 8.11
11] Cold Wind To Valhalla 4.12
12] Too Old To Rock'n'Roll 5.29
13] Songs From The Wood 4.52
14] Heavy Horses 9.03
15] Black Sunday 6.40
16] Broadsword 4.54
CD 2 "AT THE CARNEGIE HALL: LIVE IN NEW YORK 1970"
Ian Anderson Martin Barre Glenn Cornick Clive Bunker John Evans
1] Nothing Is Easy 6.05
2] My God 11.10
3] With You There To Help Me 6.46
4] A Song For Jeffrey 5.45
5] To Cry You A Song 7.59
6] Sossity, You're A Woman 2.15
7] Reasons For Waiting 3.55
8] We Used To Know 3.18
9] Guitar Solo (Barre) 8.23
10] For A Thousand Mothers 4.47
CD 3 "THE BEACONS BOTTOM TAPES"
Ian Anderson Martin Barre Dave Pegg Doane Perry Andy Giddings
Produced by Ian Anderson except 'Cheerio' (Dave Pegg) and 'Protect
And Survive' (Martin Barre)
Recorded November / December 1992
1] So Much Trouble (Brownie McGee) 2.28 [Ian Anderson solo]
2] My Sunday Feeling 3.56
3] Someday The Sun Won't Shine For You 2.00 [Ian Anderson solo]
4] Living In The Past 3.25 [Ian Anderson solo]
5] Bouree 3.32 [Ian Anderson with Andy Giddings]
6] With You There To Help Me 6.11
7] Thick As A Brick 9.00
8] Cheerio 3.58 [Dave Pegg solo]
9] A New Day Yesterday 8.01
10] Protect And Survive 3.05 [Martin Barre solo]
11] Jack-A-Lynn 4.56
12] The Whistler 2.50
13] My God 10.01

14] Aqualung 7.32
CD 4 "POT POURRI – LIVE ACROSS THE WORLD & THROUGH THE
YEARS"
1] To Be Sad Is A Mad Way To Be 3.56 [Stockholm 1969]
2] Back To The Family 3.35 [Stockholm 1969]
3] A Passion Play Extract 3.18 [Paris 1975]
4] Wind Up / Locomotive Breath / Land Of Hope And Glory 11.48 [Lon-
don 1977]
5] Seal Driver 5.36 [Hamburg 1982]
6] Nobody's Car 4.02 [London 1984]
7] Pussy Willow 4.58 [London 1984]
8] Budapest 10.49 [Leysin, Switzerland 1991]
9] Nothing Is Easy 5.16 [Leysin, Switzerland 1991]
10] Kissing Willie 3.38 [Tallin, Estonia 1991]
11] Still Loving You Tonight 5.00 [London 1991]
12] Beggar's Farm 5.21 [Washington, USA 1992]
13] Passion Jig 2.00 [Chicago 1992]
14] A Song For Jeffrey 3.26 [Chicago 1992]
15] Living In The Past 3.24 [Montreal 1992]

THE BEST OF JETHRO TULL – The Anniversary
Collection 2CD June 1993
CHRYSALIS CDCHR 6001 (CD and cassette only)
CD 1
1] A Song For Jeffrey 3.18 (from This Was)
2] Beggar's Farm 4.17 (from This Was)
3] A Christmas Song 3.06 (from Living In The Past)
4] A New Day Yesterday 4.08 (from Stand Up)
5] Bouree 3.45 (from Stand Up)
6] Nothing Is Easy 4.22 (from Stand Up)
7] Living In The Past 3.20 (from Living In The Past)
8] To Cry You A Song 6.13 (from Benefit)
9] Teacher 3.59 (from Living In The Past)
10] Sweet Dream 4.00 (from Living In The Past)
11] Cross Eyed Mary 4.07 (from Aqualung)
12] Mother Goose 3.51 (from Aqualung)
13] Aqualung 6.35 (from Aqualung)
14] Locomotive Breath 4.24 (from Aqualung)
15] Life Is A Long Song 3.18 (from Living In The Past)
16] Thick As A Brick extract 3.00 (from Thick As A Brick)
17] A Passion Play extract 3.46 (from A Passion Play)
18] Skating Away On The Thin Ice Of The New Day 3.52 (from Warchild)
19] Bungle In The Jungle 3.34 (from Warchild)
CD 2
1] Minstrel In The Gallery 6.10 (from Minstrel In The Gallery)
2] Too Old To Rock'n'Roll; Too Young To Die 5.39 (from Too Old To
Rock'n'Roll)
3] Songs From The Wood 4.54 (from Songs From The Wood)
4] Jack In The Green 2.28 (from Songs From The Wood)
5] The Whistler 3.32 (from Songs From The Wood)
6] Heavy Horses 8.55 (from Heavy Horses)
7] Dun Ringill 2.40 (from Stormwatch)
8] Fylingdale Flyer 4.31 (from A)
9] Jack-A-Lynn 4.41 (from 20 Years Of Jethro Tull)
10] Pussy Willow 3.53 (from The Broadsword And The Beast)
11] Broadsword 4.58 (from The Broadsword And The Beast)
12] Under Wraps #2 4.14 (from Under Wraps)
13] Steel Monkey 3.33 (from Crest Of A Knave)
14] Farm On The Freeway 6.28 (from Crest Of A Knave)
15] Jump Start 4.52 (from Crest Of A Knave)
16] Kissing Willie 3.29 (from Rock Island)
17] This Is Not Love 3.53 (from Catfish Rising)

NIGHTCAP – The Unreleased Masters 1973-1991 2CD
November 1993
CHRYSALIS CDCHR 6057 (CD only)
Produced by Ian Anderson
All songs written by Ian Anderson
All previously unreleased except where indicated
CD 1 (My Round) Chateau D'Isaster Tapes 1973

Ian Anderson Martin Barre John Evans Jeffrey Hammond Hammond Barrie Barlow
1] First Post 1.57
2] Animelee 2.37
3] Tiger Toon 1.36
4] Look At The Animals 5.10
5] Law Of The Bungle 2.32
6] Law Of The Bungle Part II 5.25
7] Left Right 5.01
8] Solitaire 1.27 (from Warchild)
9] Critique Oblique 9.05
10] Post Last 5.34
11] Scenario 3.25 (from 20 Years Box Set)
12] Audition 2.34 (from 20 Years Box Set)
13] No Rehearsal 5.07 (from 20 Years Box Set)
CD 2 (Your Round) – Unreleased & Rare
1] Paradise Steakhouse 3.59 (1974)
2] Sea Lion II 3.18 (1974)
3] Piece Of Cake 3.37 (1990) (1993 CD single track)
4] Quartet 2.41 (1974)
5] Silver River Turning 4.49 (1990) (1993 CD single track)
6] Crew Nights 4.31 (1981)
7] The Curse 3.35 (1981)
8] Rosa On The Factory Floor 4.35 (1990) (1993 CD single track)
9] A Small Cigar 3.38 (1975)
10] Man Of Principle 3.55 (1988) (1993 CD single track)
11] Commons Brawl 3.23 (1981)
12] No Step 3.36 (1981)
13] Drive On The Young Side Of Life 4.11 (1981)
14] I Don't Want To Be Me 3.28 (1990) (1993 CD single track)
15] Broadford Bazaar 3.37 (1978)
16] Lights Out 5.14 (1981)
17] Truck Stop Runner 3.45 (1991) (1993 CD single track)
18] Hard Liner 3.45 (1989) (1993 vinyl single track)

IN CONCERT June 1995
Recorded Live at the Hammersmith Odeon, London 9-10-91
Ian Anderson Martin Barre Dave Pegg Maartin Allcock Doane Perry
Produced by Pete Ritzema
All songs written by Ian Anderson
WINDSONG WINCD 070 (CD only)
Tracks
1] Minstrel In The Gallery / Cross Eyed Mary 4.00
2] This Is Not Love 4.00
3] Rocks On The Road 6.30
4] Heavy Horses 7.33
5] Tall Thin Girl 3.28
6] Still Loving You Tonight 4.40
7] Thick As A Brick 7.48
8] A New Day Yesterday 5.45
9] Blues Jam 3.00
10] Jump Start 6.30

ROOTS TO BRANCHES September 1995
Ian Anderson Martin Barre Andy Giddings Doane Perry Dave Pegg Steve Bailey (bass)
Produced by Ian Anderson
All songs written by Ian Anderson
CHRYSALIS CHR 6109 (CD, Double LP)
Tracks
1] Roots To Branches 5.12
2] Rare And Precious Chain 3.34
3] Out Of The Noise 3.24
4] This Free Will 4.04
5] Valley 6.08
6] Dangerous Veils 5.33
7] Beside Myself 5.49
8] Wounded, Old And Treacherous 7.50
9] At Last, Forever 7.55
10] Stuck In The August Rain 4.06
11] Another Harry's Bar 6.22.
#20 in the UK. #114 in USA.

THROUGH THE YEARS March 1977
EMI GOLD 7243 8 55505 2 2 (CD only)
1] Living In The Past (Live) 5.07 [from A Little Light Music]
2] Wind Up 6.04 [from Aqualung]
3] Warchild 4.33 [from Warchild]
4] Dharma For One 4.11 [from This Was]
5] Acres Wild 3.22 [from Heavy Horses]
6] Budapest 10.00 [from Crest Of A Knave]
7] The Whistler 3.30 [from Songs From The Wood]
8] We Used To Know 3.55 [from Stand Up]
9] Beastie 3.57 [from The Broadsword And The Beast]
10] Locomotive Breath (live) 6.37 [from Live – Bursting Out]
11] Rare And Precious Chain 3.34 [from Roots To Branches]
12] Quizz Kid 5.08 [from Too Old To Rock'n'Roll]
13] Still Loving You Tonight [from Catfish Rising]
Yet another compilation, this time at budget price. Sadly lacking in detailed sleeve notes, but a fine selection of material and a striking cover made it a worthwhile release.

A JETHRO TULL COLLECTION March 1997
DISKY RECORDS DC 8786 12 (CD only)
Strictly speaking this was not a UK release, but imports were so heavy that it was easier to find this in UK shops than the UK version, "Through The Years". Controversially, it was also much cheaper than the UK release! Track listing is the same, but with a completely different running order. Different cover too.

THE JOHN EVAN BAND – "LIVE '66" November 1990
Ian Anderson (vocals) John Evans (organ) Bo Ward (bass) Ritchie Dharma (drums) Neil Smith (guitar) Tony Wilkinson (sax) Neil Valentine (sax)
Produced by Neil Smith and Adrian Wagner
A NEW DAY RECORDS AND CD1 (CD and cassette only)
1] Twine Time (Williams / Wright) 4.11
2] Hold On I'm Coming (Porter / Haynes) 3.57
3] Let The Good Times Roll (Theard / Moore) 3.25
4] Don't Fight It (Pickett / Cropper) 3.29
5] Respect (Redding) 3.09
6] Water (Penn / Hall / Franck) 4.00
7] Everything's Gonna Be Alright (Mitchell) 3.23
8] Mr Pitiful (Cropper / Redding) 3.17
9] Boot-leg (Axton / Dunn / Hayes / Jackson) 2.59
10] Stupidity (Burke) 2.55
11] Pink Champagne (Liggins) 4.41
12] I Want You (G.Bond) 2.00
13] Wade In The Water (J.Griffin) 3.37
14] Work Song (Brown Jr. / Adderley) 3.49
15] Shake (Cooke) 3.34
16] Twine Time (Williams / Wright) 4.12
17] Last Night (Mar-Keys) 0.50
This limited edition of 500 CDs was the first release on A New Day, and available only to subscribers to the magazine. It now changes hands for £100 and more.
The sound quality is of bootleg standard only, but as a historical document it is priceless. From the introduction by the clearly perplexed club host through Ian Anderson's undisguised near contempt for the audience, it is a fascinating glimpse at the band that just two years later was to become Jethro Tull. Worth a listen if only to hear Ian Anderson, soul singer, speaking with a northern accent! Highlights from Ian: "Thank you, you're very kind... it's obviously just the wrong kind of music here". "This is called Everything's Gonna Be Alright... which it obviously isn't". (To the rest of the band) "These people are laughing at me! They think there's something wrong with me!"

IAN ANDERSON – "WALK INTO LIGHT" November 1983
Ian Anderson Peter John Vettese
Produced by Ian Anderson
CHRYSALIS CDL 1443
1] Fly By Night (Anderson / Vettese) 3.51
2] Made In England (Anderson) 4.57

3] Walk Into Light (Anderson) 3.08
4] Trains (Anderson / Vettese) 3.18
5] End Game (Anderson) 3.17
6] Black And White Television (Anderson) 3.35
7] Toad In The Hole (Anderson) 3.22
8] Looking For Eden (Anderson) 3.40
9] User-Friendly (Anderson / Vettese) 3.59
10] Different Germany (Anderson / Vettese) 5.22
Reached #78 in the UK chart.
Licensed to and re-issued on CD by BGO in 1997 (BGO CD350).

IAN ANDERSON – "DIVINITIES: TWELVE DANCES WITH GOD" September 1995

Ian Anderson Andy Giddings
With Doane Perry (percussion), Douglas Mitchell (clarinet), Christopher Cowie (oboe), Jonathon Carrey (violin), Nina Greslin (cello), Randy Wigs (harp), Sid Gander (french horn), Dan Redding (trumpet).
Produced by Ian Anderson
Written by Ian Anderson with additional material by Andy Giddings
EMI 5 55262 2 (CD and cassette only)
1] In A Stone Circle 3.25
2] In Sight Of The Minaret 3.54
3] In A Black Box 3.24
4] In The Grip Of Stronger Stuff 2.48
5] In Maternal Grace 3.21
6] In The Moneylender's Temple 3.19
7] In Defence Of Faiths 3.11
8] At Their Father's Knee 5.43
9] En Afrique 2.54
10] In The Olive Garden 2.50
11] In The Pay Of Spain 4.05
12] In The Times Of India (Bombay Valentine) 8.09

Albums featuring exclusive tracks by JETHRO TULL / IAN ANDERSON

"RATTLESNAKE GUITAR – The Music Of Peter Green" 1996
COAST TO COAST RECORDS CTC 0202 Double CD.
Excellent tribute to Peter Green, featuring two tracks with a Jethro Tull connection:
MAN OF THE WORLD 2.54 by Ian Anderson (with Andy Giddings, Pete McKenzie & Pete Brown
THE SAME WAY 3.44 by Mick Abrahams (in fact by Blodwyn Pig)
THE ROLLING STONES ROCK AND ROLL CIRCUS 1996
ABCKO RECORDS 1268-2
Recorded December 1968. Jethro Tull perform "A Song For Jeffrey" 'live'. In fact only Ian Anderson is singing live, to a pre-recorded backing track.
MESSAGE TO LOVE: ISLE OF WIGHT FESTIVAL 1970 Dec. 1995
ESSENTIAL EDF 327.
Jethro Tull perform "My Sunday Feeling" live.
MARK CRANEY & FRIENDS "SOMETHING WITH A PULSE" 1997
LAUGHING GULL RECORDS LG002 (CD only) Available in the UK via A New Day.
BLACK SUNDAY 7.05 Performed by Jethro Tull, live in Los Angeles, November 1980.
SONG FOR JEFFREY 3.50 Performed by Ian Anderson, with Martin Barre and Andy Giddings.
Studio recording, March 1997.
THE DEREK LAWRENCE SESSIONS Take 3 1991
5 CD set released by LINE RECORDS in Germany. Volume 1 included "Aeroplane" by Jethro (Tull) Toe. More interestingly volume 3 included this otherwise unavailable gem from 1967, recorded at the same session. It was also available on the 5 track CD sampler (LICD 9.01138 E)
BLUES FOR THE 18th (Anderson / Barnard) 2.53. by Jethro Tull.
FAIRPORT CONVENTION "THE THIRD LEG" 1988
Double cassette pack of recorded highlights of Fairport's set at Cropredy 1987. Includes Ian Anderson,
Martin Barre, Dave Pegg and chums playing "Serenade To A Cuckoo"

JETHRO TULL UK SINGLES

MGM MGM 1384 AEROPLANE / SUNSHINE DAY February 1968
ISLAND WIP 6043 A SONG FOR JEFFREY / ONE FOR JOHN GEE September 1968
ISLAND WIP 6048 LOVE STORY / A CHRISTMAS SONG [#29] November 1968
ISLAND WIP 6056 LIVING IN THE PAST / DRIVING SONG [#3] May 1969
CHRYSALIS WIP 6070 SWEET DREAM / 17 [#9] October 1969
CHRYSALIS WIP 6077 THE WITCH'S PROMISE / TEACHER [#4] January 1970
CHRYSALIS WIP 6081 INSIDE / ALIVE AND WELL AND LIVING IN May 1970
CHRYSALIS WIP 6098 LICK YOUR FINGERS CLEAN / UP TO ME (unissued 1970)
CHRYSALIS WIP 6106 LIFE IS A LONG SONG / UP THE POOL / DR. BOGENBROOM / FROM LATER / NURSIE [#18] July 1971
CHRYSALIS CHS 2054 BUNGLE IN THE JUNGLE / BACK DOOR ANGELS October 1974
CHRYSALIS CHS 2075 MINSTREL IN THE GALLERY / SUMMERDAY SANDS Sept. 1975
CHRYSALIS CHS 2081 LIVING IN THE PAST / REQUIEM January 1976
CHRYSALIS CHS 2086 TOO OLD TO ROCK'N'ROLL: TOO YOUNG TO DIE / RAINBOW BLUES March 1976
CHRYSALIS CXP 2 RING OUT SOLSTICE BELLS / MARCH THE MAD SCIENTIST / A CHRISTMAS SONG / PAN DANCE [#28] November 1976
CHRYSALIS CHS 2135 THE WHISTLER / STRIP CARTOON February 1977
CHRYSALIS CHS 2214 MOTHS / LIFE IS A LONG SONG March 1978 (The unissued BELTANE was originally planned as the b-side)
CHRYSALIS CHS 2260 A STITCH IN TIME (3m.30s) / SWEET DREAM (Live) July 1978
CHRYSALIS CHS 2260 A STITCH IN TIME (4m.20s) / SWEET DREAM (Live) July 1978
CHRYSALIS CHS 2378 NORTH SEA OIL / ELEGY October 1978
CHRYSALIS CHS 2394 HOME / KING HENRY'S MADRIGAL / WARM SPORRAN / RING OUT SOLSTICE BELLS November 1979
CHRYSALIS CHS 2468 WORKING JOHN,WORKING JOE / FYLINGDALE FLYER Oct 1980
CHRYSALIS CHS 2619 BROADSWORD / FALLEN ON HARD TIMES May 1982
CHRYSALIS CHSP 2619 BROADSWORD / FALLEN ON HARD TIMES (Picture Disc)
CHRYSALIS TULL 1 LAP OF LUXURY / ASTRONOMY September 1984
CHRYSALIS TULLD 1 LAP OF LUXURY / ASTRONOMY / AUTOMOTIVE ENGINEERING / TUNDRA (gatefold 7" double pack)
CHRYSALIS TULLX 1 LAP OF LUXURY / ASTRONOMY / AUTOMOTIVE ENGINEERING / TUNDRA (12" single)
CHRYSALIS TULL 2 CORONACH / JACK FROST AND THE HOODED CROW June 1986
CHRYSALIS TULLX 2 CORONACH / JACK FROST AND THE HOODED CROW / LIVING IN THE PAST / ELEGY (12" single)
OLD GOLD OG 9673 LIVING IN THE PAST / THE WITCH'S PROMISE March 1987
CHRYSALIS TULL 3 STEEL MONKEY / DOWN AT THE END OF YOUR ROAD Sep 1987
CHRYSALIS TULLP 3 Tracks as TULL 3 (shaped picture disc)

CHRYSALIS TULLX 3 STEEL MONKEY / DOWN AT THE END OF YOUR ROAD / TOO MANY TOO / I'M YOUR GUN (12" single)

CHRYSALIS ZTULL 3 STEEL MONKEY / DOWN AT THE END OF YOUR ROAD / TOO MANY TOO / I'M YOUR GUN (cassette single in 7" pack)

CHRYSALIS TULL 4 SAID SHE WAS A DANCER / DOGS IN THE MIDWINTER Jan 1988

CHRYSALIS TULLP 4 Tracks as TULL 4 (shaped picture disc)

CHRYSALIS TULLX 4 SAID SHE WAS A DANCER / DOGS IN THE MIDWINTER / THE WAKING EDGE (12" single)

CHRYSALIS TULLCD 4 SAID SHE WAS A DANCER / DOGS IN THE MIDWINTER / DOWN AT THE END OF YOUR ROAD / TOO MANY TOO (CD)

CHRYSALIS TULL 5 ANOTHER CHRISTMAS SONG / Intro*- A CHRISTMAS SONG* (* recorded live in the dressing room, Zurich) November 1989

CHRYSALIS TULLX 5 ANOTHER CHRISTMAS SONG / Intro- A CHRISTMAS SONG*/ CHEAP DAY RETURN* / MOTHER GOOSE* / Outro- LOCOMOTIVE BREATH*) (12")

CHRYSALIS TULLCD 5 Tracks as TULLX 5 (CD)

CHRYSALIS TULLPCD 1 PART OF THE MACHINE / STORMY MONDAY BLUES / LICK YOUR FINGERS CLEAN / MINSTREL IN THE GALLERY / FARM ON THE FREEWAY (picture CD. All tracks from box set) June 1988

CHRYSALIS TULL 6 THIS IS NOT LOVE / NIGHT IN THE WILDERNESS August 1981

CHRYSALIS TULLX 6 THIS IS NOT LOVE / NIGHT IN THE WILDERNESS / JUMP START (live in Philadelphia 1987) (12")

CHRYSALIS TULLCD 6 Tracks as TULLX 6 (CD)

CHRYSALIS TULLXMC 6 THIS IS NOT LOVE / NIGHT IN THE WILDERNESS (cassette)

CHRYSALIS TULLCD 7 ROCKS ON THE ROAD Boxed 2 CD set. March 1992

Track details:- (CD 1) Rocks On The Road [from Catfish Rising]
Jack-a-Lynn [home demo recording from 1981]
Tall Thin Girl [live at WMMR Philadelphia 1991]
Fat Man [live on Rockline 26-8-91]
(CD 2) Rocks On The Road [live at WMMR Philadelphia 1991]
Bouree [live at WMMR Philadelphia 1991]
Mother Goose / Jack-a-Lynn [live in New York 20-8-91]
Aqualung / Locomotive Breath [live in New York 20-8-91]

CHRYSALIS TULLX 7 ROCKS ON THE ROAD / JACK-A-LYNN (demo) / AQUALUNG – LOCOMOTIVE BREATH (live) (12" picture disc)

CHRYSALIS TULLMC 7 ROCKS ON THE ROAD / BOUREE (live) / MOTHER GOOSE – JACK-A-LYNN (live) (cassette)

CHRYSALIS CHS 3970 LIVING IN THE PAST / HARDLINER (7") (#32) June 1993

CHRYSALIS 12CHS 3970 LIVING IN THE PAST (4 dance mixes) (12")

CHRYSALIS CD3970 (CD1) LIVING IN THE (SLIGHTLY MORE RECENT) PAST (live in Montreal, 1992) / SILVER RIVER TURNING / ROSA ON THE FACTORY FLOOR / I DON'T WANT TO BE ME (CD2) LIVING IN THE PAST / TRUCK STOP RUNNER / PIECE OF CAKE / MAN OF PRINCIPLE

IAN ANDERSON SINGLE

CHRYSALIS CHS 2746 FLY BY NIGHT / END GAME November 1983
With the two box sets, almost all of Tull's single tracks, both A-sides and B-sides, are available on albums. The exceptions are:
17: a shortened version of this track was included on the 20th anniversary box set. Ian Anderson really didn't want to include it, but gave in to pressure for the sake of completion. Infuriatingly though he could not bring himself to include the full 6 minute version, so it fades out halfway through!
A Stitch In Time: the 3.30 version is on the 20th box set. The 4.20 version is only available on the 7"..
The Zurich Dressing Room Tapes: The bonus tracks on the 'Another Christmas Song' singles, recorded backstage in Zurich, are only available on those singles.
Jump Start live in Philadelphia 1987: is only available on the 'This Is Not Love' single.

Night In The Wilderness: is only available as a single track, or on the Japanese 'Catfish Rising' CD.
"Rocks On The Road" bonus tracks: the bonus tracks on all formats of the single were recorded live during a radio station promo tour. Only available on the singles, except 'Bouree' which can be found on "Acoustic Aid" (KOME 98.5), a benefit CD for the AIDS foundation, in memory of Freddie Mercury.

MARTIN BARRE – "A SUMMER BAND" 1993

Martin Barre (guitars), Maggie Reeday & Joy Russell (lead vocals), Mark Tucker (guitar), Craig Milverton (keyboards), Tom Glendinning (drums), Matt Pegg (bass), Rob Darnell (percussion, harmonica, vocals).
Produced by Mark Tucker and Martin Barre
Recorded live in July 1992.
PRESSHOUSE RECORDS MBSBCD 92 CD & cassette only
1] Ain't That Peculiar (Holland/Whitfield) 3.49
2] Too Tired (Johnny Guitar Watson / Maxwell Davis / Saul Bihari) 3.09
3] Born Under A Bad Sign (Booker T Jones / William Bell) 3.05
4] One Love (Bett / Carpenter) 5.45
5] Georgia (Carmichael / Gorrell) 4.56
6] Cold Feet (Albert King) 2.22
7] Better Lying Down (Grace Slick) 3.59
8] I Shot The Sheriff (Bob Marley) 3.29
9] Barefootin' (Robert Parker) 3.21
10] Mustang Sally (Wilson Picket) 4.30
11] Nutbush City Limits (Ike & Tina Turner) 2.52
12] Faith Healer (A.Harvey / H.McKenna) 5.52
Limited edition of 500 CDs and cassettes, available only through A New Day magazine.

MARTIN BARRE – "A TRICK OF MEMORY" June 1994

Martin Barre (guitars and vocals), Andy Giddings (keyboards), Marc Parnell (drums), Rob Darnell (percussion), Matt Pegg (bass), Mel Collins (sax), Nick Pentelow (sax), Maggie Reeday (vocals), Richard Sidwell and Steve Sidwell (trumpets), Maartin Allcock (double bass), Ric Sanders (violin).
Produced by Martin Barre and Mark Tucker
All songs written by Martin Barre
ZYX 20282-2 (CD and cassette only)
1] Bug 4.08
2] Way Before Your Time 4.36
3] Bug Bee 0.49
4] Empty Café 2.08
5] Suspicion 4.24
6] I Be Thank You 2.17
7] A Blues For All Reasons 7.16
8] A Trick Of Memory 4.28
9] Steal 4.48
10] Another View 1.45
11] Cold Heart 5.21
12] Bug C 0.51
13] Morris Minus 3.06
14] In The Shade Of The Shadow 4.11
Martin Barre took objection to the original cover produced by ZYX, and had it withdrawn and redesigned at his own expense. The original cover has a head and shoulders photo of Barre, and the legend "Guitarist Of Jethro Tull" printed alongside his name. The later cover has a full length shot of Barre and a less Teutonic typeface!

MARTIN BARRE – "THE MEETING" January 1996

Martin Barre (guitars), Maggie Reeday (vocals), John Noyce (bass), Andy Murray (keyboards), Darren Mooney, Gerry Conway, Doane Perry, Dave Mattacks, Marc Parnell (drums), Matt Pegg (bass), Miles Bould (percussion), Mel Collins (sax).
Produced by Martin Barre and Mark Tucker
All songs written by Martin Barre
PRESSHOUSE RECORDS (CD only)
1] The Meeting 4.27
2] The Potion 5.17
3] Outer Circle 5.53
4] I Know Your Face 5.14
5] Misere 5.58

6] Time After Time 5.40
7] Spanner 6.52
8] Running Free 5.14
9] Tom's 3.55
10] Dreamer 3.20
11] The Audition 3.17

First 1,000 copies were on the Presshouse label and sold through A New Day magazine before Imago Records in America took over. The original CD features Paul Cox singing 'Running Free'. A new vocal from Maggie Reeday was used on the Imago CD "for better continuity".

JOHN CARTER with MARTIN BARRE – "SPIRIT FLYING FREE" March 1997

John Carter (vocals), Martin Barre (guitars & flutes), John Noyce (bass), Dave Pegg (bass), Paul Burgess (drums), Chris Leslie (violin), Nigel Neill (keyboards), Mark Tucker (guitar, Maggie Reeday, Joy Russell, Ian Francis (backing vocals).
Produced by Martin Barre
All songs written by John Carter except where indicated
A NEW DAY RECORDS AND CD16 (CD and cassette only)
1] The Student 4.17
2] Winter Setting 3.29
3] No Easy Way 6.45
4] Spirit Flying Free 4.13
5] Melody Of Words 2.43
6] Laugh It Off 5.50
7] Don't Mess Around With Me 4.15
8] I Can't Forget 3.10
9] Exciting Eyes 3.18
10] I'll Make A Stand This Time (John Carter / Martin Barre) 3.50
11] Your Dry Land 5.07

THREAD – "THREAD" 1996

Doane Perry (drums & percussion) Vince DiCola (keyboards) Ellis Hall (vocals)
With Mark Boals, John De Faria and Rocket Ritchotte (guitars), Rick Livingstone (vocals).
Produced by Thread
All songs written by Vince DiCola and Doane Perry with additional material by Rick Livingstone
LAUGHING GULL RECORDS PHD8-96 Distributed in the UK by A New Day
1] Live At The Scene 7.02
2] Hands Of Kindness (Excerpt) 4.55
3] Another Mean Day 4.59
4] Just Out Of Reach 5.38
5] Rage 4.42
6] Secrets Of The Game 4.44
7] Rainbow Suite 14.49

VARIOUS – "TO CRY YOU A SONG: A Collection Of Tull Tales" 1996

Produced by Peter Morticelli and Mike Varney. Assisted by Robin Black.
All songs written by Ian Anderson except where indicated.
MAGNA CARTA RR 8872.2 (CD only) Distributed by ROADRUNNER in the UK.
1] A Tull Tale (T.Gardner) 2.25 performed by Magellan featuring Stan Johnson
2] Aqualung 8.09 performed by Magellan
3] Up The Pool 3.01 performed by Roy Harper
4] Nothing Is Easy 4.17 performed by John Wetton, Mick Abrahams, Clive Bunker, Glenn Cornick,
Ian McDonald, Phil Manzanera, Robert Berry.
5] Mother Goose 4.23 performed by Lief Sorbye
6] Minstrel In The Gallery 5.22 performed by Robert Berry and Lief Sorbye.
7] One Brown Mouse 3.15 performed by Echolyn
8] Cat's Squirrel (trad.arr. Abrahams) 5.52 performed by Mick Abrahams, Mike Summerland, Charlie
Musselwhite, Derek Trucks, Clive Bunker, Robert Berry.

9] To Cry You A Song 5.10 performed by Glenn Hughes, Mick Abrahams, Clive Bunker, Glenn
Cornick, Derek Sherinian, Robert Berry
10] A New Day Yesterday 3.39 performed by Robby Steinhardt, Mick Abrahams, Clive Bunker, Glenn
Cornick, Phil Manzanera, Ian McDonald, Robert Berry, Mike Wible.
11] Teacher 3.59 performed by Wolfstone & Mick Abrahams, Clive Bunker, Glenn Cornick
12] Living In The Past 3.21 performed by Keith Emerson,Mick Abrahams,Clive Bunker,Glenn Cornick
13] Locomotive Breath 4.32 performed by Tempest with Robert Berry
14] Life's A Long Song 2.45 performed by Dave Pegg and Matt Pegg.

WILD TURKEY – "BATTLE HYMN" 1972

Glenn Cornick (bass) Tweke Lewis (Guitar) Gary Pickford Hopkins (vocals, guitar) Jon Blackmore (guitar, vocals) Jeff Jones (percussion)
Original album CHRYSALIS CHR 1002
Current CD EDSEL EDCD 333

WILD TURKEY – "TURKEY" 1973

Glenn Cornick (bass) Tweke Lewis (Guitar) Gary Pickford Hopkins (vocals, guitar) Jon Blackmore (guitar, vocals) Jeff Jones (percussion)
Original album CHRYSALIS CHR 1010
Current CD EDSEL EDCD 424

WILD TURKEY – "STEALER OF YEARS" 1996

Glenn Cornick (bass, mandolin, whistle) Tweke Lewis (Guitar) Gary Pickford Hopkins (vocals, guitar) Brian Thomas (drums, percussion)
HTD RECORDS HTD CD 58 (CD only)
The original Turkey reformed 23 years on. Against all the odds, they turned out a really good album!

CLIVE BUNKER – "AWAKENING" 1998

Clive Bunker (vocals, percussion) Andy Glass (guitars) Jim Rodford (bass) John Bartrum (sax)
Dave Lennox (keyboards) Martin Barre (guitars) Ian Anderson (flute) Vikki Clayton (b.v)
Produced by Andy Glass and Clive Bunker
All songs written by Clive Bunker
A NEW DAY RECORDS AND CD 21
1] Swayo 3.20
2] Fantasy 3.40
3] Awakening 4.15
4] Penang 3.34
5] Certain Feeling 8.00
6] Monotone Thing 2.50
7] Do We Know Where We're Going? 4.53 with Martin Barre on guitar
8] Chichicastenango 3.30
9] Wrong Programme 5.59
10] Good Times 4.15 with Martin Barre on guitar
11] Strange Riff 4.25 with Martin Barre on guitar, Ian Anderson on flute

SOLSTICE – "CIRCLES" December 1996

Andy Glass Clive Bunker Marc Elton Emma Brown Craig Sunderland
A NEW DAY RECORDS AND CD 13
Cult new-age prog rockers returned in '96 with their finest work to date, aided by master drummer Clive Bunker. By pure coincidence, band leader and guitarist Andy Glass was the engineer on Mick Abrahams' "One" CD, which Ian Anderson played on. Anderson was so impressed with that finished album that he subsequently hired Glass as Tull's live sound engineer. A good gig for Andy Glass, but sadly it put a temporary end to the Solstice renaissance due to Tull's heavy touring schedule. However, a brand new Solstice album is scheduled for release in August 1998, again featuring Clive Bunker.

ALBUMS WITH MAJOR CONTRIBUTIONS BY JETHRO TULL MEMBERS

JACKIE LYNTON'S PIN-BOARD WIZARDS 1998

A NEW DAY RECORDS AND CD14 (CD only)
Veteran rocker Lynton returned to the studio after a gap of 15 years, with many rock legends guesting with his band. Rick Parfitt, Big Jim Sullivan, Mick Moody, Dick Taylor, Big Al Hodge and Mike Summerland helped out, and several tracks on the CD feature Jethro Tull members, past and present:
2] Let It Rock (Berry) with Ian Anderson on flute.
3] If You Wanna Get A Band Together (Lynton) with Martin Barre and Mick Abrahams on guitar, Clive Bunker on drums.
5] Losing Ground (Lynton) with Martin Barre on guitar
6] Odd Socks Blues (Lynton) with Mick Abrahams on guitar
7] Hi Lilly Hi Lo (Deutsch-Kaper-Bronislav) with Mick Abrahams on guitar
9] Getting By Blues (Lynton) with Mick Abrahams on guitar, Clive Bunker on drums.
11] You Gotta Go (Lynton) with Ian Anderson on harmonica
12] Shut Up, I'm Playing Me Guitar (Lynton / Rees / Wizards) with Martin Barre & Mick Abrahams on guitar, Clive Bunker on drums.
13] How Much Do You Cry? (Lynton / Abrahams) with Mick Abrahams on guitar.

THE SIX AND VIOLENCE – "LETTUCE PREY – UK DB EDITION" 1996

A NEW DAY RECORDS AND CD 9 (CD only)
Ian Anderson plays flute on two tracks by this outrageous thrash hardcore band from New York. He also recites a very brief poem at the end of the poignant ballad, 'Bursting Bladder'! This special UK edition of the CD includes two bonus tracks, incredible versions of Tull's 'Nothing Is Easy' and a medley of Tull tunes based around 'Sunshine Day'.

MADDY PRIOR – "WOMAN IN THE WINGS" 1978

Original album CHR 1185
Current CD BGO CD215 (1994)
Produced by Ian Anderson, David Palmer and Robin Black
All songs written by Maddy Prior. Arrangements by David Palmer
Tracks
1] Woman In The Wings 5.21 Barrie Barlow (drums), John Glascock (bass), David Palmer (keybds).
2] Cold Flame 3.41 Barrie Barlow (drums), Martin Barre (guitar solo)
3] Mother And Child 1.55 with David Palmer (keyboards)
4] Gutter Geese 3.33 Ian Anderson (flute), Barrie Barlow (drums).
5] Rollercoaster 3.46 with Ian Anderson (backing vocals).
6] Deep Water 2.19
7] Long Shadows 3.35 with Barrie Barlow (drums), John Glascock (bass).
8] I Told You So 2.34 with Barrie Barlow (drums)
9] Rosettes 3.31 with Barrie Barlow (drums), John Glascock (bass)
10] Catseyes 2.47 with Barrie Barlow (drums), John Glascock (bass), Shona Anderson (backing vcls)
11] Baggy Pants 2.57
With the exception of John Evans, the complete Jethro Tull line-up appear on the album, although no one track actually features them all together. Ian Anderson's wife, Shona, sings on one track.

MICK ABRAHAMS "ONE" 1996

Ian Anderson reunited in the studio with Mick Abrahams for the first time since 1968. See details in the Mick Abrahams / Blodwyn Pig section

A CLASSIC CASE 1985

"The London Symphony Orchestra Plays The Music Of Jethro Tull"
The London Symphony Orchestra, Conducted by David Palmer
With Ian Anderson Martin Barre Dave Pegg Peter Vettese Paul Burgess
Produced by David Palmer
Written by Ian Anderson except where indicated. Arranged by David Palmer
RCA RED SEAL RCD1 7067
1] Locomotive Breath 4.21

2] Thick As A Brick 4.29
3] Elegy (David Palmer) 3.46
4] Bouree (J.S.Bach / Anderson) 3.12
5] Fly By Night (Anderson / Vettese) 4.14
6] Aqualung 6.24
7] Too Old To Rock'n'Roll: Too Young To Die 3.30
8] Teacher / Bungle In The Jungle / Rainbow Blues / Locomotive Breath 4.02
9] Living In The Past 3.34
10] War Child 5.03
A European and American release on CD and vinyl that was very hard to find in the UK. Fortunately the budget label Music For Pleasure issued it on CD as "Classic Jethro Tull" (CDMFP 5989) in 1993.
The Red Seal album includes lengthy sleeve notes from respected Sunday Times music critic Derek Jewell. A patchy album, although it does have it's moments. Unfortunately nothing on the album can live up to the standard set by the final track, War Child – a fact that is even acknowledged in the sleeve notes.
A Classic Case was the first of a series of orchestral rock albums arranged and conducted by David Palmer. The series is still going strong, with the likes of Yes, Genesis, Pink Floyd, The Beatles and Queen getting the orchestral treatment. There are rumours that Led Zeppelin and The Rolling Stones might be next in line.
Other DAVID PALMER albums
WE KNOW WHAT WE LIKE – The Music of GENESIS
RCA RED SEAL RK 86242 1987
Ian Anderson guests briefly on flute on "I Know What I Like".
OBJECTS OF FANTASY – The Music Of PINK FLOYD
RCA VICTOR RD87960 1989
SYMPHONIC MUSIC OF YES RCA VICTOR 09026-61938-2 1993
ORCHESTRAL Sgt. PEPPERS EMI MFP 307682 1994
PASSING OPEN WINDOWS – A Symphonic Tribute to QUEEN
Sony Classical SK 62851 1997
"TALLIS"
Album recorded 1979-1981, still unreleased. Mostly original material from David Palmer, with a couple of classical pieces reworked by the band.
Musicians include:
David Palmer John Evans Barrie Barlow John Glascock Bill Worrall David Bristow
There are tentative plans to release this post-Tull album through A New Day, with the proceeds going to the charity LUPUS. The master tapes have been located, and as soon as time permits Robin Black and David Palmer intend to clean them up and remaster them for CD. It's been a long time coming, but with luck this lost gem will eventually see the light of day before the next Millenium!

Other Guest Appearances by IAN ANDERSON

Flute on "Home", the only studio track on an otherwise live double album by Roy Harper, "Flashes From The Archives Of Oblivion" (1974). When "Flashes" was released on CD it was shortened to fit on one CD, and "Home" was dropped. It was subsequently added to Roy Harper's "Valentine" CD.
Flute on "Under The Greenwood Tree" by Brian Protheroe, on the album "And You And I" (1976).
Flute on "All Along You Knew" by Honeymoon Suite, on the album "The Big Prize" (1985).
Flute on "On Tuesday" by Men Without Hats, on the album "Pop Goes The World" (1987).
Flute on "Yes We Can", a single by Artists United For Nature (1989). Typically 'sincere' super-group anthem "To save the rain forests", featuring Brian May, Joe Cocker, Jennifer Rush, Chris Thompson, Chaka Khan and many more.
Flute on "Crazy Love – Aqualung Remix", a 12" single by Nixon (1990). Not a sample, but real time playing from Ian in dance mode! Great fun, but a bugger to find in the shops!
Flute on "Love So True" by Bomb The Bass, on the album "Unknown Territory" (1991). Ian Anderson gets a writer's credit on both mixes of "Love So True" on the album, but his flute can only be heard on the 12" mix. Apparently a sample from "My God", but it's so unrecognisable that it begs the question "Why bother?" A cheaper option would surely have

been a session flautist! Incidentally, the flute sample on "Winter In July (Ubiquity Mix)" sounds remarkably like Anderson too.

Flute on "Play Minstrel Play" by Blackmore's Night, on the album "Shadow Of The Moon" (1997).

Flute on "Strange Riff" by Clive Bunker, on the album "Awakening" (1998). See full CD details elsewhere.

Flute on "These Fifty Years" by Roy Harper, on the album "The Dream Society" (1998).

THE MANDOKI CONNECTION

Ian Anderson has contributed to several tracks, over three albums, for Leslie Mandoki's People, an occasional super group. His 1993 CD "People" features Ian on the following tracks:

Hold Onto Your Dreams – vocals and flute

I Dance Through My Dreams – flute

Mother Europe – vocals and flute

His 1997 CD "People In Room #8" features Ian on the following tracks:

Let The Music Show You The Way – vocals and flute

On And On – flute

Back To Budapest (Mandoki / Anderson) – flute. (A live jam from Anderson and Mandoki, recorded in Budapest in 1996). This track is also included on Man Doki - "The Jazz Cuts", also 1991.

Hold On To Your Dreams (Yes, again! Same version as on 'People') – vocals and flute.

Other Guest Appearances by MARTIN BARRE

Guitar on four tracks on Chick Churchill album "You And Me" (1973)

Guitar on John Wetton album "Caught In The Crossfire" (1980)

Guitar on two tracks on "Just For The Halibut", a cassette only release by Five Furious Fish (1995)

Guitar on three tracks on Vikki Clayton album "Movers and Shakers" (1997)

Guitar on Clive Bunker album "Awakening" (1998). See details elsewhere.

Guitar on Spirit Of The West album (1998).

Martin has played many other sessions on guitar, flute and even sax, but refuses to discuss them for some reason!

BLODWYN PIG / MICK ABRAHAMS DISCOGRAPHY

BLODWYN PIG "Dear Jill" / "Sweet Caroline"
May 1969 Island WIP 6059 (7" single)

BLODWYN PIG – "AHEAD RINGS OUT" August 1969

Mick Abrahams (gtr, vcls) Jack Lancaster (flute, violin, sax) Andy Pyle (bass) Ron Berg (drums)
Produced by Andy Johns
Original album: ISLAND ILPS 9101
Current CD (1989) BEAT GOES ON BGO CD54 (Also Pic CD BGO CD 54(P)
1] It's Only Love (Abrahams) 3.23
2] Dear Jill (Abrahams) 5.15
3] Sing Me A Song That I Know (Abrahams) 3.07
4] The Modern Alchemist (Lancaster) 6.20
5] Up And Coming (Abrahams / Lancaster / Pyle / Berg) 5.25
6] Leave It With Me (Lancaster) 4.51
7] The Change Song (Abrahams) 3.39
8] Backwash (Abrahams / Lancaster / Pyle / Berg) 0.50
9] Ain't Ya Coming Home Babe? (Abrahams / Lancaster / Pyle) 5.35
The standard CD omits 'Backwash' from the credits on the back cover, although it is listed on the back cover of the picture CD. The CD inlay incorrectly times 'Backwash' at 3.39 and 'Ain't Ya Coming Home Babe?' at 6.52. Ron Berg is listed in all writing credits as 'Burp'!
BLODWYN PIG "Walk On The Water"/ "Summer Day"
September 1969 Island WIP 6069 (7" single)
BLODWYN PIG – "Same Old Story" / "Slow Down"
January 1970 Chrysalis WIP 6078 (7" single)

BLODWYN PIG – "GETTING TO THIS" April 1970

Mick Abrahams (gtr, vcls) Jack Lancaster (flute, violin, sax) Andy Pyle (bass) Ron Berg (drums)
With Mick Waller (piano)
Produced by Andy Johns

Original album: CHRYSALIS ILPS 9122
Current CD (1990) BEAT GOES ON BGO CD81
1] Drive Me (Abrahams) 3.19
2] Variations On Nainos (Abrahams) 3.47
3] See My Way (Abrahams) 5.04
4] Long Bomb Blues (Abrahams) 1.07
5] The Squirreling Must Go On (Abrahams / Pyle) 4.22
6] San Francisco Sketches (Lancaster) 8.11
   a] Beach Scape [b] Fisherman's Wharf [c] Telegraph Hill [d] Close The Door, I'm falling out of the room
7] Worry (Pyle) 3.43
8] Toys (Abrahams) 3.03
9] To Rassman (Berg) 1.29
10] Send Your Son To Die (Abrahams) 4.25
11] Summer Day (Abrahams / Pyle) 3.48
12] Walk On The Water (Abrahams) 3.42
Tracks 11 & 12 were not on the original album, but added to the CD.

MICK ABRAHAMS – "(A Musical Evening With) MICK ABRAHAMS" 1971

Mick Abrahams (guitar, vocals) Ritchie Dharma (drums) Bob Sargeant (keyboards, guitar, vocals) Walt Monaghan (bass, vocals)
Produced by Chris Thomas
Original album: CHRYSALIS CHR 9147
Current CD (1992) BEAT GOES ON BGO CD95
1] Greyhound Bus (Abrahams) 4.53
2] Awake (Abrahams) 8.51
3] Winds Of Change (Abrahams) 4.52
4] Why Do You Do Me This Way (Abrahams / Sargeant) 3.33
5] Big Queen (Abrahams) 4.29
6] Not To Rearrange (Abrahams / Sargeant) 3.27
7] Seasons (Abrahams) 15.02

MICK ABRAHAMS BAND – "AT LAST" 1972

Mick Abrahams (guitar, vocals) Ritchie Dharma (drums) Bob Sargeant (keyboards, guitar, vocals) Walt Monaghan (bass, vocals) Jack Lancaster (flute, sax, clarinet)
Produced by Chris Thomas
Original album: CHRYSALIS CHR 1005
Current CD (1991) EDSEL ECDC 335
1] When I Get Back (Abrahams / Sargeant) 5.02
2] Absent Friends (Sargeant) 4.47
3] Time Now To Decide (Abrahams) 2.26
4] Whole Wide World (Abrahams) 3.51
5] Up And Down [Part One] (Abrahams) 2.00
6] Up And Down [Part Two] (Abrahams) 2.15
7] Maybe Because (Abrahams) 8.00
8] The Good Old Days (Sargeant) 4.12
9] You'll Never Get It From Me (Sargeant) 3.36

MICK ABRAHAMS – "HAVE FUN LEARNING THE GUITAR WITH MICK ABRAHAMS" 1974

SRT 73313 (Vinyl only)
A tutorial album knocked out by Abrahams in 'a quiet period'. Not surprisingly it has not been re-issued on CD.

BLODWYN PIG – "A TASTE OF THINGS TO COME" 1989

Mick Abrahams (guitar, vocals) Dick Heckstall-Smith (sax) Clive Bunker (drums) Bruce Boardman (keyboards) Andy Pyle (bass)
Private issue demo tape. Limited edition of 50 copies
1] Black Night [live]
2] So Much Trouble [live]
3] I Wonder Who [live]
4] Cat's Squirrel [live]
5] Rock Me [live]
6] Looking For Love [studio]

JETHRO TULL

MICK ABRAHAMS – "ROADROLLER" 1990
Private issue studio album on cassette only. Limited edition of 500. See "All Said And Done" CD

MICK ABRAHAMS – "ALL SAID AND DONE" 1991
Mick Abrahams (guitar, vocals) Clive Bunker (drums) Nigel Pegrum (drums) Dave Lennox (keyboards) Pete Fensome (bass) Andy Pyle (bass) Bruce Boardman (keyboards) Gordon Murphy (sax) Dick Heckstall-Smith (sax)
Produced by Nigel Pegrum
ELITE 007CD (CD and cassette only)
1] Road Roller (Abrahams) 3.04
2] Watch Your Step (B.Parker) 3.48
3] Billy The Kid (trad.arr. Abrahams) 3.31
4] Let Me Love You Baby (W.Dixon) 3.10
5] Black Night (J M Robinson) 6.21
6] All Tore Down (Abrahams) 5.20
7] Redways Of Milton Keynes (Abrahams) 3.56
8] Long Gone (Abrahams / Murphy) 3.12
9] Rock Me Right (Abrahams) 3.22
10] So Much Trouble (B McGhee) 2.48
11] Dear Jane (Abrahams) 3.58
12] I Wonder Who (Alexis Korner) 6.51
13] All Said And Done (Abrahams / Murphy) 3.14
14] Cat's Squirrel (trad.arr. Abrahams) 11.25
This CD includes 11 of the 12 tracks on the 'Roadroller' cassette, plus tracks 4 and 14. 'All Said And Done' on Roadroller is a live cut, replaced by a studio recording on the CD.

MICK ABRAHAMS' BLODWYN PIG – "LIES" 1993
Mick Abrahams (guitar, vocals) Mike Summerland (bass) Graham Walker (drums) Dave Lennox (keyboards) Nick Payne (sax, harmonica) Jackie Challoner (backing vocals)
Produced by Mick Abrahams
All songs written by Mick Abrahams except where indicated
A NEW DAY RECORDS AND CD 3 (CD and cassette only)
1] Lies 4.40
2] The Night Is Gone 3.51
3] [Deep Down] Recession Blues 4.18
4] Latin Girl 3.00
5] Gnatz 2.18
6] Funny Money 4.06
7] Witness [To A Crime Of Love] 2.58
8] Aby's Lean 2.43
9] Victim (B B King) 4.42
10] Love Won't Let You Down 5.06
11] Dead Man's Hill 4.18
12] Maggie Rose 3.24
A New Day collector's edition, limited to 1,000 copies, included a 16pp booklet. Subsequently issued on several labels in the UK, Europe and America.

MICK ABRAHAMS' BLODWYN PIG "LIVE: ALL TORE DOWN" 1994
Mick Abrahams (gtr,vcl) Mike Summerland (bass) Graham Walker (drums) Dave Lennox (keybds)
Recorded live in Germany 1993
INDIGO RECORDS IGOCD 2011
1] It's Only Love (Abrahams) 3.02
2] All Tore Down (Abrahams) 4.32
3] Lies (Abrahams) 4.57
4] Billy The Kid (trad.arr. Abrahams) 6.27
5] I Wonder Who (Doyle) 10.33
6] The Victim (Rebennack / Pomus) 5.29
7] Cat's Squirrel (trad.arr Abrahams) 17.02
8] Slow Down (Williams) 3.32
9] Dead Man's Hill (Abrahams) 11.08

MICK ABRAHAMS – "ONE" March 1996
Mick Abrahams (guitar, vocals) Ian Anderson (flute, harmonica, mandolin)

Produced by Mick Abrahams
A NEW DAY RECORDS AND CD 7 (CD and cassette only)
1] Driftin' Blues (Johnson) 3.03 with Ian Anderson on harmonica
2] Do Re Mi (Guthrie) 3.08
3] Mystery Train (Parker / Phillips) 2.42
4] Thirteen Question Method (Berry) 2.33
5] Gnatz (Abrahams) 2.28
6] How Long Blues (Leadbetter) 3.19 (with Ian Anderson on harmonica)
7] My Uncle (Parsons) 2.02
8] Jesus On The Mainline (trad.arr. Abrahams) 3.03
9] Saunton Strut (Abrahams) 2.37
10] How Can A Poor Man Stand Such Times And Live? (A.Alexander) 3.08
11] Just Passing By (Abrahams) 1.42
12] Billy The Kid (trad.arr. Abrahams) 5.00 with Ian Anderson on mandolin
13] Lawdy Miss Clawdy (L.Price) 2.12
14] Old Mother Nicotine (Abrahams) 5.48 with Ian Anderson on flute

MICK ABRAHAMS – "MICK'S BACK" July 1996
Mick Abrahams (guitar, vocals) Tim Franks (drums) Dave Baldwin (keyboards) John Price (bass) Norman Beaker (guitar) Lenni (sax) John Hulme (trumpet) Sheila Gott (backing vocals)
INDIGO DELUX IGOXCD 501 (CD only)
1] The River's Invitation (Mayfield) 3.29
2] Bad Feeling (Abrahams) 3.46
3] Cold Women With Warm Hearts (Rice) 3.26
4] Time To Love (Abrahams) 4.58
5] Leaving Home Blues (Abrahams) 3.55
6] Long Grey Mare (Green) 5.52
7] You'd Be A Millionaire (Bland / Pea / Evans) 4.20
8] Send Me Some Lovin' (Marascatco / Price) 3.51
9] Yolanda (Moore) 3.40
10] Little Red Rooster (Dixon) 4.07
11] Ain't No Love In The Heart Of The City (Price / Walsh) 3.39
12] So Much Hard Luck (Abrahams) 4.44
13] Skyline Drive (Abrahams) 3.29

BLODWYN PIG – "PIG IN THE MIDDLE" December 1996
Mick Abrahams (guitar, vocals) Mike Summerland (bass) Graham Walker (drums)
With Clive Bunker (percussion), Mick Parker (keyboards), Nick Payne (sax, harmonica), Jackie Challoner & Lorenza Johnson (backing vocals)
Produced by Robin Black
All songs written by Mick Abrahams
A NEW DAY RECORDS AND CD 10 (CD and cassette only)
1] Raining Again 4.53
2] You Got It Wrong 4.25
3] Going Down 4.37
4] Whisky Dreams 4.50
5] Goodbye 5.44
6] I'm Bored 2.36
7] Modern Day TV Blues 2.45
8] Mo' Bad News 4.42
9] Hard Wind 4.41
10] Fire In The Hole 3.19
11] Nervous Blues 7.07
BLODWYN PIG – "Going Down / Goodbye" 1996
Mick Abrahams (guitar, vocals) Mike Summerland (bass) Graham Walker (drums)
Produced by Robin Black
4 track CD single with 2 radio edits from 'Pig In The Middle' and 2 new studio tracks.
A NEW DAY RECORDS AND CD 11 (CD only)
1] Going Down [Radio Edit] (Abrahams) 3.45
2] Goodbye [Radio Edit] (Abrahams) 3.57
3] Hound Dog (Leiber & Stoller) 2.22
4] Drive Me (Abrahams) 2.50

BLODWYN PIG – "THE MODERN ALCHEMIST" 1997

Mick Abrahams (gtr, vcls) Jack Lancaster (flute, violin, sax) Andy Pyle (bass) Ron Berg (drums)
Recorded live in 1970. Sound quality no better than a good bootleg.
INDIGO RECORDS IGOXCD 507 (CD only)
1] It's Only Love (Abrahams) 3.44
2] The Modern Alchemist (Lancaster) 10.43
3] The Change Song (Abrahams) 3.43
4] Summers Day (Abrahams / Pyle) 4.21
5] Dear Jill (Abrahams) 5.01
6] See My Way (Abrahams) 6.51
7] Drive Me (Abrahams) 3.45
8] Slow Down (Williams) 6.07
9] Ain't Ya Coming Home Babe? (Abrahams / Lancaster / Pyle) 4.24
10] Mr. Green's Blues (Abrahams) 3.54
11] Cat's Squirrel (trad.arr. Abrahams) 7.48
Tracks are listed in the wrong order on the CD tray card and inlay.

MICK ABRAHAMS BAND – "LIVE IN MADRID" 1997

Recorded live in 1974. Sound quality slightly better than "Modern Alchemist".
INDIGO RECORDS IGOCD 2065 (CD only)
1] Let's Get Down To Business (Abrahams) 4.18
2] Wanna Know How To Love (Abrahams) 6.40
3] Let Me Love You Baby (Dixon) 3.55
4] Stay With Me (Abrahams) 3.36
5] Automobile (Abrahams) 4.14
6] Blues (Abrahams) 8.30
7] Steel Blues (Abrahams) 6.07
8] Cat's Squirrel (trad.arr. Abrahams) 16.03
9] Guitar Boogie (Abrahams) 3.26
10] Rock Me (Jackson) 4.39

BLODWYN PIG – "THE FULL PORKY, Live In London 1991" 1998

Mick Abrahams (guitar, vocal) Jim Leverton (bass) Gordon Murphy (sax) Graham Walker (drums) Dave Lennox (keyboards)
A NEW DAY RECORDS AND CD 20 (CD only)
1] It's Only Love 3.10
2] Black Night Is Falling 6.44
3] All Tore Down 4.58
4] Billy The Kid 7.35
5] It'll Be Me 3.39
6] Cat's Squirrel 9.43
7] Before You Accuse Me 6.39
8] All Said And Done 3.09
9] I Wonder Who Baby 9.24
10] Got My Mojo Working 7.16
11] Slow Down 5.16
12] Roadroller 6.27
Limited edition of 1,000 CDs.

HOUSE OF SATIRE – THE DOOMSDAY CLOCK" 1997

SATIRE CD 1 (CD only)
A concept album written by Mark Law, performed by an all-star line up including Mick Abrahams, Clive Bunker, Rod Argent, Rob Burns, Graeme Edge, Tracy Graham, Robin Lumley, Mick Parker, Nick Payn, Jim Rodford and Steve Stapley. There were tentative plans for an ambitious stage show to tour the UK based on the album, starring Mick Abrahams in several roles, but to date nothing has materialised.

Appendix 3   Gigography

The following list has been compiled from many sources, and is as complete as possible using the information to hand. However, with such a massive list there are inevitably inaccuracies and omissions beyond the control of the author. Thanks to various unknown and uncredited sources, and particularly to Steve Parkhouse and Colin Harper.

1968		
2 FEB	LONDON MARQUEE CLUB	UK
9 FEB	LONDON MARQUEE CLUB	UK
16 FEB	LONDON MARQUEE CLUB	UK
15 MAR	LONDON MARQUEE CLUB	UK
18 MAR	CROYDON STAR HOTEL	UK
26 MAR	LONDON CROMWELLIAN	UK
30 MAR	LONDON MARQUEE CLUB	UK
15 APR	LONDON MARQUEE CLUB	UK
16 APR	LONDON WOOD GREEN FISHMONGERS ARMS	UK
22 APR	CROYDON STAR HOTEL	UK
3 MAY	LONDON MARQUEE CLUB	UK
5 MAY	ASCOT THE QUEENS STAG HOUNDS	UK
18 MAY	LONDON MARQUEE CLUB	UK
20 MAY	LONDON THE NAGS HEAD	UK
31 MAY	LONDON MARQUEE CLUB	UK
14 JUN	LONDON MARQUEE CLUB	UK
15 JUN	WEST HAMP STEAD KLOOKS KLEEK	UK
18 JUN	WEST HAMPSTEAD KLOOKS KLEEK	UK
21 JUN	SCARBOROUGH CANDLE LIGHT CLUB	UK
28 JUN	LONDON MARQUEE CLUB (2 SHOWS)	UK
29 JUN	LONDON HYDE PARK	UK
5 JUL	LONDON MARQUEE CLUB	UK
11 JUL	WEALDSTONE RAILWAY HOTEL	UK
19 JUL	LONDON MARQUEE CLUB	UK
20 JUL	MANCHESTER THE MAGIC VILLAGE	UK
26 JUL	LONDON MARQUEE CLUB	UK
4 AUG	BIRMINGHAM MOTHERS	UK
7 AUG	LONDON THE MANOR HOUSE	UK
9 AUG	LONDON MARQUEE CLUB	UK
11 AUG	SUNBURY KEMPTON PARK	UK
21 AUG	BIRMINGHAM MOTHERS	UK
23 AUG	LONDON MARQUEE CLUB	UK
24 AUG	LONDON MARQUEE CLUB (2 SHOWS)	UK
28 AUG	LONDON THE COUNTRY CLUB NW3	UK
29 AUG	WEALDSTONE RAILWAY HOTEL	UK
7 SEP	MANCHESTER THE MAGIC VILLAGE	UK
9 SEP	LONDON THE NAGS HEAD	UK
20 SEP	LONDON MARQUEE CLUB	UK
21 SEP	BIRMINGHAM MOTHERS	UK
23 SEP	LONDON EDMONTON COOKS FERRY INN	UK
23 SEP	LONDON WHETSTONE THE BLACK BULL	UK
11 OCT	LONDON MARQUEE CLUB	UK
15 OCT	LONDON ROYAL ALBERT HALL	UK
16 OCT	TOLWORTH THE TOBY JUG	UK
22 OCT	LONDON WOOD GREEN FISHMONGERS ARMS	UK
24 OCT	LEYTONSTONE RED LION HOTEL	UK
29 OCT	BIRMINGHAM CROWN HOTEL	UK
1 NOV	DUNSTABLE CALIFORNIA BALLROOM	UK
2 NOV	LONDON UNIVERSITY COLLEGE	UK
2 NOV	LONDON CHALK FARM ROUNDHOUSE	UK
5 NOV	WEST HAMPSTEAD KLOOKS KLEEK	UK
9 NOV	GLASTONBURY TOWN HALL	UK
15 NOV	LONDON HORNSEY WOOD TAVERN	UK
24 NOV	BIRMINGHAM MOTHERS	UK
26 NOV	LONDON MARQUEE CLUB	UK
30 NOV	LONDON SCHOOL OF ECONOMICS	UK
12 DEC	LONDON STONES ROCK'N'ROLL CIRCUS TV	UK
20 DEC	LONDON MARQUEE CLUB	UK
30 DEC	PENZANCE WINTER GARDENS	UK
1969		
2 JAN	PLYMOUTH VAN DYKE CLUB	UK
3 JAN	BOURNEMOUTH RITZ	UK
5 JAN	NOTTINGHAM BOAT CLUB	UK
6 JAN	BATH PAVILION	UK
8 JAN	TOLWORTH TOBY JUG	UK
9 JAN	STOCKHOLM KONCERTHAUS (2 SHOWS)	SWE
10 JAN	COPENHAGEN FALCONER THEATER	DEN
11 JAN	NORWICH GALA	UK
12 JAN	REDCAR JAZZ CLUB	UK
14 JAN	LONDON, SPEAKEASY CLUB	UK
15 JAN	KEELE UNIVERSITY	UK
16 JAN	WOLVERHAMPTON, LAFAYETTE CLUB	UK
18 JAN	MANCHESTER UNIVERSITY	UK
24 JAN	NEW YORK FILLMORE EAST	USA
25 JAN	NEW YORK FILLMORE EAST	USA
31 JAN	DETROIT, GRANDEE BALLROOM	USA
1 FEB	DETROIT, GRANDEE BALLROOM	USA
2 FEB	DETROIT, GRANDEE BALLROOM	USA
7 FEB	CHICAGO KINETIC PLAYGROUND	USA
8 FEB	CHICAGO KINETIC PLAYGROUND	USA
9 FEB	MINNEAPOLIS, LABOR TEMPLE	USA
13 FEB	BOSTON TEA PARTY	USA
14 FEB	BOSTON TEA PARTY	USA
15 FEB	BOSTON TEA PARTY	USA
16 FEB	BOSTON TEA PARTY	USA
20 FEB	NEW HAVEN STONE BALLROOM	USA
21 FEB	NEW HAVEN STONE BALLROOM	USA
22 FEB	NEW HAVEN STONE BALLROOM	USA
23 FEB	NEW HAVEN STONE BALLROOM	USA
1 MAR	ALEXANDRIA CITY HALL	USA
7 MAR	SEATTLE, EAGLES BALLROOM	USA
8 MAR	SEATTLE, EAGLES BALLROOM	USA
9 MAR	SEATTLE, EAGLES BALLROOM	USA

13 MAR	SAN FRANCISCO FILLMORE WEST	USA
14 MAR	SAN FRANCISCO FILLMORE WEST	USA
15 MAR	SAN FRANCISCO FILLMORE WEST	USA
16 MAR	SAN FRANCISCO FILLMORE WEST	USA
21 MAR	PASADENA ROSE PALACE	USA
22 MAR	PASADENA ROSE PALACE	USA
23 MAR	SACRAMENTO ROSE PALACE	USA
28 MAR	PHOENIX AQUARIUS THEATER	USA
29 MAR	PHOENIX AQUARIUS THEATER	USA
31 MAR	LOS ANGELES, AQUARIUS THEATER	USA
5 APR	PITTSBURGH	USA
6 APR	EVANSVILLE	USA
7 APR	DETROIT, GRANDEE BALLROOM	USA
8 APR	DETROIT, GRANDEE BALLROOM	USA
9 APR	BOSTON TEA PARTY	USA
11 APR	NEW YORK FILLMORE EAST	USA
3 MAY	FOLKSTONE, LEAS CLIFF HALL	UK
6 MAY	MANCHESTER FREE TRADE HALL	UK
7 MAY	PARIS PALAIS DES SPORTS	FRA
8 MAY	LONDON ROYAL ALBERT HALL	UK
9 MAY	BRISTOL, COLSTON HALL	UK
13 MAY	PORTSMOUTH GUILD HALL	UK
14 MAY	NEWCASTLE CITY HALL	UK
15 MAY	BIRMINGHAM TOWN HALL	UK
17 MAY	NORWICH, GALA BALLROOM	UK
23 MAY	ABERGAVENEY	UK
24 MAY	COVENTRY	UK
28 MAY	DUBLIN NATIONAL STADIUM	IRE
29 MAY	BELFAST ULSTER HALL	UK
30 MAY	CORK	IRE
31 MAY	WESTON SUPER MARE	UK
4 JUN	NOTTINGHAM SHERWOOD ROOMS	UK
5 JUN	WORTHING ASSEMBLY HALL	UK
6 JUN	PLYMOUTH VAN DYKE CLUB	UK
7 JUN	DAGENHAM ROUNDHOUSE	UK
9 JUN	CAMBRIDGE	UK
12 JUN	HULL LOCARNO	UK
13 JUN	SUNDERLAND BAY HOTEL	UK
14 JUN	MALVERN WINTER GARDENS	UK
15 JUN	WOLVERHAMPTON LAFAYETTE CLUB	UK
17 JUN	MIDDLESBOROUGH	UK
21 JUN	DEVONSHIRE DOWNS NEWPORT POP FESTIVAL	USA
24 JUN	DETROIT	USA
28 JUN	MIAMI JAZZ FESTIVAL	USA
3 JUL	NEW YORK FILLMORE EAST	USA
4 JUL	NEWPORT JAZZ FESTIVAL	USA
5 JUL	PORTLAND CITY HALL	USA
11 JUL	LAUREL SPRINGS, NEWPORT JAZZ FESTIVAL	USA
12 JUL	PHILADELPHIA, NEWPORT JAZZ FESTIVAL	USA
15 JUL	MONTICELLO	USA
16 JUL	MONTICELLO	USA
17 JUL	MONTICELLO	USA
18 JUL	CHICAGO KINETIC PLAYGROUND	USA
19 JUL	CHICAGO KINETIC PLAYGROUND	USA
22 JUL	STONEYBROOK UNIVERSITY	USA
23 JUL	BOSTON TEA PARTY	USA
24 JUL	BOSTON TEA PARTY	USA
25 JUL	BOSTON TEA PARTY	USA
26 JUL	BRUNSWICK NEWPORT JAZZ FESTIVAL	USA
28 JUL	NEW YORK CENTRAL PARK	USA
1 AUG	STA BARBARA VENTURA CTY FAIRGROUNDS	USA
2 AUG	SEATTLE EAGLES BALLROOM	USA
3 AUG	SEATTLE EAGLES BALLROOM	USA
8 AUG	SAN BERNADINO SWING AUDITORIUM	USA
9 AUG	ANAHEIM CONVENTION CENTER	USA
10 AUG	SAN DIEGO SPORTS ARENA	USA
12 AUG	SAN FRANCISCO FILLMORE WEST	USA
14 AUG	SAN FRANCISCO FILLMORE WEST	USA
15 AUG	SAN ANTONIO	USA
16 AUG	HOUSTON	USA
25 SEP	NEWCASTLE CITY HALL	UK
26 SEP	EDINBURGH, USHER HALL	UK
27 SEP	DUBLIN, NATIONAL STADIUM	IRE
29 SEP	BELFAST, ULSTER HALL	UK
1 OCT	LONDON, ROYAL ALBERT HALL	UK
2 OCT	MANCHESTER FREE TRADE HALL	UK
3 OCT	BRIGHTON DOME	UK
6 OCT	HULL CITY HALL	UK
7 OCT	LEEDS TOWN HALL	UK
8 OCT	BIRMINGHAM TOWN HALL	UK
10 OCT	AMSTERDAM CONCERTGEBOUW	NED
11 OCT	ANTWERP TOWN HALL	BEL
12 OCT	PARIS CITY HALL	FRA
15 OCT	SHEFFIELD CITY HALL	UK
19 OCT	CAMBRIDGE REX CINEMA	UK
20 OCT	SOUTHAMPTON GUILDHALL	UK
21 OCT	BRISTOL COLSTON HALL	UK
23 OCT	LEICESTER DE MONTFORT HALL	UK
25 OCT	PLYMOUTH GUILDHALL	UK
26 OCT	OXFORD TOWN HALL	UK
29 OCT	NORWICH, ST ANDREWS HALL	UK
14 NOV	MADISON DANE COUNTY COLISEUM	USA
15 NOV	SAN DIEGO COMMUNITY CONCOURSE	USA
20 NOV	SAN FRANCISCO FILLMORE WEST	USA
21 NOV	SAN FRANCISCO FILLMORE WEST	USA
22 NOV	SAN FRANCISCO FILLMORE WEST	USA
23 NOV	SAN FRANCISCO FILLMORE WEST	USA
26 NOV	SANTA MONICA CIVIC AUDITORIUM	USA
27 NOV	SAN DIEGO	USA
28 NOV	DETROIT RIVIERA THEATRE	USA
29 NOV	DETROIT RIVIERA THEATRE	USA
30 NOV	PHILADELPHIA SPECTRUM	USA
5 DEC	NEW YORK FILLMORE EAST (2 SHOWS)	USA
6 DEC	NEW YORK FILLMORE EAST (2 SHOWS)	USA
7 DEC	AMHERST UNIV OF MASSACHUSETTS	USA
8 DEC	BOSTON TEA PARTY	USA
9 DEC	BOSTON TEA PARTY	USA
10 DEC	KANSAS CITY SOLDIERS & SAILORS AUD	USA
11 DEC	HOUSTON MUSIC HALL (2 SHOWS)	USA
12 DEC	SAN ANTONIO MUNICIPAL AUDITORIUM	USA
13 DEC	AUSTIN	USA
14 DEC	CHICAGO ARAGON BALLROOM	USA
1970		
16 JAN	ODENSE	DEN
17 JAN	COPENHAGEN K.B. HALLEN	DEN
19 JAN	HELSINKI	FIN
20 JAN	STOCKHOLM KONGLIGLA TENNIS HALLEN	SWE
21 JAN	GOTHENBERG KONSERTHUSET	SWE
22 JAN	GOTHENBERG KONSERTHUSET	SWE
21 FEB	FRANKFURT JAHRHUNDERTHALLE	GER

Date	Venue	Country
5 APR	NUREMBERG	GER
7 APR	HAMBURG MUSICHALLE	GER
17 APR	DENVER MAMMOTH GARDENS	USA
18 APR	DENVER MAMMOTH GARDENS	USA
19 APR	LONG BEACH ARENA	USA
20 APR	HONOLULU CIVIC AUDITORIUM	USA
22 APR	SANTA BARBARA	USA
24 APR	SAN BERNARDINO SWING AUDITORIUM	USA
25 APR	SAN DIEGO CONVENTION HALL	USA
26 APR	SANTA CLARA	USA
28 APR	HONOLULU	USA
30 APR	SAN FRANCISCO FILLMORE WEST	USA
1 MAY	SAN FRANCISCO FILLMORE WEST	USA
2 MAY	SAN FRANCISCO FILLMORE WEST	USA
3 MAY	DEVONSHIRE DOWNS	USA
7 MAY	TUSCON	USA
8 MAY	PHOENIX	USA
9 MAY	LAS VEGAS	USA
10 MAY	ST LOUIS	USA
13 MAY	DALLAS	USA
14 MAY	HOUSTON MUSIC HALL	USA
15 MAY	AUSTIN	USA
16 MAY	MIAMI UNIVERSITY	USA
17 MAY	CAPE KENNEDY	USA
20 MAY	HARTFORD	USA
21 MAY	NEW YORK FILMORE EAST	USA
22 MAY	NEW YORK FILMORE EAST	USA
23 MAY	NEW YORK FILMORE EAST	USA
24 MAY	MONTREAL THE AUTOSTADE	CAN
28 MAY	DELAWARE SELBY STADIUM	USA
29 MAY	DETROIT EAST TOWN THEATER	USA
30 MAY	DETROIT EAST TOWN THEATER	USA
31 MAY	MINNEAPOLIS	USA
5 JUN	CHICAGO ARAGON BALLROOM	USA
6 JUN	CLEVELAND	USA
3 JUL	SOUTHAMPTON	USA
7 JUL	TANGLEWOOD	USA
8 JUL	PHILADELPHIA SPECTRUM	USA
10 JUL	BOSTON TEA PARTY	USA
11 JUL	BOSTON TEA PARTY	USA
13 JUL	SHADY GROVE	USA
14 JUL	DETROIT	USA
17 JUL	NEW YORK RANDALLS ISLAND FESTIVAL	USA
18 JUL	NEW ORLEANS WAREHOUSE	USA
22 JUL	WEST PALM BEACH	USA
24 JUL	TAMPA	USA
25 JUL	MIAMI	USA
26 JUL	JACKSONVILLE	USA
27 JUL	WESTBURY	USA
28 JUL	PORCHESTER CAPITOL THEATER	USA
3 AUG	NEW YORK CENTRAL PARK	USA
5 AUG	NEW YORK FILLMORE EAST	USA
7 AUG	TORONTO FESTIVAL	CAN
9 AUG	GOOSE LAKE PARK	USA
10 AUG	DENVER RED ROCKS AMPHITHEATER	USA
11 AUG	VANCOUVER COLISEUM	USA
15 AUG	WISCONSIN LAKE GENEVA	USA
16 AUG	CHICAGO ARAGON BALLROOM	USA
30 AUG	ISLE OF WIGHT FESTIVAL	UK
23 SEP	SHEFFIELD CITY HALL	UK
24 SEP	NOTTINGHAM ALBERT HALL	UK
25 SEP	BIRMINGHAM TOWN HALL (2 SHOWS)	UK
27 SEP	NEWCASTLE CITY HALL	UK
28 SEP	LEICESTER DE MONTFORT HALL	UK
30 SEP	ABERDEEN MUSIC HALL	UK
1 OCT	DUNDEE CAIRD HALL	UK
2 OCT	GLASGOW PLAYHOUSE CINEMA	UK
3 OCT	MANCHESTER FREE TRADE HALL	UK
4 OCT	BRISTOL COLSTON HALL	UK
9 OCT	SOUTHAMPTON GUILDHALL	UK
10 OCT	PARIS OLYMPIA	FRA
13 OCT	LONDON ROYAL ALBERT HALL	UK
16 OCT	SACRAMENTO	USA
17 OCT	BERKLEY COMMUNITY THEATER	USA
18 OCT	LOS ANGELES FORUM	USA
20 OCT	PHOENIX	USA
22 OCT	SAN BERNARDINO	USA
23 OCT	CORVALLIS	USA
24 OCT	SEATTLE	USA
29 OCT	DETROIT	USA
30 OCT	PITTSBURGH	USA
31 OCT	SYRACUSE WAR MEMORIAL	USA
1 NOV	RICHMOND	USA
3 NOV	WILKES BARRE COMERFORD THEATRE (2)	USA
4 NOV	NEW YORK CARNEGIE HALL	USA
5 NOV	PROVIDENCE	USA
6 NOV	MANCHESTER	USA
7 NOV	EAST LANSING MICHIGAN STATE UNIVERSITY	USA
8 NOV	ST LOUIS	USA
9 NOV	COLUMBUS	USA
10 NOV	DEREA	USA
11 NOV	CANTON	USA
12 NOV	BUFFALO	USA
13 NOV	SCHENECTADY	USA
14 NOV	ROCHESTER	USA
15 NOV	PLATTSBURGH	USA

1971

Date	Venue	Country
7 JAN	ODENSE	DEN
7 JAN	ODENSE	DEN
8 JAN	ARHUS	DEN
9 JAN	COPENHAGEN K.B. HALLEN	DEN
10 JAN	GOTHENBURG	SWE
11 JAN	OSLO	NOR
12 JAN	BERGEN KOUSERPALAST	NOR
14 JAN	STOCKHOLM	SWE
15 JAN	COPENHAGEN TIVOLI KONSERTSAL	DEN
16 JAN	HOLSTED	DEN
17 JAN	HAMBURG MUSIKHALLE	GER
18 JAN	DUSSELDORF RHEINHALLE	GER
19 JAN	STUTTGART SPORTHALLE BOBLINGEN	GER
20 JAN	NUREMBERG	GER
21 JAN	VIENNA KONZERTHAUS	AUT
22 JAN	MUNICH DEUTCHES MUSEUM	GER
23 JAN	FRANKFURT KONGRESSHAUS	GER
24 JAN	BERLIN DEUTSCHLANDHALLE	GER
25 JAN	WOLLSBURG STADTHALLE	GER
26 JAN	MUNSTER MUNSTERLANDHALLE	GER
27 JAN	DORTMUND WESTFALENHALLE	GER
28 JAN	HEIDELBERG STADTHALLE	GER
29 JAN	FREIBURG STADTHALLE	GER

30 JAN	MONTREUX	SWI		18 OCT	NEW YORK MADISON SQUARE GARDEN	USA
1 FEB	MILAN TEATRO SMERALDO	ITA		19 OCT	CORVALLIS GILL COLISEUM	USA
2 FEB	ROME	ITA		20 OCT	LOWELL TECHNICAL COLLEGE	USA
26 FEB	LONDON GAUMONT STATE THEATRE (2 SHOWS)	UK		21 OCT	PITTSBURGH CIVIC ARENA	USA
28 FEB	LONDON GAUMONT STATE THEATRE (2 SHOWS)	UK		22 OCT	DETROIT	USA
3 MAR	BRIGHTON DOME	UK		23 OCT	COLUMBUS VETERANS AUDITORIUM	USA
5 MAR	BOURNEMOUTH WINTER GARDENS	UK		24 OCT	DAYTON	USA
7 MAR	PLYMOUTH GUILDHALL (2 SHOWS)	UK		25 OCT	TOLEDO SPORTS ARENA	USA
11 MAR	LEEDS TOWN HALL	UK		26 OCT	CHICAGO AMPHITHEATRE	USA
12 MAR	STOKE ON TRENT VICTORIA GUILDHALL	UK		27 OCT	NEW HAVEN ARENA	USA
13 MAR	LIVERPOOL MOUNTFORD HALL (2 SHOWS)	UK		30 OCT	ROCHESTER WAR MEMORIAL	USA
14 MAR	BLACKPOOL OPERA HOUSE	UK		31 OCT	BINGHAMPTON	USA
19 MAR	EDINBURGH EMPIRE THEATRE	UK		1 NOV	BUFFALO	USA
20 MAR	SUNDERLAND EMPIRE THEATRE (2 SHOWS)	UK		6 NOV	DURHAM	USA
1 APR	MINNEAPOLIS	USA		10 NOV	FLINT	USA
2 APR	CHICAGO CIVIC OPERA HOUSE	USA		11 NOV	MEMPHIS	USA
3 APR	ST LOUIS	USA		12 NOV	LOUISVILLE CONVENTION CENTER	USA
4 APR	BALTIMORE	USA		13 NOV	CLEVELAND PUBLIC HALL	USA
13 APR	ATLANTA	USA		14 NOV	ALBANY	USA
14 APR	MILWAUKEE UHLEIN (2 SHOWS)	USA		15 NOV	BOSTON TEA GARDENS	USA
16 APR	MIAMI	USA		18 NOV	NEW YORK MADISON SQUARE GARDEN	USA
17 APR	MIAMI	USA		**1972**		
18 APR	ROANOKE	USA		6 JAN	HOLSTED	DEN
20 APR	DETROIT	USA		8 JAN	COPENHAGEN K.B. HALLEN (2 SHOWS)	DEN
24 APR	WEST LONG BRANCH	USA		9 JAN	GOTHENBURG KONSERTHUSET	SWE
25 APR	STONEYBROOK	USA		10 JAN	OSLO KONSERTHUSET	NOR
26 APR	GREENVILLE	USA		11 JAN	STOCKHOLM	SWE
27 APR	PORT CHESTER	USA		14 JAN	LUND	SWE
29 APR	DELHI	USA		15 JAN	COPENHAGEN TIVOLI KONSERTSAL	DEN
1 MAY	PHILADELPHIA	USA		16 JAN	COPENHAGEN TIVOLI KONSERTSAL	DEN
2 MAY	KUTZTOWN	USA		17 JAN	MUNSTER MUNSTERLANDHALLE	GER
4 MAY	NEW YORK	USA		18 JAN	BERLIN DEUTSCHLANDHALLE	GER
5 MAY	NEW YORK FILLMORE EAST	USA		19 JAN	HAMBURG CONGRESS CENTRUM HALLE	GER
9 JUN	SALT LAKE CITY SALT PALACE	USA		20 JAN	LUBECK HANSAHALLE	GER
10 JUN	DENVER RED ROCKS AMPHITHEATER	USA		21 JAN	ESSEN GRUGAHALLE	GER
11 JUN	ALBUQUERQUE	USA		22 JAN	OFFERBURG STADTHALLE	GER
12 JUN	HONOLULU HIC ARENA	USA		23 JAN	NUREMBERG	GER
16 JUN	SAN DIEGO	USA		24 JAN	VIENNA KONZERHAUS	AUT
17 JUN	SAN DIEGO	USA		26 JAN	LUDWIGSHAFEN FREDERICH EBERTHALLE	GER
18 JUN	LOS ANGELES FORUM	USA		27 JAN	HANNOVER KUPPELSAAL	GER
19 JUN	ANAHEIM CONVENTION CENTER	USA		28 JAN	OFFENBURG OBERHEIMHALLE	GER
20 JUN	BERKLEY COMMUNITY THEATER	USA		29 JAN	ZURICH HALLENSTADION	SWI
24 JUN	EDMONTON	CAN		30 JAN	BERNE FESTHALLE	SWI
25 JUN	VANCOUVER	CAN		31 JAN	MILAN	ITA
26 JUN	SEATTLE COLISEUM	USA		1 FEB	ROME PALASPORT	ITA
27 JUN	NEW HAVEN	USA		2 FEB	NAPOLI	ITA
29 JUN	KANSAS CITY AUDITORIUM	USA		3 FEB	BOULOGNE	FRA
30 JUN	OKLAHOMA CITY STATE FAIRGROUNDS	USA		4 FEB	NOVARA PALASPORT	ITA
1 JUL	SAN ANTONIO	USA		5 FEB	LYONS PALAIS DES SPORTS	FRA
2 JUL	DALLAS MEMORIAL COLISEUM	USA		6 FEB	PARIS	FRA
3 JUL	HOUSTON	USA		11 FEB	ROTTERDAM DE DOELEN	NED
4 JUL	NEW ORLEANS	USA		12 FEB	AMSTERDAM CONCERTGEBOUW	NED
5 JUL	VANCOUVER COLISEUM	CAN		2 MAR	PORTSMOUTH GUILDHALL	UK
9 JUL	WILDWOOD	CAN		3 MAR	EXETER ABC	UK
10 JUL	ASBURY PARK CONVENTION HALL	USA		4 MAR	PLYMOUTH GUILDHALL	UK
11 JUL	ALEXANDRIA ROLLER RINK	USA		5 MAR	BRISTOL COLSTON HALL	UK
29 JUL	PORT CHESTER	USA		6 MAR	BIRMINGHAM TOWN HALL	UK
15 OCT	ST PETERSBURG BAYFRONT CENTER	USA		7 MAR	NEWCASTLE CITY HALL	UK
16 OCT	SPRINGFIELD CIVIC CENTER	USA		8 MAR	YORK CENTRAL HALL	UK
17 OCT	COLUMBIA	USA		10 MAR	BOURNEMOUTH WINTER GARDENS	UK

11 MAR	SHEFFIELD CITY HALL	UK		17 JUN	LAS VEGAS	USA
13 MAR	NORWICH ST ANDREWS HALL	UK		18 JUN	DALLAS MEMORIAL COLISEUM	USA
14 MAR	LEICESTER DE MONTFORT HALL	UK		19 JUN	FORT WORTH	USA
15 MAR	BRADFORD ST GEORGES HALL	UK		20 JUN	SAN ANTONIO	USA
16 MAR	STOKE ON TRENT VICTORIA HALL	UK		21 JUN	EL PASO	USA
17 MAR	STOCKTON ABC CINEMA	UK		22 JUN	ALBUQUERQUE	USA
19 MAR	WOLVERHAMPTON CIVIC HALL	UK		23 JUN	LOS ANGELES	USA
20 MAR	OXFORD TOWN HALL	UK		24 JUN	LOS ANGELES	USA
21 MAR	LONDON ROYAL ALBERT HALL	UK		25 JUN	SAN DIEGO SPORTS ARENA	USA
22 MAR	LONDON ROYAL ALBERT HALL	UK		26 JUN	TUCSON	USA
24 MAR	EDINBURGH EMPIRE THEATRE	UK		27 JUN	PHOENIX	USA
25 MAR	DUNDEE CAIRD HALL	UK		28 JUN	SALT LAKE CITY SALT PALACE	USA
26 MAR	GLASGOW PLAYHOUSE CINEMA	UK		29 JUN	HONOLULU HIC ARENA	USA
27 MAR	LIVERPOOL STADIUM	UK		30 JUN	DENVER COLISEUM	USA
28 MAR	MANCHESTER FREE TRADE HALL	UK		5 JUL	AUKLAND TOWN HALL	NZ
29 MAR	LONDON ROYAL ALBERT HALL	UK		7 JUL	MELBOURNE	AUS
14 APR	MONTREAL	CAN		9 JUL	MELBOURNE	AUS
15 APR	ITHACA	USA		11 JUL	SYDNEY HORDEN PAVILLION	AUS
16 APR	SYRACUSE	USA		14 JUL	BRISBANE FESTIVAL HALL	AUS
17 APR	FRANKFURT	USA		15 JUL	TOKYO KOSEINEMHIN HALL	JAP
18 APR	LORAIN	USA		16 JUL	TOKYO BUDOKAN	JAP
19 APR	FAYETTEVILLE	USA		17 JUL	TOKYO BUDOKAN	JAP
20 APR	RALIEGH	USA		13 OCT	BUFFALO MEMORIAL AUDITORIUM	USA
21 APR	TUSCALOOSA	USA		14 OCT	ROCHESTER WAR MEMORIAL	USA
22 APR	HAMPTON NORFOLK SCOPE	USA		15 OCT	BANGOR AUDITORIUM	USA
23 APR	SALEM	USA		16 OCT	SPRINGFIELD CIVIC CENTER	USA
24 APR	BOWLING GREEN	USA		17 OCT	PITTSBURGH	USA
25 APR	MORGANTOWN	USA		18 OCT	CHARLESTON	USA
26 APR	BLACKSBURG	USA		19 OCT	COLUMBUS	USA
27 APR	ATLANTA	USA		21 OCT	CLEVELAND	USA
28 APR	ATHENS UNIVERSITY OF GEORGIA	USA		22 OCT	MEMPHIS	USA
29 APR	WEST PALM BEACH	USA		23 OCT	LITTLE ROCK BARTON COLISEUM	USA
30 APR	MIAMI	USA		24 OCT	NASHVILLE MUNICIPAL AUDITORIUM	USA
1 MAY	NEW ORLEANS	USA		25 OCT	LOUISVILLE CONVENTION CENTER	USA
2 MAY	INDIANAPOLIS	USA		26 OCT	BOWLING GREEN	USA
3 MAY	MADISON DANE COUNTY COLISEUM	USA		27 OCT	JACKSON	USA
4 MAY	CARBONDALE SOUTHERN ILLINOIS UNIVERSITY	USA		28 OCT	BATON ROUGE	USA
5 MAY	ST LOUIS KIEL CONVENTION HALL	USA		29 OCT	MACON	USA
6 MAY	KNOXVILLE	USA		30 OCT	PHILADELPHIA	USA
7 MAY	CHICAGO	USA		31 OCT	PHILADELPHIA	USA
8 MAY	DETROIT	USA		1 NOV	BOSTON TEA GARDENS	USA
9 MAY	CINCINNATI THE GARDENS	USA		2 NOV	BOSTON TEA GARDENS	USA
10 MAY	HERSHEY	USA		3 NOV	ST PETERSBURG BAYFRONT CENTER	USA
11 MAY	PHILADELPHIA	USA		4 NOV	MIAMI BEACH CONVENTION HALL	USA
12 MAY	BOSTON TEA GARDENS	USA		5 NOV	JACKSONVILLE	USA
13 MAY	NASSAU VETERANS MEMORIAL COLISEUM	USA		6 NOV	WAYNE	USA
14 MAY	NASSAU VETERANS MEMORIAL COLISEUM	USA		8 NOV	DETROIT COBO HALL	USA
2 JUN	QUEBEC COLISEUM	CAN		9 NOV	DETROIT COBO HALL	USA
3 JUN	OTTAWA CIVIC CENTER	CAN		10 NOV	CHICAGO STADIUM	USA
4 JUN	TORONTO MAPLE LEAF GARDENS	CAN		11 NOV	CHICAGO STADIUM	USA
6 JUN	MILWAUKEE ARENA	USA		12 NOV	BALTIMORE CIVIC CENTER	USA
7 JUN	DULUTH	USA		13 NOV	NEW YORK MADISON SQUARE GARDEN	USA
8 JUN	EDMONTON THE GARDENS	CAN		**1973**		
9 JUN	CALGARY STAMPEDE CORRAL	CAN		2 FEB	FRANKFURT FESTHALLE	GER
10 JUN	VANCOUVER PACIFIC COLISEUM	CAN		4 FEB	ZURICH HALLENSTADION	SWI
11 JUN	SEATTLE	USA		2 MAR	GOTHENBURG	SWE
12 JUN	PORTLAND	USA		4 MAR	COPENHAGEN TIVOLI KONSERTSAL	DEN
14 JUN	OKLAHOMA CITY STATE FAIRGROUNDS	USA		6 MAR	HAMBURG CONGRESS CENTRUM HALLE	GER
15 JUN	KANSAS CITY MUNICIPAL AUDITORIUM	USA		7 MAR	HAMBURG	GER
16 JUN	OAKLAND	USA		8 MAR	MUNSTER MUNSTERLANDHALLE	GER

9 MAR	DUSSELDORF	GER	3 SEP	MADISON		USA
11 MAR	BERLIN DEUTSCHLANDHALE	GER	4 SEP	CHICAGO STADIUM		USA
13 MAR	MUNICH	GER	5 SEP	CHICAGO STADIUM		USA
15 MAR	VIENNA	AUT	6 SEP	DETROIT COBO ARENA		USA
16 MAR	ROME	ITA	8 SEP	CLEVELAND PUBLIC ARENA		USA
18 MAR	BOLOGNA PALASPORT	ITA	9 SEP	CLEVELAND		USA
19 MAR	BOLOGNA PALASPORT	ITA	10 SEP	ROCHESTER		USA
20 MAR	MILAN	ITA	11 SEP	PITTSBURGH CIVIC ARENA		USA
26 MAR	DUSSELDORF PHILLIPSHALLE	GER	12 SEP	PITTSBURGH		USA
4 MAY	TUSCALOOSA	USA	13 SEP	DETROIT COBO HALL		USA
5 MAY	CLEMSON	USA	14 SEP	DETROIT		USA
7 MAY	HERSHEY	USA	15 SEP	MILWAUKEE ARENA		USA
9 MAY	OXFORD, OH	USA	18 SEP	NEW ORLEANS		USA
11 MAY	HAMPTON NORFOLK SCOPE	USA	19 SEP	NEW ORLEANS		USA
13 MAY	KNOXVILLE	USA	20 SEP	MOBILE		USA
14 MAY	LOUISVILLE CONVENTION CENTER	USA	21 SEP	JACKSONVILLE		USA
15 MAY	EAST LANSING MSU TENISON FIELD HOUSE	USA	22 SEP	ST PETERSBURG BAYFRONT CENTER		USA
16 MAY	MEMPHIS	USA	23 SEP	MIAMI		USA
17 MAY	DENVER HOFSTRA UNIVERSITY	USA	24 SEP	MIAMI JAI ALAI FRONTON		USA
18 MAY	RICHMOND	USA	26 SEP	ROANOKE		USA
19 MAY	GREENSBORO	USA	27 SEP	SPRINGFIELD CIVIC CENTER		USA
20 MAY	ATLANTA	USA	28 SEP	BOSTON TEA GARDENS		USA
21 MAY	NASHVILLE	USA	29 SEP	BOSTON TEA GARDENS		USA
22 MAY	INDIANAPOLIS	USA	**1974**			
23 MAY	ST LOUIS KIEL CONVENTION HALL	USA	25 JUL	ADELAIDE CENTINAL HALL		AUS
24 MAY	ST LOUIS KIEL CONVENTION HALL	USA	28 JUL	MELBOURNE FESTIVAL HALL		AUS
29 MAY	KITCHENER	USA	30 JUL	SYDNEY OPERA HOUSE		AUS
30 MAY	TORONTO MAPLE LEAF GARDENS	CAN	31 JUL	SYDNEY OPERA HOUSE		AUS
31 MAY	OTTOWA	CAN	1 AUG	BRISBANE FESTIVAL HALL		AUS
2 JUN	MONTREAL FORUM	CAN	2 AUG	BRISBANE FESTIVAL HALL		AUS
22 JUN	LONDON EMPIRE POOL WEMBLEY	UK	3 AUG	SYDNEY HORDERN PAVILION		AUS
23 JUN	LONDON EMPIRE POOL WEMBLEY	UK	4 AUG	SYDNEY HORDERN PAVILION		AUS
30 JUN	BUFFALO MEMORIAL AUDITORIUM	USA	5 AUG	SYDNEY HORDERN PAVILION		AUS
4 JUL	KANSAS CITY MUNICIPAL AUDITORIUM	USA	7 AUG	DETROIT COBO HALL		USA
7 JUL	BERKLEY COMMUNITY THEATRE	USA	8 AUG	DETROIT COBO HALL		USA
8 JUL	ALBUQUERQUE	USA	10 AUG	AUKLAND		NZ
9 JUL	DENVER COLISEUM	USA	11 AUG	AUKLAND		NZ
10 JUL	OKLAHOMA CITY STATE FAIR ARENA	USA	12 AUG	CHRISTCHURCH TOWN STAGE HALL		NZ
12 JUL	DALLAS MEMORIAL AUDITORIUM	USA	13 AUG	CHRISTCHURCH TOWN STAGE HALL		NZ
14 JUL	HOUSTON	USA	23 AUG	TOKYO NHK HALL		JAP
15 JUL	HOUSTON	USA	24 AUG	TOKYO NHK HALL		JAP
16 JUL	FORT WORTH CONVENTION CENTER	USA	25 AUG	TOKYO NHK HALL		JAP
18 JUL	LOS ANGELES	USA	26 AUG	TOKYO NHK HALL		JAP
19 JUL	SAN DIEGO SPORTS ARENA	USA	28 AUG	TOKYO NHK HALL		JAP
20 JUL	LOS ANGELES FORUM	USA	12 OCT	ROTTERDAM AHOY HALL		NED
21 JUL	LOS ANGELES FORUM	USA	13 OCT	BRUSSELS VORST NATIONAL		BEL
22 JUL	LOS ANGELES FORUM	USA	14 OCT	BRUSSELS VORST NATIONAL		BEL
23 JUL	OAKLAND	USA	16 OCT	GLENOBLE		FRA
24 JUL	VANCOUVER COLISEUM	CAN	17 OCT	GLENOBLE		FRA
25 JUL	SEATTLE COLISEUM	USA	18 OCT	MARSEILLE		FRA
26 JUL	SEATTLE COLISEUM	USA	23 OCT	MADRID		ESP
27 JUL	SEATTLE	USA	24 OCT	MADRID		ESP
28 JUL	SALT LAKE CITY SALT PALACE	USA	9 NOV	EDINBURGH USHER HALL		UK
26 AUG	BALTIMORE	USA	10 NOV	EDINBURGH USHER HALL		UK
27 AUG	BALTIMORE	USA	11 NOV	GLASGOW APOLLO CENTRE		UK
28 AUG	NEW YORK MADISON SQUARE GARDEN	USA	12 NOV	GLASGOW APOLLO CENTRE		UK
29 AUG	NEW YORK MADISON SQUARE GARDEN	USA	13 NOV	NEWCASTLE ODEON		UK
30 AUG	PROVIDENCE CIVIC CENTER	USA	14 NOV	LONDON RAINBOW THEATRE		UK
31 AUG	NASSAU COLISEUM	USA	15 NOV	LONDON RAINBOW THEATRE		UK
1 SEP	UNIONDALE	USA	16 NOV	LONDON RAINBOW THEATRE		UK

17 NOV	LONDON RAINBOW THEATRE	UK	13 MAR	BOSTON TEA GARDENS	USA
18 NOV	BRISTOL COLSTON HALL	UK	30 MAR	BERLIN DEUTSCHLANDHALLE	GER
19 NOV	BIRMINGHAM ODEON	UK	1 APR	KIEL OSTSEEHALLE	GER
20 NOV	BIRMINGHAM ODEON	UK	6 APR	FRANKFURST FESTHALLE	GER
21 NOV	LIVERPOOL EMPIRE THEATRE	UK	7 APR	COLOGNE SPORTHALLE	GER
22 NOV	MANCHESTER OPERA HOUSE	UK	8 APR	ESSEN GRUGAHALLE	GER
23 NOV	MANCHESTER OPERA HOUSE	UK	9 APR	KARLSRUHE SCHARTZWALDHALLE	GER
24 NOV	OXFORD NEW THEATRE	UK	10 APR	LUDWIGSHAFEN EBERTHALLE	GER
25 NOV	CARDIFF CAPITOL	UK	11 APR	FRANKFURT FESTHALLE	GER
26 NOV	SOUTHAMPTON GAUMONT THEATRE	UK	13 APR	FRANKFURT FESTHALLE	GER
30 NOV	GOTHENBURG	SWE	14 APR	FRANKFURT FESTHALLE	GER
1 DEC	MALMO	SWE	15 APR	BELGRADE PIONIR HALL	YUG
2 DEC	LUND OLYMPEN	SWE	16 APR	LINZ	AUT
4 DEC	COPENHAGEN FALKONERTEATRET	DEN	17 APR	VIENNA WIENSTADTHALLE	AUT
5 DEC	COPENHAGEN FALKONERTEATRET	DEN	18 APR	MUNICH OLYMPIAHALLE	GER
1975			20 APR	ZURICH HALLENSTADION	SWI
17 JAN	ASHVILLE CIVIC CENTER	USA	29 JUN	HAMBURG CONGRESS CENTRUM HALL	GER
19 JAN	TUSCALOOSA	USA	30 JUN	MUNSTER MUNSTERLANDHALLE	GER
20 JAN	ATLANTA THE OMNI	USA	1 JUL	MUNSTER MUNSTERLANDHALLE	GER
21 JAN	MEMPHIS MID SOUTH COLISEUM	USA	2 JUL	DUSSELDORF	GER
22 JAN	OKLAHOMA CITY STATE FAIRGROUNDS	USA	3 JUL	BOBLINGEN SPORTSHALLE BOBLINGEN	GER
23 JAN	FORT WORTH	USA	5 JUL	PARIS	FRA
24 JAN	SAN ANTONIO	USA	24 JUL	VANCOUVER	CAN
26 JAN	TULSA ASSEMBLEY CENTER	USA	26 JUL	TOLEDO PONTIAC STADIUM	USA
27 JAN	DALLAS TERRANT CTY CONVENTION CENTER	USA	27 JUL	SEATTLE COLISEUM	USA
28 JAN	KANSAS CITY KEMPER ARENA	USA	28 JUL	OAKLAND	USA
29 JAN	ST LOUIS THE ARENA	USA	1 AUG	DALLAS MEMORIAL AUDITORIUM	USA
31 JAN	SAN DIEGO SPORTS ARENA	USA	2 AUG	HOUSTON COLISEUM	USA
1 FEB	SAN DIEGO SPORTS ARENA	USA	3 AUG	NEW YORK MADISON SQUARE GARDEN	USA
2 FEB	FRESNO	USA	5 AUG	NASHVILLE MUNICIPAL AUDITORIUM	USA
3 FEB	LOS ANGELES FORUM	USA	10 AUG	GREENSBORO	USA
4 FEB	LOS ANGELES FORUM	USA	11 AUG	LOUISVILLE THE GARDENS	USA
5 FEB	TUCSON	USA	13 AUG	RICHMOND COLISEUM	USA
6 FEB	EL PASO	USA	15 AUG	ROANOKE	USA
8 FEB	LOS ANGELES FORUM	USA	16 AUG	CHARLOTTE	USA
9 FEB	LOS ANGELES FORUM	USA	17 AUG	MACON	USA
10 FEB	LOS ANGELES FORUM	USA	18 AUG	HUNTSVILLE CIVIC CENTER	USA
16 FEB	MADISON	USA	19 AUG	COLUMBUS	USA
17 FEB	MINNEAPOLIS	USA	20 AUG	KNOXVILLE	USA
18 FEB	CHAMPAIGN	USA	21 AUG	JOHNSON CITY	USA
19 FEB	CHICAGO	USA	23 AUG	JACKSON, MS	USA
20 FEB	CHICAGO STADIUM	USA	24 AUG	LITTLE ROCK	USA
21 FEB	CLEVELAND	USA	25 AUG	JACKSON, IN	USA
23 FEB	NIAGARA FALLS CONVENTION CENTER	USA	26 AUG	MOBILE	USA
24 FEB	SYRACUSE	USA	27 AUG	ST PETERSBURG BAYFRONT CENTER	USA
25 FEB	PHILADELPHIA	USA	28 AUG	MIAMI JAI ALAI FRONTON	USA
26 FEB	PHILADELPHIA	USA	29 AUG	MIAMI JAI ALAI FRONTON	USA
27 FEB	HERSHEY	USA	30 AUG	TAMPA LAKELAND	USA
28 FEB	HAMPTON VALLEY	USA	3 SEP	EAST LANSING	USA
2 MAR	NEW HAVEN	USA	26 SEP	BUFFALO WAR MEMORIAL AUDITORIUM	USA
3 MAR	NASSAU	USA	27 SEP	BUFFALO WAR MEMORIAL AUDITORIUM	USA
4 MAR	NASSAU	USA	28 SEP	VANCOUVER PACIFIC COLISEUM	CAN
5 MAR	PITTSBURGH	USA	29 SEP	MONTREAL FORUM	CAN
6 MAR	PROVIDENCE CIVIC CENTER	USA	1 OCT	WASHINGTON	USA
7 MAR	NEW YORK MADISON SQUARE GARDEN	USA	2 OCT	BINGHAMPTON	USA
8 MAR	PHILADELPHIA SPECTRUM	USA	4 OCT	CINCINNATI	USA
9 MAR	BALTIMORE CIVIC CENTER	USA	5 OCT	DETROIT COBO ARENA	USA
10 MAR	NEW YORK	USA	6 OCT	DETROIT COBO ARENA	USA
11 MAR	SPRINGFIELD CIVIC CENTER	USA	7 OCT	TORONTO MAPLE LEAF GARDENS	CAN
12 MAR	BOSTON TEA GARDENS	USA	8 OCT	KALAMAZOO WINGS STADIUM	USA

9 OCT	DETROIT COBO ARENA	USA
12 OCT	EAST LANSING	USA
13 OCT	DES MOINES VETERANS STADIUM	USA
15 OCT	EVANSTON MAGAW HALL	USA
16 OCT	DEKALB EVANS FIELD HOUSE	USA
17 OCT	TERRE HAUTE INDIANA STATE UNIVERSITY	USA
18 OCT	MANHATTAN	USA
19 OCT	MORRISON	USA
21 OCT	BLOOMINGTON HORTON FIELD HOUSE	USA
22 OCT	TOLEDO	USA
23 OCT	EASTON	USA
26 OCT	IONA CITY	USA
27 OCT	MILWAUKEE ARENA	USA
28 OCT	MADISON	USA
29 OCT	ORNAKA	USA
2 NOV	ATHENS	USA
1976		
1 MAY	BRUSSELS VOREST NATIONAL	BEL
3 MAY	PARIS	FRA
5 MAY	ROTTERDAM AHOY HALL	NED
8 MAY	STOCKHOLM KONSERTHUSET	SWE
9 MAY	STOCKHOLM KONSERTHUSET	SWE
10 MAY	COPENHAGEN TIVOLI KONSERTSAL	SWE
12 MAY	HAMBURG CONGRESS CENTRUM HALLE	GER
14 MAY	FRANKFURT	GER
15 MAY	MUNICH OLYMPIAHALLE	GER
16 MAY	ZURICH HALLENSTADION	GER
18 MAY	BARCELONA	ESP
20 MAY	MADRID PABELLON DEPORTIVO	ESP
15 JUL	PROVIDENCE CIVIC CENTER	USA
16 JUL	HARTFORD COLT PARK	USA
18 JUL	WASHINGTON CAPITAL CENTER	USA
19 JUL	PHILADELPHIA	USA
21 JUL	BOSTON TEA GARDENS	USA
23 JUL	NEW YORK SHEA STADIUM	USA
25 JUL	DETROIT PONTIAC STADIUM	USA
27 JUL	CINCINNATI RIVERFRONT COLISEUM	USA
28 JUL	LOUISVILLE CONVENTION CENTER	USA
29 JUL	ATLANTA	USA
31 JUL	TAMPA STADIUM	USA
3 AUG	CLEVELAND	USA
5 AUG	CHICAGO STADIUM	USA
6 AUG	CHICAGO STADIUM	USA
7 AUG	ST LOUIS KIEL AUDITORIUM	USA
8 AUG	KANSAS CITY ARROWHEAD STADIUM	USA
10 AUG	DALLAS MOODY COLISEUM	USA
12 AUG	DENVER	USA
13 AUG	SALT LAKE CITY SALT PALACE	USA
15 AUG	LOS ANGELES MEMORIAL COLISEUM	USA
16 AUG	SAN DIEGO BALBOA STADIUM	USA
18 AUG	OAKLAND ARENA	USA
20 AUG	PORTLAND	USA
21 AUG	SEATTLE COLISEUM	USA
23 AUG	EDMONTON	CAN
25 AUG	CALGARY STAMPEDE CORRAL	CAN
1977		
14 JAN	PASADENA CIVIC AUDITORIUM	USA
15 JAN	PASADENA CIVIC AUDITORIUM	USA
16 JAN	LOS ANGELES DOROTHY CHANDLER PAVILION	USA
19 JAN	DETROIT MASONIC AUDITORIUM	USA
20 JAN	DETROIT MASONIC AUDITORIUM	USA
22 JAN	NEW YORK RADIO CITY MUSIC HALL	USA
23 JAN	NEW YORK RADIO CITY MUSIC HALL	USA
1 FEB	ABERDEEN CAPITOL THEATRE	UK
2 FEB	GLASGOW APOLLO THEATRE	UK
3 FEB	NEWCASTLE CITY HALL	UK
4 FEB	MANCHESTER APOLLO	UK
5 FEB	MANCHESTER APOLLO	UK
6 FEB	BIRMINGHAM ODEON	UK
7 FEB	LIVERPOOL EMPIRE THEATRE	UK
9 FEB	SOUTHAMPTON GAUMONT THEATRE	UK
10 FEB	LONDON GOLDERS GREEN HIPPODROME (TV)	UK
11 FEB	LONDON HAMMERSMITH ODEON	UK
12 FEB	LONDON HAMMERSMITH ODEON	UK
13 FEB	LONDON HAMMERSMITH ODEON	UK
14 FEB	BRISTOL COLSTON HALL	UK
1 MAR	OAKLAND COLISEUM	USA
3 MAR	SEATTLE COLISEUM	USA
4 MAR	EUGENE	USA
5 MAR	PULLMAN	USA
6 MAR	MISSOULA	USA
8 MAR	DENVER	USA
9 MAR	OMAHA CITY AUDITORIUM ARENA	USA
10 MAR	COLUMBIA	USA
11 MAR	CINCINNATI	USA
12 MAR	EVANSTON	USA
13 MAR	ST LOUIS	USA
14 MAR	NASHVILLE	USA
15 MAR	MEMPHIS MIDSOUTH COLISEUM	USA
16 MAR	LOUISVILLE GARDENS	USA
17 MAR	CHICAGO	USA
18 MAR	PEORIA	USA
19 MAR	COLUMBUS	USA
21 MAR	DETROIT	USA
22 MAR	DETROIT	USA
23 MAR	CLEVELAND RICHFIELD COLISEUM	USA
24 MAR	TORONTO MAPLE LEAF GARDENS	CAN
25 MAR	MONTREAL	CAN
26 MAR	OTTAWA	CAN
28 MAR	BOSTON TEA GARDENS	USA
29 MAR	BUFFALO WAR MEMORIAL AUDITORIUM	USA
30 MAR	SYRACUSE	USA
31 MAR	NEW HAVEN VETERAN MEMORIAL COLISEUM	USA
1 APR	NEW HAVEN VETERAN MEMORIAL COLISEUM	USA
6 APR	ANAHEIM CONVENTION CENTER	USA
7 APR	ANAHEIM CONVENTION CENTER	USA
8 APR	SAN DIEGO SPORTS ARENA	USA
9 APR	LONG BEACH ARENA	USA
10 APR	LAS VEGAS ALLADIN THEATRE	USA
11 APR	MIAMI SPORTATORIUM	USA
16 APR	NUREMBERG MESSECENTRUM	GER
17 APR	MUNICH OLYMPIAHALLE	GER
18 APR	FRANKFURT FESTHALLE	GER
19 APR	HANNOVER EILENFRIEDEHALLE	GER
20 APR	COLOGNE SPORTHALLE	GER
21 APR	ESSEN GRUGAHALLE	GER
22 APR	BREMEN	GER
23 APR	BERLIN DEUTSCHLANDHALLE	GER
24 APR	BERLIN DEUTSCHLANDHALLE	GER
24 MAY	STOCKHOLM KONSERTHUSET	SWE

25 MAY	GOTHENBURG	SWE		9 MAY	LONDON HAMMERSMITH ODEON	UK
27 MAY	COPENHAGEN FALKONERTEATRET	DEN		10 MAY	LONDON HAMMERSMITH ODEON	UK
29 MAY	HAMBURG	GER		11 MAY	LONDON HAMMERSMITH ODEON	UK
30 MAY	SAARBRUCKEN SAALANDHALLE	GER		13 MAY	THE HAGUE CONGRESGEBOUW	NED
31 MAY	PARIS PALAIS DES CONGRESS	FRA		14 MAY	BRUSSELS VORST NATIONAL	BEL
2 JUN	ROTTERDAM AHOY HALL	NED		15 MAY	COLOGNE SPORTHALLE	GER
3 JUN	BRUSSELS VOREST NATIONAL	BEL		16 MAY	BREMERHAVEN STADTHALLE	GER
5 JUN	BASEL ST JAKOB STADIUM	SWI		17 MAY	MUNSTER MUNSTERLANDHALLE	GER
6 JUN	INNSBRUCK	AUT		18 MAY	BERLIN DEUTSCHLANDHALLE	GER
7 JUN	LINZ SPORTHALLE	AUT		20 MAY	ESSEN GRUGAHALLE	GER
8 JUN	VIENNA STADTHALLE	AUT		21 MAY	LUDWIGSHAFEN FREDERICH EBERTHALLE	GER
4 SEP	PERTH ENTERTAINMENT CENTER	AUS		22 MAY	LUDWIGSHAFEN FREDERICH EBERTHALLE	GER
5 SEP	PERTH ENTERTAINMENT CENTER	AUS		23 MAY	BOBLINGEN SPORTHALLE	GER
7 SEP	ADELAIDE	AUS		25 MAY	STRASBOURG	GER
9 SEP	MELBOURNE	AUS		26 MAY	SAARBRUCKEN SAARLANDHALLE	GER
10 SEP	MELBOURNE	AUS		27 MAY	MUNICH OLYMPIAHALLE	GER
11 SEP	MELBOURNE	AUS		28 MAY	BERNE FESTHALLE	SWI
12 SEP	MELBOURNE	AUS		29 MAY	RUSSELSHEIM WALTER KUBEL HALLE	GER
14 SEP	SYDNEY HORDEN PAVILLION	AUS		30 MAY	RUSSELSHEIM WALTER KUBEL HALLE	GER
15 SEP	SYDNEY HORDEN PAVILLION	AUS		31 MAY	HANNOVER KUPPELSALLE	GER
17 SEP	BRISBANE FESTIVAL HALL	AUS		2 JUN	KIEL OSTSEEHALLE	GER
19 SEP	SYDNEY	AUS		4 JUN	BIRMINGHAM ODEON	UK
20 SEP	SYDNEY	AUS		5 JUN	MANCHESTER APOLLO	UK
4 NOV	MIAMI JAI ALAI FRONTON	USA		1 OCT	HAMPTON VALLEY	USA
5 NOV	MIAMI JAI ALAI FRONTON	USA		2 OCT	WASHINGTON CAPITAL CENTER	USA
6 NOV	ST PETERSBURG BAYFRONT CENTER	USA		3 OCT	PHILADELPHIA SPECTRUM	USA
7 NOV	ATLANTA THE OMNI	USA		4 OCT	PHILADELPHIA	USA
8 NOV	NEW ORLEANS	USA		6 OCT	BOSTON TEA GARDENS	USA
9 NOV	HOUSTON SAM HOUSTON COLISEUM	USA		7 OCT	BOSTON TEA GARDENS	USA
10 NOV	DALLAS MEMORIAL AUDITORIUM	USA		8 OCT	NEW YORK MADISON SQUARE GARDEN	USA
11 NOV	DALLAS MEMORIAL AUDITORIUM	USA		9 OCT	NEW YORK MADISON SQUARE GARDEN	USA
12 NOV	OKLAHOMA CITY	USA		11 OCT	NEW YORK MADISON SQUARE GARDEN	USA
13 NOV	KANSAS CITY MUNICIPAL AUDITORIUM	USA		12 OCT	PROVIDENCE CIVIC CENTER	USA
14 NOV	MILWAUKEE ARENA	USA		13 OCT	MONTREAL FORUM	CAN
15 NOV	ST PAUL	USA		15 OCT	TORONTO MAPLE LEAF GARDENS	CAN
16 NOV	MADISON	USA		16 OCT	BUFFALO WAR MEMORIAL AUDITORIUM	USA
18 NOV	SPRINGFIELD CIVIC CENTER	USA		17 OCT	DETROIT COBO HALL	USA
19 NOV	SPRINGFIELD CIVIC CENTER	USA		18 OCT	DETROIT COBO HALL	USA
20 NOV	HEMPSTEAD NASSAU COLISEUM	USA		19 OCT	ST LOUIS CHECKERDOME	USA
21 NOV	WASHINGTON CAPITAL CENTER	USA		20 OCT	MEMPHIS	USA
22 NOV	NORFOLK	USA		21 OCT	HUNTSVILLE ALABAMA	USA
23 NOV	GREENSBORO COLISEUM	USA		23 OCT	CHICAGO STADIUM	USA
24 NOV	LEXINGTON	USA		24 OCT	TOLEDO	USA
25 NOV	DAYTON	USA		25 OCT	CINCINNATI RIVERFRONT COLISEUM	USA
27 NOV	PORTLAND CIVIC CENTER	USA		26 OCT	PITTSBURGH CIVIC ARENA	USA
28 NOV	HARTFORD	USA		27 OCT	CLEVELAND RICHFIELD COLISEUM	USA
29 NOV	NEW YORK	USA		28 OCT	KALAMAZOO WING STADIUM	USA
30 NOV	NEW YORK MADISON SQUARE GARDEN	USA		30 OCT	NEW HAVEN VETERAN MEMORIAL COLISEUM	USA
1 DEC	ROCHESTER	USA		31 OCT	NEW HAVEN VETERAN MEMORIAL COLISEUM	USA
2 DEC	WILMINGTON	USA		1 NOV	SYRACUSE WAR MEMORIAL	USA
3 DEC	BINGHAMPTON	USA		2 NOV	ROCHESTER	USA
4 DEC	PROVIDENCE CIVIC CENTER	USA		7 NOV	DENVER MC NICHOLS ARENA	USA
5 DEC	PHILADELPHIA SPECTRUM	USA		8 NOV	SALT LAKE CITY SALT PALACE ARENA	USA
6 DEC	BOSTON TEA GARDENS	USA		9 NOV	RENO CENTENNIAL COLISEUM	USA
1978				10 NOV	TEMPE	USA
1 MAY	EDINBURGH USHER HALL	UK		12 NOV	OAKLAND STADIUM	USA
2 MAY	GLASGOW APOLLO CENTRE	UK		13 NOV	LOS ANGELES INGLEWOOD FORUM	USA
3 MAY	MANCHESTER APOLLO	UK		14 NOV	LOS ANGELES INGLEWOOD FORUM	USA
7 MAY	LONDON RAINBOW THEATRE	UK		15 NOV	LONG BEACH AUDITORIUM	USA
8 MAY	LONDON RAINBOW THEATRE	UK		16 NOV	LONG BEACH AUDITORIUM	USA

JETHRO TULL

17 NOV	LONG BEACH AUDITORIUM	USA
1979		
1 APR	ALBUQUERQUE	USA
2 APR	TAMPA	USA
3 APR	SAN DIEGO	USA
4 APR	FRESNO SELLAND ARENA	USA
6 APR	OGDEN	USA
7 APR	POCATELLO	USA
8 APR	BILLINGS THE METRA	USA
10 APR	SEATTLE COLISEUM	USA
11 APR	VANCOUVER	CAN
12 APR	PORTLAND	USA
14 APR	EDMONTON	CAN
15 APR	CALGARY STAMPEDE CORRAL	CAN
17 APR	ST PAUL MET CENTER	USA
18 APR	CEDAR FALLS UNIDOME	USA
19 APR	MILWAUKEE ARENA	USA
20 APR	MADISON DANE COUNTY COLISEUM	USA
21 APR	LINCOLN	USA
23 APR	KANSAS CITY KEMPER ARENA	USA
24 APR	WICHITA	USA
25 APR	OKLAHOMA CITY THE MYRIAD	USA
26 APR	LUBBOCK COLISEUM	USA
28 APR	HOUSTON SAM HOUSTON COLISEUM	USA
29 APR	HOUSTON SAM HOUSTON COLISEUM	USA
30 APR	FORT WORTH COUNTY CONVENTION CENTER	USA
1 MAY	SAN ANTONIO CONVENTION CENTER	USA
2 OCT	JACKSONVILLE COLISEUM	USA
5 OCT	TORONTO MAPLE LEAF GARDENS	CAN
6 OCT	QUEBEC COLISEUM	CAN
7 OCT	MONTREAL FORUM	CAN
9 OCT	NEW HAVEN COLISEUM	USA
10 OCT	NEW HAVEN COLISEUM	USA
12 OCT	NEW YORK MADISON SQUARE GARDENS	USA
15 OCT	PROVIDENCE CIVIC CENTER	USA
16 OCT	PHILADELPHIA SPECTRUM	USA
17 OCT	PHILADELPHIA SPECTRUM	USA
18 OCT	WASHINGTON CAPITAL CENTER	USA
19 OCT	PORTLAND	USA
20 OCT	ROCHESTER	USA
21 OCT	BOSTON TEA GARDENS	USA
22 OCT	NASSAU	USA
24 OCT	DETROIT	USA
25 OCT	PITTSBURGH	USA
26 OCT	CLEVELAND	USA
27 OCT	CINCINNATI	USA
29 OCT	CHICAGO	USA
30 OCT	NASHVILLE	USA
31 OCT	MEMPHIS MIDSOUTH COLISEUM	USA
1 NOV	ATLANTA OMNI	USA
2 NOV	JACKSONVILLE	USA
3 NOV	LAKELAND CIVIC CENTER	USA
4 NOV	MIAMI HOLLYWOOD SPORTATORIUM	USA
5 NOV	HOLLYWOOD SPORTATORIUM	USA
6 NOV	BIRMINGHAM	USA
7 NOV	CARBONDALE	USA
8 NOV	ST LOUIS	USA
9 NOV	OMAHA CITY AUDITORIUM	USA
10 NOV	DENVER MCNICHOLS ARENA	USA
12 NOV	LAS VEGAS	USA
13 NOV	LONG BEACH ARENA	USA
14 NOV	LONG BEACH ARENA	USA
15 NOV	LONG BEACH ARENA	USA
16 NOV	SANTA MONICA CIVIC AUDITORIUM	USA
17 NOV	SAN DIEGO SPORTS ARENA	USA
18 NOV	OAKLAND COLISEUM	USA
1980		
13 MAR	DRAMMEN	NOR
14 MAR	STOCKHOLM ISSTADION	SWE
16 MAR	THE HAGUE CONGRESGEBOUW	NED
17 MAR	BRUSSELS VORST NATIONAAL	BEL
18 MAR	SAARBRUCKEN SAARLANDHALLE	GER
19 MAR	LUDWIGSHAFEN FREDERICH EBERTHALLE	GER
20 MAR	MUNSTER MUNSTERLANDHALLE	GER
22 MAR	BERLIN DEUTSCHLANDHALLE	GER
23 MAR	HAMBURG CONGRESS CENTRUM HALLE	GER
24 MAR	HANNOVER KUPPELSAALE	GER
25 MAR	KASSEL EISSPORTHALLE	GER
26 MAR	COLOGNE SPORTHALLE	GER
28 MAR	BREMEN STADTHALLE	GER
29 MAR	DUSSELDORF PHILLIPSHALLE	GER
30 MAR	ESSEN GRUGAHALLE	GER
31 MAR	BOBLINGEN SPORTHALLE BOBLINGEN	GER
1 APR	MUNICH OLYMPIAHALLE	GER
2 APR	FRANKFURT FESTHALLE	GER
3 APR	ZURICH HALLENSTADION	SWI
4 APR	DIJON PALAIS DES SPORTS	FRA
8 APR	GLASGOW APOLLO CENTRE	UK
9 APR	MANCHESTER ABC APOLLO	UK
10 APR	LONDON HAMMERSMITH ODEON	UK
11 APR	LONDON HAMMERSMITH ODEON	UK
12 APR	LONDON HAMMERSMITH ODEON	UK
13 APR	LONDON HAMMERSMITH ODEON	UK
14 APR	LONDON HAMMERSMITH ODEON	UK
4 OCT	SALISBURY	USA
5 OCT	WASHINGTON CAPITAL CENTRE	USA
6 OCT	HARTFORD CIVIC CENTER	USA
7 OCT	UTICA MEMORIAL AUDITORIUM	USA
8 OCT	NEW YORK MADISON SQUARE GARDEN	USA
9 OCT	NEW YORK MADISON SQUARE GARDEN	USA
10 OCT	PROVIDENCE CIVIC CENTER	USA
11 OCT	BOSTON TEA GARDENS	USA
12 OCT	NASSAU COLISEUM	USA
13 OCT	PHILADELPHIA SPECTRUM	USA
15 OCT	CLEVELAND	USA
16 OCT	CINCINNATI RIVERFRONT COLISEUM	USA
17 OCT	SAGINAW CIVIC CENTER	USA
18 OCT	MILWAUKEE ARENA	USA
19 OCT	CHICAGO	USA
20 OCT	ST PAUL	USA
22 OCT	DETROIT COBO HALL	USA
23 OCT	KALAMAZOO WINGS STADIUM	USA
24 OCT	CHAMPAIGN	USA
25 OCT	LOUISVILLE THE GARDENS	USA
26 OCT	ST LOUIS CHECKERDOME	USA
28 OCT	KANSAS CITY MUNICIPAL AUDITORIUM	USA
29 OCT	TULSA ASSEMBLY CENTER	USA
30 OCT	NORMAN	USA
31 OCT	DALLAS REUNION ARENA	USA
1 NOV	SAN ANTONIO	USA

2 NOV	HOUSTON	USA	30 APR	FREIBURG STADTHALLE	GER
3 NOV	HOUSTON	USA	2 MAY	ROME 7UP THEATRE	ITA
4 NOV	ALBUQUERQUE TINGLEY COLISEUM	USA	3 MAY	BOLOGNA PALASPORT	ITA
5 NOV	DENVER MCNICHOLS ARENA	USA	4 MAY	GENOVA PALASPORT	ITA
7 NOV	SAN BERNARDINO SWING AUDITORIUM	USA	5 MAY	PADOVA PALAZZO DELLO SPORT	ITA
8 NOV	FRESNO SELLAND ARENA	USA	6 MAY	NICE THEATREDE VERDUR	FRA
9 NOV	OAKLAND COLISEUM	USA	7 MAY	BARCELONA MUNICIPAL DE DEPORTES	ESP
10 NOV	SAN DIEGO	USA	8 MAY	MADRID REAL MADRID INDOOR HALL	ESP
11 NOV	LOS ANGELES SPORTS ARENA	USA	9 MAY	SAN SEBASTIAN VELODROMO DE AUNETA	ESP
12 NOV	LOS ANGELES SPORTS ARENA	USA	11 MAY	ROTTERDAM AHOY HAL	NED
20 NOV	LONDON ROYAL ALBERT HALL	UK	13 MAY	LONDON WEMBLEY ARENA	UK
21 NOV	LONDON ROYAL ALBERT HALL	UK	14 MAY	EDINBURGH PLAYHOUSE	UK
1981			15 MAY	NEWCASTLE CITY HALL	UK
1 FEB	BRUSSELS VORST NATIONAL	BEL	16 MAY	BIRMINGHAM NATIONAL EXHIBITION CENTRE	UK
2 FEB	BOBLINGEN SPORTHALLE	GER	17 MAY	ST AUSTELL CORNWALL COLISEUM	UK
3 FEB	FRANKFURT FESTHALLE	GER	19 MAY	INVERNESS ICE RINK	UK
4 FEB	ROTTERDAM AHOY HALL	NED	29 MAY	DORTMUND WESTFALENHALLE	GER
5 FEB	DORTMUND WESTFALENHALLE	GER	29 MAY	DORTMUND WESTFALENHALLE	GER
7 FEB	GOTHENBURG SCANDINAVIUM	SWE	21 JUL	LONDON DOMINION THEATRE (3 SONGS)	UK
8 FEB	COPENHAGEN FORUM	SWE	28 AUG	WAKEFIELD NOSTEL PRIORY	UK
9 FEB	HAMBURG CONGRESS CENTRUM HALLE	GER	1 SEP	BARCELONA PLAZA DE TOROS	ESP
10 FEB	HAMBURG CONGRESS CENTRUM HALLE	GER	4 SEP	NORFOLK COLISEUM	USA
11 FEB	HANNOVER MESSESPORTPALAST	GER	4 SEP	WIESBADEN REINWIESSEN	GER
12 FEB	BREMERHAVEN STADTHALLE	GER	5 SEP	NURNBERG FESTIVAL	GER
13 FEB	MUNSTER MUNSTERLANDHALLE	GER	9 SEP	COLUMBIA MERRIWEATHER POST PAVILION	USA
14 FEB	COLOGNE SPORTHALLE	GER	10 SEP	ROCHESTER WAR MEMORIAL HALL	USA
16 FEB	BERLIN DEUTSCHLANDHALLE	GER	11 SEP	BLOSSOM MUSIC CENTER	USA
17 FEB	HOF FREIHEITSHALLE	GER	12 SEP	HOFFMAN ESTATES	USA
18 FEB	AUGSBURG SPORTHALLE	GER	14 SEP	CLARKSON PINE KNOB MUSIC CENTER	USA
19 FEB	PASSAU NIBELUNGENHALLE	GER	15 SEP	CLARKSON	USA
20 FEB	MUNICH R SEDLMAYERHALLE	GER	16 SEP	DAYTON	USA
21 FEB	LUDWIGSHAFEN FREDERICH EBERTHALLE	GER	17 SEP	PITTSBURGH CIVIC ARENA	USA
22 FEB	SAARBRUCKEN SAARLANDHALLE	GER	18 SEP	UNIONDALE	USA
23 FEB	PARIS HIPPODROME	FRA	19 SEP	GLEN FALLS	USA
24 FEB	LYONS PALAIS DES SPORTS	FRA	21 SEP	PHILADELPHIA SPECTRUM	USA
1982			22 SEP	BUFFALO WAR MEMORIAL AUDITORIUM	USA
1 APR	OSLO KONSERTHUT	NOR	23 SEP	TORONTO MAPLE LEAF GARDENS	CAN
2 APR	STOCKHOLM ISSTADION	SWE	24 SEP	MONTREAL FORUM	CAN
3 APR	COPENHAGEN TIVOLI KONSERTSAL	SWE	26 SEP	QUEBEC CITY COLISEUM	CAN
4 APR	BREMEN STADTHALLE	GER	28 SEP	NEW HAVEN VETERAN MEMORIAL COLISEUM	USA
5 APR	BERLIN DEUTSCHLANDHALLE	GER	29 SEP	PORTLAND	USA
6 APR	MUNICH OLYMPIAHALLE	GER	30 SEP	EAST RUTHERFORD MEADOWLANDS ARENA	USA
7 APR	LUDWIGSHAFEN FREDERICH EBERTHALLE	GER	1 OCT	BINGHAMTON BROOME COUNTY ARENA	USA
8 APR	HAMBURG CONGRESS CENTRUM HALLE	GER	2 OCT	WORCESTER CENTRUM	USA
9 APR	HANNOVER	GER	3 OCT	PROVIDENCE CIVIC CENTRE	USA
10 APR	HAMBURG CONGRESS CENTRUM HALLE	GER	5 OCT	HAMPTON VALLEY	USA
11 APR	COLOGNE SPORTHALLE	GER	6 OCT	CHARLOTTE COLISEUM	USA
12 APR	ESSEN GRUGAHALLE	GER	7 OCT	ATLANTA OMNI	USA
13 APR	SAARBRUCKEN SAARLANDHALLE	GER	8 OCT	GAINSVILLE	USA
14 APR	LYONS PALAIS DES SPORTS	FRA	9 OCT	MIAMI HOLLYWOOD SPORTATORIUM	USA
15 APR	CERMONT-FERRAND MAISON DES SPORT	FRA	10 OCT	ST PETERSBURG BAYFRONT CENTER	USA
16 APR	DIJON PALAIS DES SPORTS	FRA	12 OCT	TALLAHASSEE LEON COUNTY ARENA	USA
19 APR	MONTPELLIER	FRA	13 OCT	NEW ORLEANS	USA
21 APR	NANTES	FRA	14 OCT	HOUSTON	USA
22 APR	PARIS	FRA	15 OCT	SAN ANTONIO	USA
25 APR	BRUSSELS VORST NATIONAAL	BEL	16 OCT	DALLAS REUNION ARENA	USA
26 APR	FRANKFURT FESTHALLE	GER	17 OCT	BOULDER FOLSOM FIELD	USA
27 APR	PASSAU NIBELUNGENHALLE	GER	19 OCT	OAKLAND COLISEUM	USA
28 APR	RAVENSBURG OBERSCHWABENHALLE	AUT	20 OCT	LOS ANGELES FORUM	USA
29 APR	BOBLINGEN SPORTHALLE	GER	21 OCT	SAN BERNARDINO	USA

22 OCT	FRESNO	USA		13 NOV	BOULDER EVENTS CENTER	USA
23 OCT	RENO	USA		14 NOV	SALT LAKE CITY SALT PALACE ARENA	USA
24 OCT	STOCKTON	USA		17 NOV	VANCOUVER PNE COLISEUM	CAN
1983				18 NOV	SEATTLE ARENA	USA
15 NOV	MUNCHEN ATLAS CIRCUS (3 SONGS)	GER		19 NOV	PORTLAND COLISEUM	USA
1984				21 NOV	SAN FRANCISCO COW PALACE	USA
30 AUG	DUNDEE CAIRD HALL	UK		22 NOV	LOS ANGELES UNIVERSAL AMPHITHEATRE	USA
1 SEP	GLASGOW APOLLO	UK		5 DEC	MELBOURNE SPORTS CENTRE	AUS
2 SEP	NEWCASTLE CITY HALL	UK		10 DEC	SYDNEY HORDON PAVILION	AUS
3 SEP	MANCHESTER APOLLO	UK		13 DEC	BRISBANE FESTIVAL HALL	AUS
4 SEP	MANCHESTER APOLLO	UK		16 DEC	SYDNEY HORDEN PAVILION	AUS
6 SEP	BIRMINGHAM NATIONAL EXHIBITION CENTRE	UK		18 DEC	MELBOURNE SPORTS CENTRE	AUS
7 SEP	LONDON HAMMERSMITH ODEON	UK		**1985**		
8 SEP	LONDON HAMMERSMITH ODEON	UK		16 MAR	BERLIN INTERNATIONAL CONGRESS CENTRUM	GER
9 SEP	LONDON HAMMERSMITH ODEON	UK		**1986**		
12 SEP	BARCELONA PALACIO MUNICIPAL DEPORTES	ESP		28 JUN	MILTON KEYNES BOWL	UK
13 SEP	MADRID CUIDAD PORTIVA DEL REAL MADRID	ESP		30 JUN	TEL AVIV YARKON PARK	ISR
14 SEP	SAN SEBASTIAN VELODROMO ANOETA	ESP		2 JUL	BUDAPEST MKT STADIUM	HUN
15 SEP	TOULOUSE PALAIS DES SPORTES	FRA		4 JUL	RINGE	DEN
16 SEP	ORANGE LES ARENAS	FRA		5 JUL	DINKELSBUHL INSELWIESE	GER
17 SEP	PARIS LE ZENITH	FRA		6 JUL	ST GOARHAUSEN LORELEI FREILICHTBUHNE	GER
18 SEP	RENNES SALLE OMNISPORT	FRA		**1987**		
21 SEP	STOCKHOLM ISSTADION	SWE		15 AUG	CROPREDY	UK
22 SEP	COPENHAGEN FALKONER THEATRET	DEN		4 OCT	EDINBURGH PLAYHOUSE	UK
24 SEP	THE HAGUE CONGRESGEBOUW	NED		5 OCT	NEWCASTLE CITY HALL	UK
25 SEP	BRUSSELS FORET NATIONAL	BEL		7 OCT	MANCHESTER ABC APOLLO	UK
26 SEP	COLOGNE SPORTHALLE	GER		8 OCT	MANCHESTER ABC APOLLO	UK
27 SEP	HEIDELBERG RHEINNECKARHALLE	GER		9 OCT	BIRMINGHAM NATIONAL EXHIBITION CENTRE	UK
28 SEP	STUTTGART SCHLEYERHALLE	GER		11 OCT	THE HAGUE CONGRESGEBOUW	UK
29 SEP	FRANKFURT FESTHALLE	GER		12 OCT	BRUSSELS CIRQUE ROYALE	BEL
30 SEP	ESSEN GRUGAHALLE	GER		14 OCT	WUERTZBURG CARL DIEM HALLE	GER
2 OCT	HAMBURG CONGRESS CENTRUM HALLE	GER		15 OCT	STUTTGART SCHLEYER HALLE	FRA
3 OCT	HAMBURG CONGRESS CENTRUM HALLE	GER		16 OCT	ZURICH HALLENSTADION	SWI
4 OCT	BERLIN INTERNATIONAL CONGRESS CENTRUM	GER		18 OCT	HAMBURG SPORTHALLE	GER
6 OCT	MUNICH OLYMPIAHALLE	GER		19 OCT	HEIDELBERG RHEIN NECKAR HALLE	GER
7 OCT	ZURICH HALLENSTADION	SWI		20 OCT	MUNICH OLYMPIAHALLE	GER
12 OCT	NEW HAVEN VETERAN MEMORIAL COLISEUM	USA		22 OCT	BERLIN INTERNATIONAL CONGRESS CENTRUM	GER
13 OCT	MEADOWLANDS BYRNE ARENA	USA		23 OCT	COLOGNE SPORTHALLE	GER
14 OCT	BINGHAMPTON BROOME COUNTY ARENA	USA		24 OCT	ESSEN GRUGAHALLE	GER
16 OCT	CLEVELAND RICHFIELD COLISEUM	USA		26 OCT	PARIS LE ZENITH	FRA
17 OCT	ROCHESTER WAR MEMORIAL COLISEUM	USA		27 OCT	FRANKFURT FESTHALLE	GER
18 OCT	BALTIMORE CIVIC CENTER	USA		29 OCT	LONDON HAMMERSMITH ODEON	UK
19 OCT	PHILADELPHIA SPECTRUM	USA		7 NOV	PROVIDENCE CIVIC CENTER	USA
20 OCT	BUFFALO WAR MEMORIAL AUDITORIUM	USA		10 NOV	TROY FIELDHOUSE	USA
21 OCT	OTTAWA CIVIC CENTER	CAN		11 NOV	BALTIMORE CIVIC CENTER	USA
22 OCT	MONTREAL FORUM	CAN		13 NOV	HEMPSTEAD NASSAU COLISEUM	USA
23 OCT	TORONTO MAPLE LEAF GARDENS	CAN		14 NOV	NEW HAVEN VETERAN MEMORIAL COLISEUM	USA
24 OCT	QUBEC COLISEUM	CAN		15 NOV	POUGHKEEPSIE MID HUDSON CIVIC CENTRE	USA
26 OCT	HEMPSTEAD NASSAU COLISEUM	USA		17 NOV	PROVIDENCE CIVIC CENTER	USA
27 OCT	PROVIDENCE CIVIC CENTER	USA		19 NOV	TORONTO MAPLE LEAF GARDENS	CAN
29 OCT	WORCESTER CENTRUM	USA		20 NOV	MONTREAL FORUM	CAN
31 OCT	PITTSBURGH CIVIC CENTER	USA		21 NOV	WORCESTER CENTRUM	USA
1 NOV	COLUMBUS VETERANS AUDITORIUM	USA		22 NOV	EAST RUTHERFORD MEADOWLANDS ARENA	USA
2 NOV	MADISON DANE COUNTY COLISEUM	USA		24 NOV	PHILADELPHIA TOWER THEATRE	USA
3 NOV	DETROIT JOE LOUIS ARENA	USA		25 NOV	PHILADELPHIA TOWER THEATRE	USA
4 NOV	CHICAGO PAVILION	USA		27 NOV	DETROIT COBO HALL	USA
5 NOV	ST PAUL CIVIC CENTRE	USA		28 NOV	CLEVELAND PUBLIC HALL	USA
8 NOV	NEW ORLEANS LAKEFRONT ARENA	USA		29 NOV	CHICAGO PAVILION	USA
9 NOV	SAN ANTONIO CONVENTION CENTER	USA		1 DEC	ST PAUL FORUM	USA
10 NOV	HOUSTON SAM HOUSTON COLISEUM	USA		2 DEC	MILWAUKEE ARENA	USA

3 DEC	ST LOUIS FOX THEATRE	USA
5 DEC	DENVER MCNICHOLS ARENA	USA
7 DEC	SALT LAKE CITY SALT PALACE ARENA	USA
9 DEC	SEATTLE ARENA	USA
10 DEC	PORTLAND SCHNITZER AUDITORIUM	USA
12 DEC	SACREMENTO ARCO ARENA	USA
13 DEC	SAN FRANCISCO CIVIC HALL	USA
14 DEC	LOS ANGELES UNIVERSAL AMPHITHEATRE	USA
15 DEC	LOS ANGELES UNIVERSAL AMPHITHEATRE	USA
16 DEC	LOS ANGELES UNIVERSAL AMPHITHEATRE	USA
1988		
1 JUN	MOUNTAIN VIEW SHORELINE AMPHITHEATRE	USA
2 JUN	CONCORD PAVILION	USA
3 JUN	LAGUNA HILLS AMPHITHEATRE	USA
5 JUN	SAN DIEGO OPEN AIR THEATER	USA
7 JUN	DENVER RED ROCKS AMPHITHEATER	USA
9 JUN	DALLAS TERRANT CONVENTION CENTER	USA
10 JUN	NEW ORLEANS ZOO AMPHITHEATER	USA
12 JUN	HOFFMAN ESTATES POPLAR CREEK THEATRE	USA
13 JUN	CUYAHOGA FALLS BLOSSOM AMPHITHEATER	USA
14 JUN	CLARKSON PINE KNOB MUSIC THEATER	USA
16 JUN	ATLANTA CHASTAIN PARK AMPHITHEATER	USA
17 JUN	MEMPHIS MUD ISLAND AMPHITHEATER	USA
19 JUN	DOSWELL KINGS DOMINION SHOWPLACE	USA
20 JUN	CINCINNATI RIVERBEND MUSIC CENTER	USA
21 JUN	COLUMBIA MERRIWEATHER POST PAVILION	USA
23 JUN	MANSFIELD GREAT WOODS CENTER	USA
24 JUN	WANTAGH JONES BEACH THEATER	USA
25 JUN	SARATOGA SPRINGS ARTS CENTER	USA
26 JUN	PHILADELPHIA MANN MUSIC CENTER	USA
27 JUN	NEW YORK THE PIER	USA
3 JUL	ROME PALAZZO DELLA CIVILTA DEL LAVORO	ITA
4 JUL	FLORENCE PALAZZA DE SANTA CROCE	ITA
5 JUL	MILAN PALSTRUSSARDT	ITA
6 JUL	CORREGIO	ITA
8 JUL	IMST TENT ON VILLAGE GREEN	AUT
9 JUL	NURENBERG VOLKSPARK DUTZENDTEICH	GER
10 JUL	FRAUENFELD OPEN AIR FESTIVAL	SWI
12 JUL	VIENNA OPEN AIR ARENA	AUT
13 JUL	BUDAPEST MTK STADIUM	HUN
15 JUL	ATHENS	GRE
16 JUL	GIESSEN VFB STADION	GER
19 JUL	LONDON WEMBLEY ARENA	UK
26 JUL	BELO HORIZONTE	BRA
2 AUG	PORTO ALLEGRE	BRA
6 AUG	SAO PAULO MARCANAZINHO	BRA
7 AUG	SAO PAULO MARCANAZINHO	BRA
8 AUG	SAO PAULO MARCANAZINHO	BRA
30 AUG	RIO DE JANEIRO	BRA
1989		
18 SEP	INVERNESS EDEN COURT THEATRE	UK
20 SEP	NEWCASTLE CITY HALL	UK
21 SEP	EDINBURGH PLAYHOUSE	UK
23 SEP	MANCHESTER ABC APOLLO	UK
24 SEP	MANCHESTER ABC APOLLO	UK
25 SEP	BIRMINGHAM NATIONAL EXHIBITION CENTRE	UK
27 SEP	LONDON HAMMERSMITH ODEON	UK
28 SEP	LONDON HAMMERSMITH ODEON	UK
29 SEP	LONDON HAMMERSMITH ODEON	UK
1 OCT	HAMBURG SPORTHALLE	GER

2 OCT	HANNOVER EILENRIEDENHALLE	GER
3 OCT	FRANKFURT FESTHALLE	GER
5 OCT	STUTTGART LIEDERHALLE	GER
6 OCT	MUNICH OLYMPIAHALLE	GER
7 OCT	WUERTZBURG KARL DIEN HALLE	GER
9 OCT	ESSEN GRUGAHALLE	GER
10 OCT	COLOGNE SPORTHALLE	GER
11 OCT	LUDWIGSHAFEN FREDERICH EBERTHALLE	GER
13 OCT	ZURICH HALLENSTADION	SWI
14 OCT	LAUSANNE HALLE DES FETES	SWI
15 OCT	MILAN PALATRUSSARDI	ITA
16 OCT	TURIN PALASPORT	ITA
23 OCT	TROY FIELDHOUSE	USA
24 OCT	ROCHESTER WAR MEMORIAL	USA
26 OCT	HAMILTON COPPS ARENA	CAN
27 OCT	MONTREAL FORUM	CAN
28 OCT	WORCESTER CENTRUM	USA
29 OCT	PORTLAND CUMBERLAND CIVIC CENTER	USA
31 OCT	NEW HAVEN COLISEUM	USA
1 NOV	PROVIDENCE CIVIC CENTER	USA
2 NOV	PHILADELPHIA SPECTRUM	USA
3 NOV	HEMPSTEAD NASSAU COLISEUM	USA
4 NOV	RICHMOND COLISEUM	USA
6 NOV	AUBURN HILLS THE PALACE	USA
7 NOV	CLEVELAND PUBLIC HALL	USA
8 NOV	PITTSBURGH PALUMBO CENTER	USA
9 NOV	EAST RUTHERFORD MEADOWLANDS ARENA	USA
11 NOV	ANN ARBOR HILL AUDITORIUM	USA
12 NOV	COLUMBUS VETERANS AUDITORIUM	USA
14 NOV	CHICAGO THEATRE	USA
15 NOV	CHICAGO THEATRE	USA
16 NOV	NORMAL REDBIRD ARENA	USA
17 NOV	ST PAUL FORUM	USA
19 NOV	CINCINNATI RIVERFRONT COLISEUM	USA
20 NOV	ST LOUIS FOX THEATRE	USA
21 NOV	HUNTSVILLE VON BRAUN CIVIC CENTER	USA
22 NOV	ATLANTA OMNI	USA
24 NOV	MIAMI JAMES L KNIGHT CENTER	USA
26 NOV	TAMPA SUN DOME	USA
28 NOV	NEW ORLEANS LAKEFRONT ARENA	USA
29 NOV	HOUSTON SUMMIT	USA
30 NOV	DALLAS STATE FAIR COLISEUM	USA
1 DEC	OKLAHOMA CITY CIVIC CENTER	USA
3 DEC	DENVER MCNICHOLS ARENA	USA
5 DEC	LOS ANGELES UNIVERSAL AMPHITHEATRE	USA
6 DEC	LOS ANGELES UNIVERSAL AMPHITHEATRE	USA
7 DEC	PHOENIX COMPTON TERRACE	USA
8 DEC	SAN DIEGO SPORTS ARENA	USA
10 DEC	SAN FRANCISCO CIVIC CENTER	USA
1990		
4 MAY	ABERDEEN CAPITOL THEATRE	UK
5 MAY	DUNDEE CAIRD HALL	UK
6 MAY	SUNDERLAND EMPIRE THEATRE	UK
8 MAY	LIVINGSTONE FORUM	UK
9 MAY	HARROGATE CENTRE	UK
10 MAY	BRADFORD ST GEORGE'S HALL	UK
11 MAY	CARLISLE SANDS CENTRE	UK
13 MAY	PRESTON GUILDHALL	UK
14 MAY	HANLEY VICTORIA HALL	UK
15 MAY	DONCASTER THE DOME	UK

17 MAY	NEWPORT CENTRE	UK
18 MAY	POOLE ARTS CENTRE	UK
19 MAY	PORTSMOUTH GUILDHALL	UK
21 MAY	NOTTINGHAM ROYAL CENTRE	UK
22 MAY	LIVERPOOL EMPIRE THEATRE	UK
24 MAY	READING THE HEXAGON	UK
25 MAY	BRIGHTON THE DOME	UK
27 MAY	BIRMINGHAM TOWN HALL	UK
28 MAY	OXFORD APOLLO	UK
25 AUG	EAST BERLIN WEISSEMSEE	GER
26 AUG	HOCKENHEIM RING	GER
27 AUG	DORTMUND BLICKPUNKTSTUDIO	GER
1 SEP	LONDON WEMBLEY STADIUM	UK
2 SEP	BERLIN LUNEBURG	GER
10 SEP	SAO PAULO OLYMPIA	BRA
11 SEP	SAO PAULO OLYMPIA	BRA
13 SEP	RIO DE JANEIRO CANECAO	BRA
14 SEP	RIO DE JANEIRO CANECAO	BRA
15 SEP	SAO PAULO IBIRAPUERA ARENA	BRA
1991		
22 JUN	ALBORG FESTIVAL	DEN
23 JUN	ROSTOCK OPEN AIR THEATRE	GER
25 JUN	DRESDEN OPEN AIR THEATRE	GER
26 JUN	HALLE EISSPORTHALLE	GER
28 JUN	HOF FREIHEITSHALLE	GER
29 JUN	COTTBUS FESTIVAL	GER
30 JUN	MAYRHOFEN FESTIVAL	AUT
2 JUL	SALZBURG FESTIVAL	AUT
3 JUL	VIENNA CASINO STADION	AUT
4 JUL	PRAGUE CITY HALL	CHZ
6 JUL	MULHOUSE PALAIS DE SPOTRS	FRA
7 JUL	REMICH PATINOIRE EISSPORTHALLE	LUX
9 JUL	ATHENS PAO STADIUM	GRE
10 JUL	LEYSIN FESTIVAL	SWI
12 JUL	ISTANBUL AMPHITHEATRE	TUR
13 JUL	ISTANBUL AMPHITHEATRE	TUR
15 JUL	ISMIR AMPHITHEATRE	TUR
16 JUL	ISTANBUL AMPHITHEATRE	TUR
17 JUL	ISTANBUL AMPHITHEATRE	TUR
20 JUL	TALLINN FESTIVAL	EST
3 OCT	MANCHESTER APOLLO	UK
4 OCT	MANCHESTER APOLLO	UK
5 OCT	BIRMINGHAM NATIONAL EXHIBITION CENTRE	UK
7 OCT	LONDON HAMMERSMITH ODEON	UK
8 OCT	LONDON HAMMERSMITH ODEON	UK
9 OCT	LONDON HAMMERSMITH ODEON	UK
12 OCT	FORLI PALASPORT	ITA
13 OCT	MILAN PALATRUSSARDI	ITA
14 OCT	VERONA PALASPORT	ITA
16 OCT	ZURICH HALLENSTADION	SWI
17 OCT	MUNICH OLYMPIAHALLE	GER
18 OCT	WUERTZBURG KARL DIEM HALLE	GER
19 OCT	ALSFELD HESSENHALLE	GER
21 OCT	ESSEN GRUGAHALLE	GER
23 OCT	HANNOVER EILENRIEDENHALLE	GER
25 OCT	MUNSTER MUNSTERLANDHALLE	GER
26 OCT	BERLIN INTERNATIONAL CONGRESS CENTRUM	GER
27 OCT	HAMBURG SPORTHALLE	GER
29 OCT	COLOGNE SPORTHALLE	GER
30 OCT	FRANKFURT FESTHALLE	GER

31 OCT	STUTTGART CONGRESSHALLE	GER
1 NOV	HAGEN STADTHALLE	GER
7 NOV	PROVIDENCE CIVIC CENTER	USA
8 NOV	PORTLAND CIVIC CENTER	USA
10 NOV	NEW YORK PARAMOUNT THEATRE	USA
11 NOV	NEW YORK PARAMOUNT THEATRE	USA
12 NOV	SYRACUSE WAR MEMORIAL	USA
14 NOV	HEMPSTEAD NASSAU COLISEUM	USA
15 NOV	ALBANY KNICKERBOCKER ARENA	USA
16 NOV	WORCESTER CENTRUM	USA
17 NOV	BURLINGTON MEMORIAL AUDITORIUM	USA
19 NOV	RICHMOND MOSQUE	USA
20 NOV	PITTSBURGH PALUMBO CENTER	USA
21 NOV	CINCINNATI SHOEMAKER CENTER	USA
22 NOV	CLEVELAND STATE UNIVERSITY	USA
24 NOV	CHICAGO THEATRE	USA
25 NOV	CHICAGO THEATRE	USA
26 NOV	DETROIT FOX THEATRE	USA
27 NOV	GRAND RAPIDS GRAND THEATRE	USA
29 NOV	ST LOUIS FOX THEATRE	USA
30 NOV	CHATTANOOGA MEMORIAL AUD	USA
1 DEC	ATLANTA FOX THEATER	USA
2 DEC	TAMPA USF SUN DOME	USA
3 DEC	MIAMI JAMES L KNIGHT CENTER	USA
6 DEC	SALT LAKE CITY DELTA CENTER	USA
7 DEC	DENVER MCNICHOLS ARENA	USA
9 DEC	SEATTLE ARENA	USA
10 DEC	VANCOUVER ORPHEUM THEATER	CAN
11 DEC	PORTLAND SCHNITZER THEATER	USA
13 DEC	DAVIS UNIVERSITY OF CALIFORNIA	USA
14 DEC	LOS ANGELES UNIVERSAL AMPHITHEATER	USA
15 DEC	LOS ANGELES UNIVERSAL AMPHITHEATER	USA
16 DEC	SAN DIEGO GOLDEN HALL	USA
17 DEC	SAN FRANCISCO CIVIC CENTER	USA
1992		
13 MAR	PLYMOUTH PAVILIONS	UK
14 MAR	WOLVERHAMPTON CIVIC HALL	UK
15 MAR	HULL CITY HALL	UK
17 MAR	EDINBURGH PLAYHOUSE	UK
18 MAR	GLASGOW ROYAL CONCERT HALL	UK
19 MAR	NEWCASTLE CITY HALL	UK
20 MAR	SHEFFIELD CITY HALL	UK
22 MAR	SWINDON OASIS	UK
23 MAR	BRISTOL HIPPODROME	UK
24 MAR	PORTSMOUTH GUILDHALL	UK
27 MAR	COPENHAGEN SAGA ROCKTEATRE	DEN
28 MAR	GOTHENBURG KONSERTHUSET	SWE
29 MAR	STOCKHOLM THE CIRCUS	SWE
30 MAR	OSLO KONSERTHUS	NOR
1 APR	SIEGEN SIEGENLANDHALLE	GER
2 APR	UTRECHT MUSIEK CENTRUM	NED
3 APR	BRUSSELS ANCIENNE BELGIQUE	BEL
5 APR	ZARAGOZA PABELLON LA CHIMENEA	ESP
7 APR	VALENCIA ARENA DISCO	ESP
8 APR	BARCELONA MUNICIPAL DE LOS DEPORTES	ESP
9 APR	MADRID DISCO UNVIERSAL AQUALUNG	ESP
10 APR	SALSONA DISCO XELSA	ESP
1 MAY	GUILDFORD CIVIC HALL	UK
2 MAY	WEMBLEY CONFERENCE CENTRE	UK
4 MAY	DORTMUND WESTFALENHALLE 2	GER

5 MAY	MANNHEIM ROSENGARTEN MUSENSAAL	GER
6 MAY	ZURICH KONGRESSHAUS	SWI
7 MAY	ZURICH PRINZREGENTHEATER	GER
9 MAY	GRAZ STEFANIENSAAL	AUT
10 MAY	PRAGUE LUCERNA HALL	CHZ
11 MAY	BERLIN METROPOLTHEATRE	GER
12 MAY	FRANKFURT ALTE OPER	GER
13 MAY	ATHENS ATTIKON THEATRE	GRE
14 MAY	ATHENS ATTIKON THEATRE	GRE
16 MAY	ANKARA TRT ARI STUDYOSU	TUR
17 MAY	ANKARA TRT ARI STUDYOSU	TUR
19 MAY	BE'ER SHEVA UNIVERSITY	ISR
21 MAY	JERUSALEM SULTAN'S POOL	ISR
23 MAY	CAESAREA AMPHITHEATRE	ISR
24 JUL	NYON FESTIVAL	SWI
25 JUL	BOLOGNA ARENA PARCO NORDE	ITA
26 JUL	FINKENSTEN BURGARENAZELT	AUT
22 SEP	IPSWICH REGENTS THEATRE	UK
23 SEP	NORTHAMPTON DERNGATE	UK
25 SEP	AKRANES SPORTS HALL	ICE
1 OCT	BOSTON ORPHEUM	USA
2 OCT	BOSTON ORPHEUM	USA
3 OCT	BOSTON ORPHEUM	USA
5 OCT	NEW YORK BEACON THEATRE	USA
6 OCT	NEW YORK BEACON THEATRE	USA
7 OCT	ALBANY PALACE THEATRE	USA
8 OCT	PHILADELPHIA TOWER THEATRE	USA
10 OCT	PHILADELPHIA TOWER THEATRE	USA
10 OCT	CHICAGO RIVIERA THEATRE	USA
11 OCT	CHICAGO RIVIERA THEATRE	USA
13 OCT	DENVER PARAMOUNT	USA
14 OCT	SAN FRANCISCO WARFIELD THEATER	USA
15 OCT	LOS ANGELES WILTERN THEATER	USA
16 OCT	LOS ANGELES WILTERN THEATER	USA
20 OCT	MEXICO CITY AUDITORIO NACIONAL	MEX
21 OCT	MEXICO CITY AUDITORIO NACIONAL	MEX
22 OCT	SEATTLE PARAMOUNT THEATRE	USA
23 OCT	VANCOUVER ORPHEUM THEATRE	CAN
24 OCT	PULLMAN BEASLEY THEATRE QUAD	CAN
26 OCT	EDMONTON JUBILEE	CAN
27 OCT	SASKATOON CENTENNIAL AUDITORIUM	CAN
28 OCT	WINNIPEG WALKER THEATRE	CAN
29 OCT	REGINA CENTRE OF THE ARTS	CAN
30 OCT	WINNIPEG WALKER THEATRE	CAN
1 NOV	DETROIT STATE THEATER	USA
2 NOV	TOLEDO MASIONIC AUDITORIUM	USA
3 NOV	TORONTO MASSEY HALL	CAN
4 NOV	TORONTO MASSEY HALL	CAN
6 NOV	OTTAWA CONGRESS CENTRE	CAN
7 NOV	QUEBEC GRAND THEATRE	CAN
8 NOV	QUEBEC GRAND THEATRE	CAN
9 NOV	MONTREAL ST DENIS THEATRE	CAN
1993		
26 APR	NEW YORK LONE STAR ROADHOUSE	USA
27 APR	PHILADELPHIA SPECTRUM	USA
25 MAY	CAMBRIDGE CORN EXCHANGE	UK
26 MAY	CROYDON FAIRFIELD HALL	UK
28 MAY	PARIS ELYSEE MONTMATRE	FRA
29 MAY	STUTTGART FREILICHTBUHNE	GER
30 MAY	GEMUNDEN SCHERENBERGHALLE	GER

31 MAY	MEMMINGEN STADTHALLE	GER
3 JUN	COLOGNE TANZBRUNNEN	GER
4 JUN	WOLFSBURG CONGRESSPARK	GER
5 JUN	KAMENZ HUTBERGBUEHNE	GER
6 JUN	HALLE EISSPORTHALLE	GER
10 JUN	DORTMUND WESTFALEN PARK	GER
11 JUN	ELSPE NATURBUHNE	GER
12 JUN	OSNABRUCK STADION BREMERBRUECKE	GER
13 JUN	LUBEK	GER
15 JUN	BRUSSELS CIRQUE ROYALE	BEL
17 JUN	UTRECHT MUSIC CENTRE	NED
18 JUN	HAMBURG STADTPARK	GER
19 JUN	FRANKFURT MUSIK-ARENA AM WALSTADION	GER
20 JUN	GREFRATH EISSPORTHALLE	GER
22 JUN	OSTRAVA VICTOVICS SPORTS HALL	CZE
23 JUN	BUDAPEST PETOFI HALL	HUN
25 JUN	ST GALLEN	SWI
26 JUN	ST WENDEL BOSENBACHSTADION	GER
27 JUN	LICHTENFELS SCHUETZENANGER	GER
30 JUN	VIENNA ARENA	AUT
1 JUL	WIESEN RAIFFEISENZELT	AUT
2 JUL	WELS STADTHALLE	AUT
3 JUL	REGENSBURG SARCHINGER WEIHER	GER
4 JUL	LIENZ TOWN SQUARE	AUT
6 JUL	TRENTO STADIO BRIAMASCO	ITA
7 JUL	MILAN ROLLING STONE	ITA
9 JUL	ROSTOCK CITY HALL	GER
11 JUL	TURKU RUISROCK	FIN
12 JUL	BERLIN TEMPODROM	GER
13 JUL	GLAUCHAU GRUENDELPARK	GER
15 JUL	MADRID	ESP
16 JUL	MADRID	ESP
17 JUL	LIVERPOOL EMPIRE	UK
18 JUL	MACDUFF TARLAIR MUSIC FESTIVAL	UK
20 AUG	HOUSTON WOODLANDS PAVILION	USA
21 AUG	DALLAS STARPLEX AMPITHEATRE	USA
23 AUG	ATLANTA LAKEWOOD AMPITHEATRE	USA
24 AUG	RALEIGH WALNUT CREEK AMPITHEATRE	USA
26 AUG	HOLMDALE GARDEN STATE ARTS CENTER	USA
27 AUG	WANTAGH JONES BEACH	USA
28 AUG	MANSFIELD GREAT WOODS	USA
30 AUG	COLUMBIA MERRIWEATHER POST	USA
31 AUG	PHILADELPHIA MANN MUSIC CENTER	USA
2 SEP	GROTON THAMES RIVER MUSIC CENTER	USA
3 SEP	DARIEN LAKE DARIEN CENTER	USA
4 SEP	TORONTO KINGSWOOD AMPITHEATRE	CAN
5 SEP	PITTSBURGH STAR LAKE	USA
8 SEP	MILWAUKEE MARCUS AMPITHEATER	USA
10 SEP	CINCINNATI RIVERBEND	USA
11 SEP	INDIANAPOLIS DEER CREEK	USA
12 SEP	CHICAGO THE WORLD MUSIC THEATRE	USA
14 SEP	ENGLEWOOD FIDDLER'S GREEN	USA
16 SEP	LOS ANGELES GREEK THEATRE	USA
17 SEP	LOS ANGELES GREEK THEATRE	USA
18 SEP	LAGUNA HILLS AMPITHEATRE	USA
19 SEP	SAN DIEGO STATE UNIVERSITY THEATRE	USA
22 SEP	TOKYO SHIBUYA ON AIR	JAP
2 OCT	POOLE ARTS CENTRE	UK
3 OCT	PORTSMOUTH GUILDHALL	UK
4 OCT	BRIGHTON DOME	UK

6 OCT	BIRMINGHAM SYMPHONY HALL	UK		1 APR	SYRACUSE LANDMARK THEATER	USA
7 OCT	NOTTINGHAM ROYAL CENTRE	UK		2 APR	BUFFALO SHEAS THEATER	USA
8 OCT	MANCHESTER APOLLO	UK		4 APR	BURLINGTON MEMORIAL AUDITORIUM	USA
9 OCT	MANCHESTER APOLLO	UK		5 APR	POUGHKEEPSIE MID HUDSON CIVIC CENTER	USA
11 OCT	GLASGOW ROYAL CONCERT HALL	UK		29 APR	BERGEN GRIEGHALLEN	NOR
12 OCT	NEWCASTLE CITY HALL	UK		1 MAY	TRONDHEIM OLAFSHALLEN	NOR
13 OCT	SHEFFIELD CITY HALL	UK		2 MAY	OSLO CENTRUM	NOR
15 OCT	LONDON HAMMERSMITH APOLLO	UK		3 MAY	STOCKHOLM CIRKUS	SWE
16 OCT	LONDON HAMMERSMITH APOLLO	UK		5 MAY	HELSINKI HOUSE OF CULTURE	FIN
17 OCT	WOLVERHAMPTON CIVIC HALL	UK		6 MAY	TURKU TYPHOON HALL	FIN
18 OCT	BRISTOL COLSTON HALL	UK		8 MAY	GOTHENBURG LISEBERGSHALLEN	SWE
20 OCT	DUBLIN STADIUM	IRE		9 MAY	LUND OLYMPEN	SWE
21 OCT	BELFAST ULSTER HALL	UK		10 MAY	COPENHAGEN FALKONER	DEN
29 OCT	SANTIAGO ESTADIO CHILE	CHI		12 MAY	GRONINGEN EVENEMENTENHAL	NED
30 OCT	VINA DEL MAR QUINTA VERGERA	CHI		13 MAY	ANTWERP QUEEN ELIZABETH HALL	BEL
1 NOV	LIMA MUELLE UNO	PERU		14 MAY	EINDHOVEN MUSIC CENTRUM	NED
4 NOV	BUENOS AIRES ESTADIO OBRAS	ARG		16 MAY	EDINBURGH USHER HALL	UK
5 NOV	BUENOS AIRES ESTADIO OBRAS	ARG		17 MAY	PRESTON GUILDHALL	UK
9 NOV	MESA AZ MESA AMPITHEATER	USA		18 MAY	BRADFORD ST GEORGES HALL	UK
10 NOV	ALBUQUERQUE NM KIVA AUDITORIUM	USA		20 MAY	HANLEY VICTORIA HALLS	UK
12 NOV	SAN ANTONIO TX MUNICIPAL AUDITORIUM	USA		21 MAY	HEREFORD LEISURE CENTRE	UK
13 NOV	TULSA OK BRADY THEATER	USA		22 MAY	YORK BARBICAN	UK
14 NOV	OKLAHOMA CITY CIVIC CENTER MUSIC HALL	USA		24 MAY	OXFORD APOLLO	UK
16 NOV	SUNRISE FL SUNRISE MUSICAL THEATRE	USA		25 MAY	IPSWICH REGENT	UK
17 NOV	SUNRISE FL SUNRISE MUSICAL THEATRE	USA		26 MAY	BRENTWOOD LEISURE CENTRE	UK
18 NOV	TAMPA SUNDOME	USA		28 MAY	KETTERING ARENA	UK
20 NOV	NEW ORLEANS SAENGER THEATER	USA		29 MAY	BASINGSTOKE ANVIL	UK
21 NOV	PENSACOLA BAYFRONT AUDITORIUM	USA		7 JUN	GRAZ	AUT
22 NOV	LITTLE ROCK ROBINSON CENTER	USA		8 JUN	KLAGENFURT	AUT
1994				10 JUN	STAVANGER	NOR
16 FEB	BOMBAY RANG BHAWAN	IND		11 JUN	OSLO (FESTIVAL)	NOR
17 FEB	BOMBAY RANG BHAWAN	IND		12 JUN	BUCHAREST (FESTIVAL)	ROM
19 FEB	BANGALORE PALACE GROUNDS	IND		10 JUL	BALINGEN (FESTIVAL)	GER
20 FEB	MADRAS Y.M.C.A. GROUNDS	IND		16 JUL	TUTBURY FESTIVAL	UK
23 FEB	HONG KONG KO SHAN THEATRE	HK		17 JUL	BERNE (FESTIVAL)	SWI
26 FEB	NEW PLYMOUTH TSB STADIUM	NZ		11 AUG	LONDON, CLAPHAM GRAND	UK
27 FEB	NEW PLYMOUTH TSB STADIUM	NZ		12 AUG	AARHUS (FESTIVAL)	DEN
1 MAR	MELBOURNE CONCERT HALL	AUS		19 AUG	BUDAPEST FESTIVAL	HUN
2 MAR	MELBOURNE CONCERT HALL	AUS		5 OCT	PRETORIA SAAMBOU BANK ARENA	SA
4 MAR	SYDNEY STATE THEATRE	AUS		6 OCT	JOHANNESBURG STANDARD BANK ARENA	SA
5 MAR	SYDNEY STATE THEATRE	AUS		7 OCT	DURBAN VILLAGE GREEN	SA
6 MAR	SYDNEY STATE THEATRE	AUS		9 OCT	CAPE TOWN THREE ARTS THEATRE	SA
7 MAR	SYDNEY STATE THEATRE	AUS		10 OCT	CAPE TOWN THREE ARTS THEATRE	SA
9 MAR	BRISBANE FESTIVAL HALL	AUS		11 OCT	CAPE TOWN THREE ARTS THEATRE	SA
10 MAR	MELBOURNE SPORTS CENTRE	AUS		13 OCT	JONANNESBURG STANDARD BANK ARENA	SA
12 MAR	ADELAIDE THEBARTON THEATRE	AUS		**1995**		
13 MAR	ADELAIDE THEBARTON THEATRE	AUS		17 MAY	BRUSSELS PASSAGE 44	BEL
14 MAR	PERTH ENTERTAINMENT CENTRE	AUS		19 MAY	HAMBURG MUSILDIALLE	GER
16 MAR	HONOLULU AFTER DARK	USA		20 MAY	MUNICH PRINZREGENTENTHEATER	GER
18 MAR	FRESNO WARNERS THEATER	USA		21 MAY	ZURICH VOLKSHAUS	SWI
19 MAR	SAN JOSE STATE EVENTS CENTER	USA		22 MAY	BERLIN HOCHSCHULE DE KUNSTE	GER
20 MAR	PORTLAND CIVIC AUDITORIUM	USA		24 MAY	LONDON SHEPHERDS BUSH EMPIRE	UK
21 MAR	SEATTLE ARENA	USA		1 JUN	BOSTON ORPHEUM THEATER	USA
22 MAR	VANCOUVER ORPHEUM	CAN		2 JUN	ROCHESTER AUDITORIUM THEATER	USA
24 MAR	CALGARY SOUTHERN JUBILEE	CAN		3 JUN	TORONTO MASSEY HALL	USA
26 MAR	WINNIPEG WALKER THEATRE	CAN		5 JUN	NEW YORK BEACON THEATRE	USA
27 MAR	WINNIPEG OR THUNDER BAY	CAN		6 JUN	TOWER THEATRE, PHILADELPHIA	USA
28 MAR	MINNEAPOLIS ORPHEUM	USA		7 JUN	CLEVELAND MUSIC HALL	USA
30 MAR	TORONTO MASSEY HALL	CAN		8 JUN	CHICAGO BISMARCK THEATER	USA
31 MAR	MONTREAL ST DENIS	CAN		9 JUN	MINNEAPOLIS STATE THEATER	USA

11 JUN	VANCOUVER ORPHEUM THEATER	USA		31 MAR	TAMPA USF DOME	USA
13 JUN	SAN FRANCISCO WARFIELD THEATER	USA		2 APR	ATLANTA FOX THEATRE	USA
14 JUN	LOS ANGELES THE PANTAGES THEATER	USA		3 APR	PENSACOLA BAYFRONT AUDITORIUM	USA
16 SEP	CARLISLE SANDS CENTRE	UK		4 APR	NEW ORLEANS SAENGER THEATRE	USA
18 SEP	GLASGOW ROYAL CONCERT HALL	UK		5 APR	SAN ANTONIO MAJESTIC THEATRE	USA
19 SEP	NEWCASTLE CITY HALL	UK		6 APR	DALLAS BRONCO BOWL	USA
21 SEP	MANCHESTER APOLLO	UK		11 MAY	CANBERRA ROYAL THEATRE	AUS
22 SEP	SHEFFIELD CITY HALL	UK		12 MAY	SYDNEY STATE THEATRE	AUS
23 SEP	NOTTINGHAM ROYAL CENTRE	UK		13 MAY	SYDNEY STATE THEATRE	AUS
25 SEP	PORTSMOUTH GUILDHALL	UK		14 MAY	SYDNEY STATE THEATRE	AUS
26 SEP	BRISTOL COULSTON HALL	UK		18 AUG	DARIEN LAKE, DARIEN LAKES CENTER	USA
27 SEP	BIRMINGHAM SYMPHONY HALL	UK		19 AUG	VAUGHAN, KINGSWOOD MUSIC THEATRE,	USA
28 SEP	CAMBRIDGE CORN EXCHANGE	UK		21 AUG	SCRANTON, MONTAGE MOUNTAIN	USA
29 SEP	LONDON HAMMERSMITH APOLLO	UK		22 AUG	HOLMDEL, GARDEN STATE ARTS CENTER	USA
2 OCT	COPENHAGEN THE CIRKUS	DEN		23 AUG	COLUMBIA, MERRIWEATHER POST PAVILION	USA
3 OCT	STOCKHOLM THE CIRKUS	SWE		25 AUG	HARTFORD, MEADOWS MUSIC THEATRE	USA
4 OCT	OLSO CENTRUM	NOR		26 AUG	MANSFIELD, GREAT WOODS CENTER	USA
6 OCT	GOTHENBURG LISEBERGSHALLEN	SWE		27 AUG	SYRACUSE, NEW YORK STATE FAIR	USA
7 OCT	LUND OLYMPEN	GER		29 AUG	HERSHEY, STAR PAVILION AT HERSHEY PARK	USA
9 OCT	BERLIN TEMPODROM	GER		30 AUG	WANTAGH, JONES BEACH THEATRE	USA
10 OCT	HANNOVER MUSICHALLE	GER		31 AUG	CAMDEN, BLOCKBUSTER/SONY CENTER	USA
11 OCT	HAMBURG CCH	GER		1 SEP	WEST HOMESTEAD, MILLER LITE RIVERPLEX	USA
13 OCT	BRUSSELS CIRQUE ROYALE	BEL		3 SEP	CLEVELAND, NAUTICA STAGE	USA
14 OCT	COLOGNE SPORTHALLE	GER		4 SEP	COLUMBUS, POLARIS AMPITHEATRE	USA
15 OCT	ESSEN GRUGAHALLE	GER		5 SEP	CLARKSTON, PINE KNOB MUSIC THEATRE	USA
17 OCT	SCHWERIN STADTHALLE	GER		6 SEP	CINCINNATI, RIVERBEND MUSIC CENTRE	USA
18 OCT	BREMEN ALADINHALLE	GER		7 SEP	TINLEY PARK, NEW WORLD MUSIC THEATRE	USA
19 OCT	UTRECHT MUZIEKCENTRUM	NED		8 SEP	MOLINE, THE MARK	USA
21 OCT	BAYREUTH OBERFRANKENHALLE	GER		10 SEP	MINNEAPOLIS, NORTHRUP AUDITORIUM	USA
22 OCT	ZURICH HALLENSTADION	SWI		11 SEP	MILWAUKEE, MARCUS AMPITHEATRE	USA
23 OCT	MANNHEIM MOZARTSAAL	GER		13 SEP	MARYLAND, RIVERPORT AMPITHEATRE	USA
25 OCT	FRANKFURT OFFENBACH STADTHALLE	GER		14 SEP	BONNER SPRINGS, SANDSTONE AMPITHEATRE	USA
26 OCT	STUTTGART LIEDERHALLE	GER		15 SEP	LITTLE ROCK, RIVERFEST AMPITHEATRE	USA
27 OCT	MUNICH SEDLMEYERHALLE	GER		18 SEP	PHOENIX, BLOCKBUSTER DESERT SKY PAV	USA
10 NOV	BOSTON ORPHEUM	USA		19 SEP	LAS VEGAS, ALADDIN HOTEL	USA
14 NOV	NEW YORK BEACON THEATRE	USA		20 SEP	SAN DIEGO, OPEN AIR THEATRE	USA
18 NOV	DETROIT FOX THEATRE	USA		21 SEP	LAGUNA HILLS, IRVINE MEADOWS	USA
19 NOV	COLUMBUS VETS. AUDITORIUM	USA		22 SEP	LOS ANGELES, UNIVERSAL AMPITHEATRE	USA
20 NOV	AKRON EJ THOMAS THEATRE	USA		24 SEP	CONCORD, CONCORD PAVILION	USA
21 NOV	CHICAGO CHICAGO THEATRE	USA		25 SEP	RENO, RENO AMPITHEATRE	USA
22 NOV	MILWAUKEE RIVERSIDE THEATRE	USA		27 SEP	GEORGE, GEORGE AMPITHEATRE	USA
24 NOV	L.A. UNIVERSAL AMPITHEATRE	USA		28 SEP	SALEM, LB DAY AMPITHEATRE	USA
1996				29 SEP	BOISE, BOISE STATE UNIVERSITY	USA
6 MAR	SANTIAGO ESTADIO SANTIAGO	CHIL		11 NOV	PLYMOUTH PAVILIONS	UK
8 MAR	BUENOS AIRES GRAN REX	ARG		13 NOV	CARDIFF ST DAVIDS HALL	UK
9 MAR	BUENOS AIRESGRAN REX	ARG		14 NOV	BOURNEMOUTH ICC	UK
10 MAR	MONTEVIDEO PALACIO	URU		16 NOV	HEREFORD LEISURE CENTRE	UK
12 MAR	PORTO ALEGRE TEATRO OSPA	BRA		17 NOV	READING HEXAGON	UK
13 MAR	CURITIBA CIRCULO MILITAR	BRA		18 NOV	BRIGHTON THE DOME	UK
14 MAR	RIO DE JANEIRO METROPOLITAN	BRA		20 NOV	BRENTWOOD CENTRE	UK
15 MAR	SAO PAULO OLYMPIA	BRA		22 NOV	BLACKBURN KING GEORGES HALL	UK
16 MAR	SAO PAULO OLYMPIA	BRA		24 NOV	YORK BARBICAN	UK
17 MAR	SAO PAULO OLYMPIA	BRA		25 NOV	BRADFORD ST GEORGES HALL	UK
19 MAR	LIMA MUELLE UNO	PER		26 NOV	NORTHAMPTON DERNGATE	UK
21 MAR	LA PAZ ESTADLO SILAS	BOL		**1997**		
23 MAR	CARACAS TEREZA CARENO	VEN		30 APR	ESBJERG	DEN
25 MAR	PHILADELPHIA ELECTRIC FACTORY	USA		1 MAY	HAYES BECK THEATRE	UK
26 MAR	PHILADELPHIA ELECTRIC FACTORY	USA		2 JUN	TUNBRIDGE WELLS ASSEMBLY HALL	UK
29 MAR	ORLANDO TUPPERWARE CONV. CTR.	USA		3 JUN	HEMEL HEMPSTEAD DACORUM PAVILION	UK
30 MAR	SUNRISE SUNRISE MUS. THEATRE	USA		5 JUN	LUXEMBOURG CITY PATINOIRE	LUX

6 JUN	UTRECHT MUSIEKCENTRUM	NED
7 JUN	BRUSSELS ANCIENNE BELGIQUE	BEL
9 JUN	POZNAN ARENA	POL
10 JUN	WARSAW COLISEUM	POL
11 JUN	KATOWICE SPODEK	POL
13 JUN	ZLINZIMNI STADIUM	CZH
14 JUN	PRESOV AMPITHEATRE	SLO
1 6 JUN	BUDAPEST PETOFI CSARNOK	HUN
17 JUN	BANSKA BYSTRICA ZIMNI SATADIUM	SLO
18 JUN	PRAGUE INDUSTRIAL PALACE	CZH
20 JUN	AUGSBURG SPORTHALLE	GER
21 JUN	MUNICH RUDI-SEDIMEYERHALLE	GER
22 JUN	WERNECK SCHLOSSPARK	GER
23 JUN	KOBLENZ RHEIN-MOSEL-HALLE	GER
24 JUN	TUBINGEN KULTURZELT	GER
26 JUN	STUTTGART FREILICHTBUHNE KILLESBERG	GER
27 JUN	NEUMARKT GROSSE JURAHALLE	GER
28 JUN	STEINBACH-LANGEN NATURTHEATER	GER
29 JUN	KORBACH HESSENTAG	GER
30 JUN	HAMM EISSPORTHALLE	GER
4 JUL	BERLIN ARENA WUHLHEIDE	GER
5 JUL	CHEMNITZ THEATERPLATZ	GER
6 JUL	DRESDEN JUNGE GARDE	GER
7 JUL	COTTBUS MESSEHALLE	GER
9 JUL	ERFURT THURINGENHALLE	GER
10 JUL	HANNOVER MUSIC HALLE	GER
11 JUL	GELSENKIRCHEN BUNDESGARTENSCHAU	**GER**
12 JUL	KOLN TANZBRUNNEN	GER
13 JUL	GIESSEN FREILICHTBUHNE SCHIFFENBERG	GER
17 JUL	KIEL OSTSEEHALLE	GER
18 JUL	MAGDEBURG CULTURPARK ROTEHORN	GER
19 JUL	RUG EN FREILICHTBUHNE BERGEN	GER
20 JUL	NEUBRANDENBURG LEICHATHLETIKHALLE	GER
21 JUL	HAMBURG STADTPARK	GER
23 JUL	FINKENSTEIN BURGRUINE	AUT
24 JUL	GRAZ SCHLOSSBERG	AUT
25 JUL	WIESEN FESTIVALTENT	AUT
26 JUL	BURG CALM	AUT
27 JUL	SPILIMBERGO(UDINE) FOLKFEST FESTIVAL	ITA
29 JUL	NAPOLI MARECHARLO	ITA
30 JUL	SUBIACO (ROME)	ITA
31 JUL	VIGEVANO (MILAN) CASTELLO	ITA
2 AUG	PENTRICH, DERBYS. ROCK & BLUES SHOW	UK
3 AUG	GUILDFORD STOKE PARK FESTIVAL	UK
7 AUG	HOLMDEL, PNC BANK ARTS CENTER	USA
8 AUG	WALLINGFORD, OAKLAND THEATER	USA
9 AUG	PROVIDENCE, THE STRAND	USA
10 AUG	BOSTON, HARBORLIGHTS	USA
12 AUG	CLARKSTON, PINE KNOB	USA
13 AUG	GRAND RAPIDS, DEVOS HALL	USA
14 AUG	CHICAGO, NAT.FLUTE CONV., GRANT PARK	USA
15 AUG	HAMPTON BEACH CASINO BALLROOM	USA
16 AUG	WANTAGH, JONES BEACH THEATER	USA
17 AUG	BALTIMORE, PIER SIX PAVILION	USA
27 SEP	NAPLES BLUES FESTIVAL	ITA
9 SEP	POUGHKEEPSIE, MID HUDSON CIVIC CENTER	USA
11 SEP	TULL CONVENTION, BURLINGTON (AFT)	USA
11 SEP	BURLINGTON, FLYNN THEATRE (EVE)	USA
12 SEP	PORTLAND, MERRILL AUDITORIUM	USA
14 SEP	QUEBEC CITY, PQ GRAND THEATRE	CAN

15 SEP	MONTREAL, ST DENIS THEATRE	CAN
16 SEP	OTTAWA, CIVIC CENTER	CAN
18 SEP	KITCHENER, LU LU'S CONCERT CLUB	CAN
19 SEP	LONDON, CENTENNIAL HALL	CAN
20 SEP	TORONTO, MASSEY HALL	CAN
22 SEP	DULUTH, DECC AUDITORIUM	USA
23 SEP	FARGO, MEMORIAL AUDITORIUM	USA
24 SEP	WIN NEPEG, WALKER THEATRE	CAN
26 SEP	CALGARY, JACK SINGER HALL	CAN
27 SEP	SASKATOON, CENTENNIAL AUDITORIUM	CAN
28 SEP	EDMONTON, NTH ALBERTA JUBILEE AUD	CAN
30 SEP	VANCOUVER, ORPHEUM	CAN
1 NOV	EUGENE, HULT CENTER	USA
2 NOV	SEATTLE, THE PARAMOUNT	USA
3 NOV	SPOKANE, OPERA HOUSE	USA
4 NOV	BELL INGHAM, MT. BAKER THEATRE	USA
6 NOV	SALT LAKE CITY, E.CENTER	USA
7 NOV	LAS VEGAS, THE JOINT	USA
8 NOV	PHOENIX, UNION HALL	USA
9 NOV	TUCSON, CENTENNIAL HALL	USA
10 NOV	ALBUQUERQUE, NM POPEJOY HALL	USA
17 NOV	SIEGEN SIEGERLANDHALLE	GER
18 NOV	OFFENBACHSTADTHALLE	GER
19 NOV	APPENWEIER SCHWARZWALDHALLE	GER
20 NOV	MANNHEIM MOZARTSAAL	GER
21 NOV	BAD KREUZNACH KONRAD-FREY HALLE	GER
1998		
18 APR	TULL CONVENTION, BEDBURG-HAU	GER
15 JUL	EL PASO, ABRAHAM CHAVES THEATRE	USA
16 JUL	SANTA FE, PAOLO SOLERI	USA
18 JUL	KANSAS, STARLIGHT AMPITHEATRE	USA
21 JUL	AUSTIN THE BACK YARD	USA
22 JUL	HOUSTON AERIAL THERATRE	USA
23 JUL	NEW ORLEANS SAENGER THEATRE	USA
24 JUL	MEMPHIS MUD ISLAND	USA
27 AUG	SANTA ANA GALAXY CONCERT THEATRE	USA
28 AUG	SANTA ANA GALAXY CONCERT THEATRE	USA
30 AUG	SAN DIEGO HUMPHREYS CONCERTS	USA
31 AUG	LOS ANGELES HOUSE OF BLUES	USA
1 SEP	LOS ANGELES HOUSE OF BLUES	USA
3 SEP	KELSEYVILLE KONOCTI FIELD AMPITHEATRE	USA
4 SEP	PORTLAND WASHINGTON GDN AMPITHEATRE	USA
5 SEP	SEATTLE BUMBERSHOOT FESTIVAL	USA
25 SEP	RICHMOND CLASSIC AMPITHEATRE	USA
26 SEP	WASHINGTON/MANASSAS NISSAN PAVILLION	USA
27 SEP	VIRGINIA BEACH GTE AMPITHEATRE	USA
29 SEP	LOUISVILLE PALACE THEATRE	USA
1 OCT	CHARLOTTE BLOCKBUSTER PAVILLION	USA
2 OCT	RALEIGH WALNUT CREEK AMPITHEATRE	USA
3 OCT	N MYRTLE BEACH HOUSE OF BLUES	USA
4 OCT	JACKSONVILLE FLORIDA THEATRE	USA
6 OCT	CLEARWATER RUTH ECKERD HALL	USA
7 OCT	WEST PALM BEACH CORAL SKY AMPITHEATRE	USA
8 OCT	LAKE BUENA VISTA HOUSE OF BLUES	USA
9 OCT	ATLANTA CHASTAIN PARK AMPITHEATRE	USA

New Titles From SAF Publishing

Wish The World Away - Mark Eitzel and the American Music Club
by Sean Body   ISBN: 0 946719 20 9
192 pages (illustrated) UK £11.95

Mark Eitzel's songs are poignant, highly personal tales, encapsulating a sense of loss and loathing, but often tinged with a bitter twist of drink-fuelled humour. Through his solo work and that of his former band American Music Club, Eitzel has been responsible for some of the most individual and memorable records of recent years. Through unrestricted access to Eitzel, former band members, associates and friends, Sean Body has written a fascinating biography which portrays an artist tortured by demons, yet redeemed by the aching beauty of his songs.

LUNAR NOTES - Zoot Horn Rollo's Captain Beefheart Experience
by Bill Harkleroad with Billy James   ISBN: 0 946719 217
160 pages (illustrated) - UK £11.95

Bill Harkleroad joined Captain Beefheart's Magic Band at a crucial time in their development. Beefheart rechristened Harkleroad as Zoot Horn Rollo and they embarked on recording one of the classic rock albums of all time - *Trout Mask Replica* - a work of unequalled daring and inventiveness. Further LPs, *Lick My Decals Off Baby* and *Clear Spot*, highlighted Zoot's skilled guitar playing and what a truly innovative band they were. For the first time we get the insider's story of what it was like to record, play and live with an eccentric genius such as Beefheart.

Meet The Residents - America's Most Eccentric Band! by Ian Shirley
ISBN: 0946 719 12 8   200 pages (illustrated) UK £11.95
Fully updated and now available again!

An outsider's view of The Residents' operations, exposing a world where nothing is as it seems. It is a fascinating tale of the musical anarchy and cartoon wackiness that has driven this unique bunch of artistic maverics forward.

"This is the nearest to an official history you are ever likely to get, slyly abetted by the bug-eyed beans from Venus themselves". **Vox**

"Few enthusiasts will want to put this book down once they start reading".
Record Collector

Digital Gothic - A Critical Discography Of Tangerine Dream
by Paul Stump   ISBN: 0946 719 18 7
160 pages (illustrated) UK £9.95

In this critical discography, music journalist Paul Stump picks his way through a veritable minefield of releases, determining both the explosive and those which fail to ignite. For the very first time Tangerine Dream's mammoth output is placed within an ordered perspective.

"It focuses fascinatingly on the pre-soporific roots of the group and their place in a cool electronic lineage which traces right up to Detroit techno". **Mojo**

"A stimulating companion to the group's music". **The Wire**

Available Now From SAF Publishing

The One and Only: Peter Perrett - Homme Fatale by Nina Antonia
ISBN: 0946 719 16 0
224 pages (illustrated). UK £11.95
An extraordinary journey through crime, punishment and the decadent times of The Only Ones. Includes interviews with Perrett and all ex-band members.
"Antonia gets everyone's co-operation and never loses her perspective on Perrett". **Mojo**
"Antonia is the ideal chronicler of Perrett's rise and fall. From his time as drug dealer, to the smack sojourn in The Only Ones, Perrett's tale is one of self-abuse and staggering selfishness". **Select**

Plunderphonics, 'Pataphysics and Pop Mechanics by Andrew Jones
ISBN: 0946 719 15 2
256 pages (illustrated) UK £12.95
Chris Cutler, Fred Frith, Henry Threadgill, Ferdinand Richard, Amy Denio, Lindsay Cooper, John Oswald, John Zorn, The Residents and many more...
"The talent assembled between Jones's covers would be interesting under any rubric. Thought provoking and stimulating". **Mojo**
"Jones's book is perhaps the first study of the growth of these techniques within the avant-garde. Packed with fascinating interviews and written with wit and insight". **Q magazine**

Kraftwerk - Man, Machine and Music by Pascal Bussy
ISBN: 0946 719 09 8
200 pages (illustrated). UK £11.95
Uniquely definitive account of Kraftwerk's history, delving beyond their publicity shunning exterior to reveal the full story behind one of the most influential bands in the history of rock music. Based on interviews with Ralf Hutter, Florian Schneider, Karl Bartos, Emil Schult and many more.
"Bussy engagingly explains why they are one of the few groups who've actually changed how music sounds". **Q magazine**
"I doubt this book will ever be bettered". **Vox**

Wrong Movements - A Robert Wyatt History by Mike King
ISBN: 0946 719 10 1
160 pages (illustrated). UK £14.95
A sumptuous and detailed journey through Robert Wyatt's 30 year career with Soft Machine, Matching Mole and as a highly respected solo artist. Packed with previously unpublished archive material and rare photos. Commentary from Wyatt himself, Hugh Hopper, Mike Ratledge, Daevid Allen, Kevin Ayers & more.
"King's careful chronology and Wyatt's supreme modesty produce a marvellously unhysterical, oddly haunting book". **Q magazine**
"Low key, likeable and lefty. Like the man himself". **iD magazine**

Available Now From SAF Publishing

No More Mr. Nice Guy - The Inside Story of the Alice Cooper Group
by original guitarist Michael Bruce and Billy James
ISBN: 0946 719 17 9   160 pages (illustrated). UK £9.95

Michael Bruce opens the lid on his years with the platinum selling group, revealing the truth behind the publicity stunts, the dead babies, the drinking, the executions and, of course, the rock 'n' roll.

"I'm Eighteen changed Alice Cooper from the group that destroyed chickens to the group that destroyed stadiums". **Village Voice.**

"It might even be argued that the band defined what it meant to be a role ridden seventies teenager". **Rolling Stone**

Wire - Everybody Loves a History by Kevin Eden
ISBN: 0946 719 07 1
192 pages (illustrated). UK £9.95

A fascinating look at one of punk's most endearing and enduring bands, including interviews with all band members. A self-analysis of the complex motivations which have often seen the various members cross the boundaries between music and art.

"Any band or their fans could feel well served by a book like Eden's". **Vox**

"Eden delivers a sharp portrayal of the punk industry's behaviour, influence and morality". **Q magazine**

TAPE DELAY by Charles Neal
ISBN: 0946 719 02 0
256 pages (illustrated). UK £11.95

Marc Almond, Cabaret Voltaire, Nick Cave, Chris & Cosey, Coil, Foetus, Neubauten, Non, The Fall, The The, Lydia Lunch, New Order, Psychic TV, Rollins, Sonic Youth, Swans, Test Department and many more...

"A virtual Who's Who of people who've done the most to drag music out of commercial confinement". **NME**

"Intriguing and interesting". **Q magazine**

Dark Entries - Bauhaus and Beyond by Ian Shirley
ISBN: 0946 719 13 6
200 pages (illustrated). UK £11.95

The full gothic rise and fall of Bauhaus, including offshoot projects Love and Rockets, Tones on Tail, Daniel Ash, David J and Peter Murphy. Ian Shirley unravels the uncompromising story of four individuals who have consistently confounded their detractors by turning up the unexpected.

"A brilliant trench-to-toilet missive of who did what, where and when. It works brilliantly". **Alternative Press**

"Solidly researched account of goth-tinged glam". **Top Magazine**

Available Now From Helter Skelter Publishing

Bob Dylan by Anthony Scaduto 1-900924-00-5 £11.95
The first and best biography of Dylan.

"Scaduto's 1971 book was the pioneering portrait of this legendarily elusive artist. Now in a welcome reprint it's a real treat to read the still-classic Bobography".
Paul Du Noyer, Q*****

"Superb on the Greenwich Village scene, insightful on the meaning of John Wesley Harding ... it's still perhaps the best book ever written on Dylan".
Peter Doggett, *Record Collector*

A Journey Through America With The Rolling Stones by Robert Greenfield   1-900924-01-3 £12.00
Definitive insider's account of the Stones' legendary 1972 US tour.

"Greenfield is afforded extraordinary access to the band... drugs... groupies. In all, it's a graphic if headache inducing document of strange days indeed".
Tom Doyle, Q****

"Sure, I was completely mad. I go crazy."
Mick Jagger

Back To The Beach - A Brian Wilson and the Beach Boys Reader edited by Kingley Abbott 1-900924-02-1 £12.99

Featuring a foreword by Brian Wilson, Back to the Beach is a collection of the best articles about the band, including a number of pieces specially commissioned for this volume.

"Pet Sounds was my inspiration for making Sgt Pepper." **Paul McCartney**

Born In The USA - Bruce Springsteen and the American Tradition by Jim Cullen 1-900924-05-6 £9.99

The first major study of Bruce Springsteen's that looks at his music in the context of his blue collar roots, and his place in American culture

"Cullen has written an excellent treatise expressing exactly how and why Springsteen translated his uneducated hicktown American-ness into music and stories that touched hearts and souls all around the world." **Q******
"This is a provocative look at one of America's cultural icons." **Newsweek**

Available Now From Helter Skelter Publishing

Like The Night -
Bob Dylan and the Road to the Manchester Free Trade Hall.
ISBN: 1 900924 07 2
192 pages (illustrated). UK £12.00
"When Dylan went electric, he both alienated the audience that had championed him and changed the face of rock music.
Lee's enjoyable and atmospheric reconstruction of this phase of Dylan's career is essential reading." **Uncut Magazine**

"CP Lee wasthere, but the point is that he can put you there too". **Greil Marcus**

XTC - The Exclusive Authorised Story Behind the Music
by XTC and Neville Farmer
ISBN: 1 900924 03 X   306 pages (illustrated). UK £12.00
Co-written by one of the most popular - and usually reclusive - cult bands of all time, this book is timed to coincide with their long-awaited new album.

"Much of what this book will reveal has been unsaid or hidden. But now journalist and friend Neville Farmer intends to weedle it out. Knowing how he can write and we can talk, people are in for an Ancient Babylonian feast of a book".
XTC's Andy Partridge

GET BACK: The Beatles' Let It Be Disaster
by Doug Sulphy and Ray Schweighhardt

AVAILABLE SOON

A detailed document of the group's breakdown seen through the prism of the Get Back recording sessions. Instead of making the planned new album, the greatest band in the world were falling apart.

"Monumental... Fascinating and revealing" **Goldmine**

If you find difficulty obtaining any title, all Helter Skelter, Firefly and SAF books are stocked by, and are available mail order from:
Helter Skelter Bookshop, 4 Denmark Street, London WC2H 8LL Tel: 0171 836 1151 Fax: 0171 240 9880.

Available From Firefly Publishing

an association between Helter Skelter and SAF Publishing

Poison Heart - Surviving The Ramones by Dee Dee Ramone and Veronica Kofman   ISBN: 0946 719 19 5
192 pages (illustrated). UK £11.95
A crushingly honest account of his life as a junkie and a Ramone.
"One of THE great rock and roll books...this is the true, awesome voice of The Ramones". **Q magazine** *****
"His story - knee deep in sex, drugs and rock and roll - is too incident packed to be anything less than gripping". **Mojo**
"A powerful work that is both confessional and exorcising" **Time Out.**

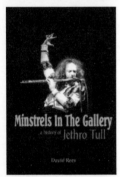

Minstrels In The Gallery - A History of Jethro Tull by David Rees
ISBN: 0 946719 22 5   224 pages (illustrated) - UK £12.99
At Last! To coincide with their 30th anniversary, a full history of one of the most popular and inventive bands of the past three decades. Born out of the British blues boom, Jethro Tull sped to almost worldwide success and superstardom. Fronted by the wild showmanship of Ian Anderson, the band were one of the biggest grossing acts of the seventies. With LPs like *Aqualung, Thick As A Brick* and *Passion Play*, Anderson mutated from the wild-eyed tramp through flute wielding minstrel to the country squire of rock n' roll. David Rees is *the* foremost authority on Jethro Tull - he has interviewed all the band members for this intriguing book.

DANCEMUSICSEXROMANCE - Prince: The First Decade
by Per Nilsen   ISBN: 0946 719 23 3
200 pages approx (illustrated). UK £tbc
For many years Per Nilsen has been a foremost authority on Prince. In this in-depth study of the man and his music, he assesses the years prior to the change of name to a symbol - a period which many consider to be the most productive and musically satisfying. Through interview material with many ex-band members and friends Nilsen paints a portrait of Prince's reign as the most exciting black performer to emerge since James Brown. In this behind the scenes documentary we get to the heart and soul of a funk maestro.

All Helter Skelter, Firefly and SAF titles can be ordered direct from the world famous Helter Skelter music bookstore which is situated at:

Helter Skelter,
4 Denmark Street, London WC2H 8LL
Tel: +44 (0) 171 836 1151   Fax: +44 (0) 171 240 9880.
Consult our website at: http://www.skelter.demon.co.uk

This store has the largest collection of music books anywhere in the world and can supply any in-print title by mail to any part of the globe. For a mail order catalogue or for wholesaling enquiries, please contact us.